TABLE OF CONTENTS

Introduction
    Randy Kirk & Lars Strandridder   i - vii
Dedication and Acknowledgements   ix - x
A Brief Interlude
    Note To Readers   xi

CHAPTERS

1: **Believing in Technology for a Better Future**
    by Elon Musk   1- 8

2: **The End of the ICE Age – Why Now? Convergence of Disruptions**
    by Randy Kirk   9 - 20

3: **Why is Elon Musk so Successful?**
    by Randy Kirk   21 - 32

4: **Tesla Inc ($TSLA)**
    by Randy Kirk   33 – 42

5: **Tesla Divisions**
    by Randy Kirk   43 - 44

6: **The Valuation Story for Tesla Vehicles**
    by Randy Kirk   45 - 49

7: **Competitive Moats**
    by Randy Kirk   51 - 52

8: **Moat: The Blank Slate**
    by Randy Kirk   53 - 54

9: **Moat: The Manufacturing Plant is the Product**
    by Randy Kirk   55 - 56

10: **Moat: He who makes the Best Battery, Wins**
    by Randy Kirk   57 - 58

11: **Moats Abound all over the Factory**
    by Randy Kirk   59 - 61

12: **Moat: Vertical Integration at Scale**
    by Randy Kirk   63 - 65

13: **Moat: Software Technology in the Car and the Factory**
    by Randy Kirk   67 - 69

14: **Moat: The Amazing Tesla Fan Base**
    by Lars Strandridder   71 - 76

15: **Moat: Data and Experience**
    by Lars Strandridder   77 - 78

16: **Moat: Already Scaled and Profitable – First Mover**
    by Randy Kirk   85 - 86

17: **Moat: The Tesla Culture – Dare We Say "Vibe?"**
    by Randy Kirk   87

18: **Moat: The Charging Station Network**
    by Randy Kirk   89 – 91

19: **Moat: Materials Innovation**
    by Randy Kirk   93

20: **Moat: The People**
    by Randy Kirk   95 - 96

21: **Moat: Elon Musk**
    by Randy Kirk   97 - 100

22: **Moat: The Mission**
    by Randy Kirk   102

23: **Moat: Cash and the Ability to Raise Way More Cash**
    by Randy Kirk   103 - 104

24: **Moat: Capital Allocation and ROI**
    by Randy Kirk   105 - 107

25: **Moat: Supply Chain Expertise**
    by Randy Kirk   109 - 112

26: **Moat: Raw Materials Sourcing**
    by Randy Kirk   113 - 114

27: **Moat: Pace of Innovation**
    by Randy Kirk   115 - 117

28: **Moat: Flexibility**
    by Randy Kirk   119 - 120

29: **Moat: Current Moats in so Many Categories**
    by Randy Kirk   121 - 122

30: **Tesla Cars and Trucks**
    by Lars Strandridder & Randy Kirk   123 - 138

31: **The Competition Is Coming**
    by Randy Kirk   139 - 157

32: **The World Needs a Lot More EVs**
    by Randy Kirk   159 - 164

33: **The Robotaxi Revolution**
    by Lars Strandridder   165 - 175

34: **The Factory IS the Product**
    by Lars Strandridder   177 - 185

35: **Beyond Agile – The Speed of Thought**
    by Lars Strandridder   187 - 198

36: **Charging Network as a Stand-Alone Business**
    by Lars Strandridder   199 - 207

37: **Disrupting the Car Insurance Business**
    by Randy Kirk   209 – 214

38: **Royalties and OEM Sales**
    by Randy Kirk   215 - 219

39: **Energy Storage – Home, Business, Local, and Utility Battery Storage**
    by Randy Kirk   221 - 234

40: **He who has the BIGGEST Battery Wins**
    by Randy Kirk   235 - 238

41: **How Tesla Uses AI to move Further and Further Ahead**
    by John Gibbs   239 - 244

42: **Tesla Solar and Home Battery Storage**
    by Brian Wang   245 - 250

43: **Valuing Tesla as a Robot Company Only**
    by Randy Kirk   251 - 259

44: **The Biggest Moat – Flexibility**
    by Randy Kirk   261 -267

45: **Coming Attractions: Dojo aaS, Used Cars, HVAC, & VTOL**
    by Randy Kirk   269 - 273

46: **The Value of SpaceX**
    by Brian Wang   275 - 280

47: **Mechazilla Launch Towers Are Giant Rocket Catching Robots**
    by Brian Wang   281 - 286

48: **Starlink as a Stand-Alone Profit Center**
    by Randy Kirk   287 - 291

49: **Starlink and your Smartphone**
    by Brian Wang   293 - 300

50: **The Boring Company: Taking Transportation into 3D Space**
    by Randy Kirk   301 - 305

51: **In the Room with Elon Musk – AI Day 2, 2022 Reflections**
    by John Gibbs   307 - 313

52: **Neuralink - Improving Brains**
    by Randy Kirk   315 - 320

53: **How Much is $1,000,000,000,000?**
    by Randy Kirk   321 - 324

54: **When will Elon Musk Reach $1T in Personal Net Worth?**
    by Randy Kirk   325 - 331
Appendix   333 - 336
    Author Biographies & Contact Information
Resources   337
41 Best Elon Musk Quotes   339 - 342

Introduction

The Future can be Awesome and Less Boring – Randy Kirk

Most of my friends and associates are business owners and professionals. They are generally solid citizens who keep up with the news and are knowledgeable about the important issues of the day. Generally, they have strong opinions about the economy, social issues, politics, and the weather and/or climate. I am, therefore, confounded when I hear one of them say:

> "I wouldn't want an electric car. They catch fire all the time."

> "The pressure to switch to renewables is driving up utility bills."

> "No way I'd put one of those Neuralink things in my head. It might get hacked."

> "Elon Musk is a big liar and showman with no actual engineering skills or knowledge."

I am an unrepentant Elon Musk fanboy. I have spent the last six years studying him, his companies, his products, and the reactions to all three. As an entrepreneur, ex-manufacturer, marketer, and futurist, I feel a certain kinship and understanding about what drives Elon and some of the ways he thinks.

My first book on Elon, *The Elon Musk Method*, has sold 20,000 copies and been translated into five languages. In that book I made the case that Elon has been gifted with a confluence of innate abilities and skills that make him unique as an entrepreneur, inventor, engineer, and marketer. I found 16 of these characteristics and laid out a case that every business owner, large or small, would benefit from emulating Elon in each of these.

In pulling together a team of writers for The Elon Musk Mission, the goal was to provide a primer on Elon, his vision, purposes, companies, products, and services that serve his mission.

We are hoping that Mission will find its way into the hands of fans, skeptics, and those who are just interested in knowing more about the real Ironman. We have set out the facts as best we can, and then asked dozens of fact-checkers to make sure we have not made material errors in our understanding. If you, dear reader, find an error, please contact the appropriate writer, and lay out your case. We will be updating Mission on a regular basis.

The book is not a simple regurgitation of the news found on hundreds of YouTube channels, podcasts, blogs, and news outlets, though these sources have been invaluable in underpinning my understanding and that of Lars, John, and Brian. We have gone one step further. You will find that most of the book has original thinking, prognostication, and totally new ways of looking at this important subject.

First, we do look at why Elon Musk is the protagonist in the story. What about his history, ways of thinking about the world, abilities, and personality have placed him in this "difficult" place. (He has described his life as harsh, not wishing to extend it, but seeing death as a future relief.)

Most of the book is centered on Tesla and its 21 startup companies. Some might argue that there are more than 21, and we don't cover all 21 in depth. We do take a deep dive look at what It is about these products, the factories as the product, and the people Musk has assembled that will seemingly result in Tesla being multiple times larger than Apple later in this decade.

Many of Tesla's detractors believe that there will eventually be demand issues for the cars. We provide a very long list of levers that Tesla can pull if demand even begins to level off. Levers not available to the competition, manufacturers of ICE (internal combustion engine) cars or at least not at the levels available to Tesla.

Others in the $TSLAQ community (individuals and groups specifically trying to criticize and undermine Tesla), claim that competition from other BEV (battery electric vehicles that have only an electric power train) makers, both existing auto companies and startups, will eventually knock Tesla off its perch and Tesla will be a future also ran. We supply another long list of moats that will keep king Tesla protected from the onslaught.

Mission next looks at SpaceX, the dominant space transportation company on earth and above earth today. SpaceX, which is not publicly traded, does not have nearly as many detractors as Tesla. SpaceX is also not disrupting major industries such as oil, natural gas, coal, energy, and auto. There are no short sellers on a mission to hurt SpaceX as there are with Tesla. There are not the same kinds of vested interests with competitive products that will lose business as Tesla gains.

However, both the space transportation business at SpaceX and the Starlink division are poised to be bigger in revenue and profits than any other current companies. You would be hard pressed to find anyone in your friend group who would be aware that SpaceX will soon be valued as the top privately held company.

Neuralink and the Boring company also have the potential to eventually be valued at multiple trillions of dollars. As these two companies are still in the early startup stages, there is less ink devoted to these two businesses.

As of this writing, Twitter is not yet a done deal. In future editions of Mission, we might add a section on Twitter.

Finally, as Lars puts it, we have a bit of fun. When will Elon Musk become the first ever trillionaire? We even have a contest with real prizes around that theme. Elon is currently the wealthiest person on earth, and he could be worth a trillion dollars by 2024, '25, '26. How does he get there? What are the immediate projections for the value of these four companies?

I'll go through the numbers and provide my own estimate(s) of how and exactly when Elon makes that mark. The information may be helpful for the contest, and/or it might be helpful for just watching the future of these companies.

You don't want to miss these final chapters!!

Introduction 2.0

The Passion Comes from the Mission, Not the Money

Lars Strandridder

How did I end up becoming a YouTuber making videos about Elon Musk and his companies?

My interest in Elon Musk and his companies started many years ago, but by 2015 I really started to dive into the world of Tesla and SpaceX and, the more I learned, the more interesting it all got.

In 2019 my wife and I bought a Tesla Model 3 long range, and at every party we went to, I didn't do much of anything else but give drives to people that wanted to try out a Tesla.

After the drive, people had a lot of questions about Tesla and electric vehicles in general.

Their questions were mostly about myths and misinformation regarding electric cars, such as how they couldn't drive in cold weather, that the battery had to be changed every 200,000km, that a Tesla would cost $200,000, or that Teslas just didn't work on road trips. All the fear, uncertainty, and doubt (FUD) that had been spread about Tesla and electric cars seemed to have worked.

Instead of talking to people about it at every single party we attended, I decided I would like to help Tesla in fighting all this fake information and lies that were being spread. I set out to show the facts about owning an electric car, and all the benefits of them. So, in July 2019, I started my YouTube channel called BestInTESLA.

I quickly took some deep dives into how Tesla was doing as a company, and how they were able to grow their production faster than any other large manufacturer in history.

Torque News - Tesla Growing Faster Than Any Large Cap Company in History
https://www.torquenews.com/14335/tesla-growing-faster-any-large-cap-company-history

And the more I learned, the more fascinated I became with Tesla and all Elon Musk's other companies that were also changing the world, like SpaceX, The Boring Company, and Neuralink.

The more I learned, the more I saw that people really had the wrong idea about these companies and especially the wrong ideas about who Elon Musk was. I saw him as a man who generally just wants to make our future exciting and our tomorrows better by helping the world to transition to a sustainable future.

How could so many people around the world hate a man that is only trying to be good?

Making The Future Awesome | vi

Well, when you are disrupting multiple industries, you are going to step on some big toes, and the owners of those toes will want to fight you and your companies.

Recognizing who it was that was perpetrating the FUD made me want to help out even more, and to tell the story of Elon Musk and his companies the way I saw them. My goal was and is to help people learn about this amazing man who is changing our world and civilization through his innovative companies that are makingced the world a better place.

That is also why I was very excited when Randy asked me if I wanted to be a co-author on a new book about Elon Musk, to try to help people understand him and his companies. I don't think anyone has ever been more misunderstood than Elon Musk. We have probably never seen a bigger misinformation campaign before than what we have seen with Tesla.

So, after 3 years of working professionally on trying to understand how Elon Musk is able to do what he does, and how Tesla is able to do the things they are doing, and how SpaceX has been able to become the only real ticket to space, I think the timing for me to help make this book couldn't be more perfect. I am super glad Randy took me with him on this journey. And I hope you will find this book helpful, inspiring, and entertaining, and that you will also feel like you will get a better understanding about Elon Musk's mission, and the impact his companies will have on the world and our civilization.

Dedication

We would like to dedicate this book to the TESLA Community. This unpaid army of volunteers spend countless hours supporting the efforts of Tesla to accelerate the world's transition to sustainable energy. They tirelessly fight the FUD, TESLAQ, and any others attempting to undermine the mission.

Acknowledgements

We wish to thank the following individuals for their tireless contributions to proof reading, fact checking, and generally helping to make the book a better read. Their ideas radically changed the entire feel of the work.

Wally Kunz – *Lead Editor*
Jim Ringold
Thomas Alan Gray
Thomas Gaudette
Peter Helander
Mike Yam
Randy Lathrop
Marvin Diercks
Christian Läntzsch
Erick Heath

Malcom Reynolds
Robert Stout
Goran Wilbran
Anthony Amenta
Peter Michelsen
Ravi Gupta
Severin Leuenberger
Pablo Flores
Pat Mcdaniel
Rich Rolan

A Brief Interlude
Notes to Readers

Thank you so much for your interest in the Elon Musk Mission. We hope you find it valuable as a fan, as someone just starting to learn about Elon Musk or any of his enterprises, or as a one stop location for the facts related to Musk.

We have recently learned that Amazon will allow us to update the book as often as we like, and even to make major changes. **Tip:** To receive automatic book updates as they become available, enable Automatic Book Update on the Preferences tab in Manage Your Content and Devices.

There are a few quirky elements to this work that could cause some readers to lose the flow from time-to-time. I'm hoping that pointing them out in advance might be of some help

First, there are four contributors to The Elon Musk Mission. Each has a different writing style. For two, English is a second language. Too much of the flavor of those personalities would have been lost if we had completely smoothed out all of those differences.

Secondly, many of the chapters have multiple writers contributing. In those chapters, we have tried to smooth out things a bit more, but you may still feel some changes in voice from paragraph to paragraph.

Thirdly, this book is filled with numbers, and most of them are very large numbers. To make the pages look better, and hopefully to make things easier to read, we have used some shortcuts.

- K or k for thousands
- M for millions
- B for billions
- T for trillions.
- Example $25M would be $25,000,000

Then there are the abbreviations. Here are some that you might find helpful.

AI – Artificial Intelligence is intelligence demonstrated by machines, as opposed to the natural intelligence displayed by animals and humans.

BEV – Battery Electric Vehicles use only batteries in the power train. Does not include hybrids.

Dojo is the neural net (an electrical network that mimics the function of a biological nervous system) training supercomputer created by Tesla to train the automated driving features on FSD and other devices (e.g., Optimus the humanoid robot).

Dojo aaS – Dojo as a Service – see SaaS

EV – Any vehicle that uses electricity for at least part of the its means of propulsion. Therefore, this would include plug in hybrids.

FSD – *Full Self Driving* – Not without controversy, this is the designation for Tesla's highest level autonomous driving solution. When fully developed Tesla says that the car outfitted with FSD will drive itself from a home garage to a

Making The Future Awesome | xii

destination parking space without touching the wheels or the pedals

IRA – Inflation Reduction Act – Congress passed a this legislation providing substantial incentives for production of electric vehicles, batteries, and mining/processing of materials for electric batteries in the US.

SaaS – *Software as a Service* – This is in reference to any app or other method which can be sold or rented on a computer type device and provide the user with a service.

S3XY – Acronym that stands for Tesla's current vehicle lineup. Model S, Model 3, Model X, and Model Y.

We have finally found a convention that seems to be the most likely, proper abbreviations for various electrical unit measures, though you'll find many variations to these on high quality internet sites.

    kW – kilowatt – 1000 watts
    MW – Megawatt – 1000 kW
    GW – Gigawatt – 1000 MW
    TW – Terawatt – 1000 GW

Add a ·h to any of the above for hour. However, we will use a more conventional kWh or MWh in this book.

Because we cover a lot of ground, and due to our having four authors involved, you will sometimes see concepts that get repeated. We have limited this as much as we thought wise. However, sometimes we felt it was better to repeat some foundational material rather than ask you to go reread another section.

We are not investment advisors, and nothing in this book is investment advice. We have worked very hard to vet the book for possible errors in fact or analysis, including having dozens of editors look through the work prior to publication.

We would be so thankful if you would take the time to leave a review. I'm sure you are aware of how important reviews are to the success of any book or product. If you like the book, we'd be extra thankful if you shared your enthusiasm in any channels where you have a voice.

We covet your comments and opinions which you can send to us individually as shown below.

Randy Kirk
RandyKirk77@gmail.com
@RandyWKirk1 on Twitter

Lars Strandridder
BestinTesla@gmail.com
@BestinTesla on Twitter

CHAPTER 1

Believing in Technology for a Better Future

by Elon Musk

The following post from Elon speaks for itself, and we felt it would be a fantastic way to begin.

Thank you for the invitation from China Cyberspace magazine. I am pleased to share with my Chinese friends some of my thoughts on the vision of technology and humanity.
Posted by Elon Musk

As technology accelerates, it may one day surpass human understanding and control. Some are optimistic and some are pessimistic. But I believe that as long as we are not complacent and always maintain a sense of urgency, the future of humanity will be bright, driven by the power of technology. It is like a self-fulfilling prophecy: if humans want to make the future good, they should take action to make it good.

I want to do everything we can to maximize the use of technology to help achieve a better future for humanity. To that end, any area that contributes to a sustainable future is worthy of our investment. Whether it's Tesla, Neuralink, or SpaceX, these companies were all founded with the ultimate goal of enhancing the future of human life and creating as much practical value for the world as possible—Tesla to accelerate the world's transition to sustainable energy,

Neuralink for medical rehabilitation, SpaceX for making interstellar connections possible.

Clean Energy: The Future of Sustainability

The starting point for my thinking about clean energy is how to create and store energy sustainably and for the long term, and how to provide a constant source of power for the future of productive life. In my view, the future of sustainable energy involves three components.

The generation of sustainable energy. The sun is like a giant fusion generator, from which humankind currently exploits a tiny amount of energy. In the long run, solar energy will become the main source of energy for human civilization. Of course, wind, hydroelectric, geothermal, and nuclear power are also useful energy supplements.

The storage of sustainable energy. Given the change of day and night and the change of weather, we need a lot of fixed battery banks to store solar and wind energy, because the sun does not shine all the time, and the wind does not blow all the time, energy needs to be stored in a large number of fixed battery banks.

Electrified transportation. Full electrification of transportation, including cars, planes, and ships. Electric rockets may be more difficult, but we may be able to manufacture the propellant used in rockets from sustainable energy sources. Eventually, the world economy will be run entirely by sustainable energy sources.

The world is on track for a sustainable energy transition, and humanity should continue to accelerate the process. The faster this transition is achieved, the less risk humanity poses to the environment and the more it will gain. When clean energy is *available, carbon sequestration and desalination will be cheaper, climate change and water shortages will be solved, and when fossil fuels are out of the picture, the skies will be cleaner, the world will be quieter, the air will be fresher, and the future will be brighter.*

Solar power, battery packs, and electric vehicles paint a rosy picture. Next, we need to focus on the limiting factors. The electrification of cars has become a consensus among nations, but battery support on a terawatt-hour scale is needed to roll out pure electric vehicles around the globe. According to our estimates, the world needs about 300 TWh of battery storage to achieve a transition to sustainable energy. The biggest difficulty in advancing sustainable energy lies in the large-scale production of lithium battery cells. Specifically, from the mining and element refining to battery cells coming off of the production line and finally assembled into battery packs, this is a complex process that is restraining the rapid development of a sustainable energy economy.

As a pioneer and innovator focusing on energy innovation technology, Tesla was founded to solve the problem of energy innovation. On the one hand, we create integrated sustainable energy products from the three segments of energy production, storage, and use; on the other hand, we are committed to redefining battery manufacturing by innovating and developing advanced battery technology to remove restrictions on battery capacity. I believe that the world will transition to a sustainable future through a combination of solar and wind energy plus battery storage and electric vehicles. I am pleased to see more and more companies joining this field. Chinese companies will be a force to be reckoned with in the cause of energy innovation.

Humanoid Robots: Doing What Humans Do

Today's cars are increasingly like smart, web-connected robots on wheels. In fact, in addition to cars, humanoid robots are also becoming a reality, with Tesla launching a general-purpose humanoid robot (Tesla Bot) in 2021. The Tesla Bot is close to the height and weight of an adult, can carry or pick up heavy objects, walk fast in small steps, and the screen on its face is an interactive interface for communication with people. You may wonder why we designed this robot with legs. Because human society is based on the interaction of a bipedal humanoid with two arms and ten fingers. So if we want a robot to adapt to its environment and be able to do what humans do, it has to be roughly the same size, shape, and capabilities as a human.

Tesla Bots are initially positioned to replace people in repetitive, boring, and dangerous tasks. But the vision is for them to serve millions of households, such as cooking, mowing lawns, and caring for the elderly.

Achieving this goal requires that robots evolve to be smart enough and for us to have the ability to mass produce robots. Our "four-wheeled robots" – cars – have changed the way people travel and even live. One day when we solve the problem of self-driving cars (i.e., real-world artificial intelligence), we will be able to extend artificial intelligence technology to humanoid robots, which will have a much broader application than cars.

We plan to launch the first prototype of a humanoid robot this year and focus on improving the intelligence of that robot and solving the problem of large-scale production. Thereafter, humanoid robots' usefulness will increase yearly as production scales up and costs fall. In the future, a home robot may be cheaper than a car. Perhaps in less than a decade, people will be able to buy a robot for their parents as a birthday gift.

It is foreseeable that with the power of robots, we will create an era of extreme abundance of goods and services, where everyone can live a life of abundance. Perhaps the only scarcity that will exist in the future is for us to create ourselves as humans.

Neuralink: Empowering the Disabled

Some of our Chinese friends may not be as familiar with Neuralink as with electric cars. These companies focus on developing computer-human brain fusion technologies, developing brain chips the size of coins, similar to wearable devices such as smartphones, except that they integrate more deeply with the user's body— recording and stimulating brain activity through implants in the cerebral cortex.

At this stage, the technology is helping injured people on an individual level. We have received many saddening letters: a 25-year-old young man was in the prime of his life when he had a motorcycle accident that left him unable to eat on his own, which is a great grief for the individual and the family. In light of this, brain-machine interface technology will be focused on curing or alleviating brain injury and other related disorders in the years to come. For example, it could help restore sensory or motor function to limbs of those with spinal injuries and mental system disorders or allow quadriplegics to use their brains to easily operate computers or cell phones.

This technology can also improve a wider range of brain injury problems, whether these disorders are congenital or accidental, or caused by age and external stressors, including severe depression, morbid obesity, sleep problems, and underlying schizophrenia, all of which are expected to be alleviated by human-computer devices. With the development of brain-machine interface technology, in the long term, this connection is expected to expand the channels of communication between the outside world and the human brain, "accessing" more brain regions and new neural data. This technology could allow humans to effectively integrate with artificial intelligence and ultimately expand new ways for humans to interact with the world, themselves, and others. Even if the goal of human-machine integration is difficult to achieve, brain-machine interface technology could be of great value in the field of medical rehabilitation.

Space Exploration: The Possibility of Cross-Planet Habitats

Finally, my greatest hope is that humans create a self-sustaining city on Mars. Many people ask me why I want to explore outer space and turn humans into multi-planetary creatures. In the vast universe, human civilization is like a faint little candle, like a little shimmering light in the void. When the sun expands one day and the Earth is no longer habitable, we can fly to a new home in a spaceship. If humans can inhabit other planets, it means that they have passed one of the conditions of the great screening of the universe, then we will become interplanetary citizens, and human civilization will be able to continue.

The first step toward interplanetary habitat is to reduce the cost of travel, which is what SpaceX was founded to do – first by building recoverable rockets and then by building reusable mega-ships with ever-increasing carrying capacity. As of earlier this year, SpaceX had successfully reused 79 rockets to deliver cargo to the space station and send ordinary people into space. We have also designed and built the largest launch vehicle in history, the Starship, which *can carry 100 passengers and supplies at a time. In the future, we plan to build at least 1,000 Starships to send groups of pioneers to Mars to build a self-sustaining city.*

As technology continues to change lives at an accelerating pace and the world evolves, life is more than simply solving one problem after another. We all want to wake up in the morning full of anticipation for the future and rejoice in what is to come. I hope more people will join us in our fight to accelerate the world's transition to sustainable energy. I also welcome more like-minded Chinese partners to join us in exploring clean energy, artificial intelligence, human-machine collaboration, and space exploration to create a future worth waiting for.

CHAPTER 2

The End of the ICE Age - Why Now? Convergence of Disruptions

by Randy Kirk

There will be no more Internal Combustion Engine (ICE) automobiles made after 2026. This is an estimate based on Tony Seba's groundbreaking studies of disruption. In order for there to be an end to ICE cars, the world will need to build 60-80 million Battery Electric Vehicles (BEV) in 2027 to meet the demand. Most (even the conservative analysts) believe that Tesla will end up with about 20% market share. This would then require Tesla to make about 15 million vehicles in 2027. That number is right in line with Elon Musk's plan to reach 20 million vehicles in 2030. Later in the book, we will spell out the specifics of how it is feasible to accomplish the end of the ice age by 2027.

Statements by ICE manufacturers like General Motors, Ford, Honda, Volkswagen, and BEV startups point to a world without ICE production between 2030 and 2035. Pick your own date, but the time is coming, and Tesla has a huge head start that we will argue is unassailable in the next decade, at least.

Tony Seba and financial guru Cathy Wood both argue that such disruptions happen due to convergences in technology. Watch the video below for a detailed explanation of how the convergence of the capabilities of batteries, displays, and integrated circuits allowed for the production of smartphones exactly when Apple and Samsung began production. A year before, it would have been impossible to make a smartphone the size and price that made it an amazing product.

Tony Seba - The Great Disruption
ttps://www.youtube.com/watch?v=Kj96nxtHdTU

The convergences that are allowing Tesla and SpaceX to create such disruption in transportation, automation, energy, and space revolve around revolutionary declines in the costs of solar, batteries, compute power, AI, and rockets. Take away any of these technological advances, and the future looks quite different.

The Human Condition

Techno King of Tesla, Elon Musk, says that "Fundamentally, if you don't have a compelling product at a compelling price, you don't have a great company." What is the driving human need that was true in 2005 and still true today that makes this the right time for electric cars, solar/wind/battery as the primary source of energy, and a robust space program?

For hundreds of years many thought leaders have been predicting that humans would use up the earth's resources, leaving the remaining population without enough food, energy, and more. While these predictions seem to have been undone by improving technology, the fast population growth of the last decade, combined with the suspicion that fossil fuels wouldn't last forever, drove a popular demand for renewable energy.

On top of this, the massive amount of carbon emissions caused by burning fossil fuels is at best causing smoggy cities and particulate issues worldwide, and potentially some very unpleasant future changes in weather, sea levels, and possible droughts and other consequences. The average citizen of the world today has some degree of fear (from moderate to existential) related to these future events.

These two converging social issues have made a future based on energy from fossil fuels seem untenable to almost anyone who is paying attention. While there are many solutions being offered for alternatives to fossil fuels, the current best hope is a combination of solar, wind, and batteries. Elon Musk has seen the future and the current social climate. He understood that if a company would lead the world to a clean, reliable, renewable/sustainable source of energy, the world would beat a path to that company's door.

CO^2 emissions, the major greenhouse gas of concern, come primarily from the current fossil fuel energy resources needed for most forms of transportation and the heating and lighting of our homes and businesses. Reduce or end the use of coal, oil, and natural gas for these purposes and the resulting impact on the future will be stunning. The burning of fossil fuels is also the major contributor to particulate pollution

For those who lived in Los Angeles in the 60's, the control of particulates at the exhaust pipe of automobiles provided a stunning change to Los Angeles skies. The next adoption of BEVs, and solar/wind/battery for energy over the 10 years will result in something far more amazing for Mexico City, Rio, Beijing, and other major cities who have varying degrees of smog interfering with life and health.

So, the timing of Musk's success revolves around multiple new technologies converging at a time when the citizens and governments of the world were looking for a new direction for energy sources, and at a time when the opportunity to lower the cost of space travel supplied an opening for a renewed push into exploration and use of space for human advancement.

Why Elon Musk?

He's been compared to Franklin, Edison, Jobs, DaVinci, Nicola Tesla, Ford, Iron Man, and Andrew Carnegie. He's been called brilliant, genius, one-in-a-generation, world changer, maverick, iconic, and best entrepreneur of all time, not to mention fool, liar, and other less respectful things.

Having studied Musk for the last six years from the perspective of a manufacturer, entrepreneur, communicator, and author of 10+ business books, I have come to this conclusion about the reasons for his incomparable success.

Elon is right at the top of multiple skill sets, any two or three of which might result in huge success in business. There may be a few other CEO's who are better at leadership, but a case could be made that he is worthy of new chapters in MBA books about leadership. There might be some who are better at creating an epic vision, but I'm hard pressed to think who that would be.

Maybe we could find someone who works harder, but 80-hour weeks back-to-back for years on end is hard to top. Possibly there is another human who can compare with Elon's ability to execute.

Some of the other wealthiest entrepreneurs would be in Musk's league, but can you say any are clearly superior? No other large market cap company in history has consistently grown as fast as Tesla.

Potentially there are others who dream bigger, and actually believe that the dream can be achieved. What dreams are bigger than moving the entire planet off fossil fuels and on to sustainable energy sources? What bigger dream than 14,400 satellites in space providing internet service to the final 2 billion people who have no connection or a very poor one? Of course, who could wonder at a bigger goal than establishing a serious working colony on the moon or 1,000,000 people taking up residence on Mars, requiring a fleet of more than 1,000 super rockets to make the trek.

How about someone who would be a better marketer? Steve Jobs had his epic Superbowl commercial. Elon doesn't advertise at all. Those who buy a Tesla appreciate the products are all the marketing that has been needed.

Ronald Reagan was called the great communicator. Musk has over 100,000,000 followers on Twitter and growing. And his ability to communicate his various visions results in hundreds of fans selling his vision for free. The top engineers graduating from the world's best engineering schools look at Tesla and SpaceX as their top hopes for employment, because they have heard the vision communicated.

Elon Musk is so quotable that he might be the most quoted person ever. Please see the Appendix for hundreds of examples of his quotes. My particular favorite: "If you want stuff, somebody has to make stuff."

What about those other leadership skills? Of course, having a vision, communicating that vision, and execution are pretty important leadership notions. But what about sleeping on the factory floor, providing direct options for bringing ideas or complaints to Elon from anyone of the 110,000 plus employees, or creating an atmosphere so charged that most of his followers are happy to sacrifice in furtherance of the cause.

Some argue that there are many engineers better than Elon Musk. But what makes a great engineer? I might argue that keeping fundamental principles in the forefront at all times would be what makes an engineer great. Or possibly one might look at the breadth of Elon's engineering prowess, from rocketry, to telecommunications, to automobile manufacturing, to artificial intelligence, to brain function to chip design, to metallurgy, to factory design, to robotics.

A thorough search of the internet doesn't shed much clarity about what makes a great engineer. Most cite curiosity, genius IQ, ability to simplify, creativity, collaborativeness, problem solving, communication skills, and future thinking.

Maybe we should review what the National Academy of Sciences on behalf of the National Academy of Engineering considers to be the most important engineering achievements of all time. This could give us some guidance. They list 20. How many of these 20 has Elon Musk already impacted in a major way, or is he providing clear leadership in the field today, or has already pronounced his intentions to make substantive change in the future:

Electrification – Tesla, the company, has made dozens of breakthroughs in battery technology, solar energy technology, and invented an entirely new way of remaking the electric grid through a distributed approach. Homes, businesses, cars, and small local utilities will all be generators and managers of electricity in the near future.

Automobile - Tesla is now the largest auto company by market cap due to the complete rethinking of how to design, build, and power a car. Coming soon will be the autonomy of automobiles which will completely revolutionize the design and layout of cities.

Airplane - The future of long-distance air travel will be SpaceX rockets flying from point-to-point anywhere on earth in 45 minutes. Elon says that he has a workable electric VTOL (Vertical Takeoff and Landing) jet on the drawing board. But he says that both he and Tesla lack the bandwidth to develop it at this time.

Water Supply and Distribution - The Boring Company will be able to create utility tunnels at a fraction of today's cost. Elon has also stated that cheap energy from solar and batteries will allow for low-cost desalination in the near future.

Electronics - Tesla automobiles are described as computers on wheels. Over the air updates is just one revolutionary electronic approach on cars.

> Utility scale battery installations use advanced electronics, called Autobidder, which allows utilities to maximize the economic benefits of solar/wind/battery installations.
>
> Electronic breakthroughs at Neuralink are pairing the brain with computers allowing for both upload of neural signals and the brain activating appliances.

Tesla has developed one of the most advanced computers in the world, Dojo.

Computers - See electronics above

Telephone - SpaceX has just announced that they will be providing connectivity with cell phones through their Starlink system.

Air Conditioning and Refrigeration - Tesla has developed an advanced heat pump transfer system for automobiles, octovalve. Elon has stated that this would be a breakthrough HVAC system for homes, but it is still a future project at this writing.

Highways - Elon has completely rethought the approach to human travel, including automation of street-vehicles, layers of high-speed tunnels, and 700 mph hyperloop trains. One result that some or all of these changes will bring will be the end of streets and highways, parking structures, and related eyesores.

Spacecraft - SpaceX is far and away the leading Spacecraft producer. They will soon have sent more payloads into orbit than the combination of all other payloads to date. Their cost to deliver payload to orbit has been reduced by over an order of magnitude, and the new Star Ship Rocket is intended to reduce payload costs by another 10 times or more. All of this is due to Musk having invented rapidly reusable spacecraft, which required the ability to land a rocket on earth, vertically, intact.

Internet - Elon saw that he could bring great broadband service to the last two billion humans on earth by creating an array of over 42,000 satellites in low earth orbit.

Health Technologies - As noted above, Neuralink goals are: Treating brain disorders and helping people who've had accidents, creating a brain-machine interface, and building toward a potential symbiosis with artificial intelligence.

Petroleum and Petrochemical Technologies - Elon's most important goal is to eliminate as much of these technologies as possible through:

- solar/wind/battery approaches.
- Laser and Fiber Optics
- Nuclear Technologies

High-performance Materials – Some, if not all, of Elon Musk's companies are creating new materials, finding new ways to use existing materials, and generally using first principles to optimize the way atoms are moved and manipulated.

Has anyone in history or currently working accomplished such a stunning array of earth-altering products and solutions to big, even existential problems?

Why Elon Musk? He says of himself that these characteristics are key: intense curiosity, willingness to work harder than anyone, voluminous reading, passion about the human species, willingness to risk everything, and persistence.

What we are really looking at is a convergence. Having Elon Musk's level of skill on any one of these characteristics will almost certainly propel an individual to achieve more of substance than 90% or more of "normal" humans. Start adding them together in a single individual, and the result is what you're witnessing.

What is your opinion? What aspect of Elon's personality, skills, or DNA have been responsible for the amazing successes that he oversees? What did we miss? Post your theory on Twitter @RandyKirk1 or @teslabest.

In summary, Elon Musk was passionate about creating a more sustainable world, and about creating another civilization for humans if humans on earth were threatened with extinction on Earth. His passion, combined with his almost superhero skills and burn-the-boats attitude are at the root of the story whose next chapter should see Elon Musk's wealth eclipsing $1T.

BUT - This analysis would be incomplete without taking a look at a counterintuitive explanation for Elon's standing at the top of the wealth leaderboard. He doesn't care about the things money buys, and his interest in acquiring wealth is merely to support the astonishing goals he has set out to accomplish.

It will cost around $1T or more to get the first major contingent of people and their needed equipment to Mars. You'd be right in speculating that going to the banks or stock market to raise $1T for that purpose would be a non-starter.

He knew you couldn't start an electric car company for the masses with any hope of success with just his modest seed money of $60M or so. Even with the help of banks, investors, or an IPO, the only way to get the job done was to start with really expensive, more-or-less hand-built cars to show the concept and create interest.

These cars needed to make money if there was going to be a less expensive luxury car that would be affordable to a much larger group of consumers. Only with the success of these cars, could there be the financial wherewithal to attempt a mass market car.

Elon placed the odds of Tesla succeeding to get to the Model 3 rollout at best just 10%. In other words, a 90% chance of failure. He placed the odds of success at SpaceX as about the same. He invested every dollar he had earned at PayPal into these two companies, and both came near to failure in the same few months of 2008.

If they had failed, he would have had a negative net worth due to loans outstanding. It wasn't about the money. If it had been, there might not have been the incredible fortitude it took to keep going during those dark days. *The passion came from the mission, not the money.*

CHAPTER 3

Why is Elon Musk so Successful?

by Randy Kirk

I devoted an entire book, *The Elon Musk Method*, to unpacking Musk's natural abilities, skill sets, management approaches, and personality that have resulted in his being the richest person on the planet. Of course, Musk is much more than that. He has successfully launched or been a critical cog in the launch of at least seven, billion-dollar businesses, one of which has been valued at over $1T and will soon be worth $10T or more.

The Elon Musk Method was written for business owners who might learn from the very visible approaches that have contributed to Elon's successes. While there may be some overlap, this first section of "The Elon Musk Mission," has a different motivation and goal. How can every human, not just entrepreneurs, learn from the Elon Musk story as we all watch it unfold?

Every human is way more than the sum of their parts such as skills, IQ, or talents. For instance, there are plenty of smart, good looking, emotionally intelligent people who have the ability to easily memorize content, and who can act on stage or in front of a camera effectively. But only a tiny fraction of those folks ever gets a significant paycheck, much less make a living at acting. Fewer still achieve stardom.

Similarly, you may know someone, as I do, who has almost no natural gifting in talents, looks, intelligence, or charm. But their gentle spirit and loving ways endear them to everyone they touch.

There are multiple other dimensions in our lives that contribute to the final story.

What is it about Elon that takes his obvious natural abilities and catapults him into such rarified air ... such success on so many levels?

Years ago, I bought a suite of signed Rockwell Lithographs. Norman Rockwell was the most popular and well-known illustrator of the 20th century. I loved his work and thought it would be cool to hang some in my home. Rockwell was near death. My real reason for buying was to make a quick buck. Artists' works always goes up after they pass. Right?

Meanwhile, a friend of mine was just crazy about wild west statuary. In particular, he loved Frederick Remington bronzes. He bought some to grace his shelves and tabletops. He had no interest in selling them or profiting from them. He just wanted to admire them.

Fast forward years or decades. His Remingtons have increased in value many times over. My Rockwells might not even fetch their purchase price. This is not a story about wisdom in selecting art for financial appreciation since the results could have been just the opposite. Rather the story illustrates the question of heart in any endeavor. It just seems so often in life that those who enter into a project with the right heart, prosper.

So, it is with Elon Musk. He is not the first, and he won't be the last entrepreneur to start a company because it is the right thing to do for humanity or some subset of humans. A smart business owner is very aware of the needs of the population the company intends to serve.

However, (and I'll tattle on myself once again) many startups are very focused on the get rich part more than they are on the hope of impacting some slice of society in a positive way. I'll let you wrestle with your own life choices and the motivation behind them.

I don't live in Elon's brain or heart, so I can't actually know all his motivations. However, from being an ardent student of his life for half a decade, I can see that there is a distinct pattern to his behavior, and I'll venture to suggest that it is a major secret to his success.

Purpose Driven

Rick Warren published what turned out to be one of the best-selling books of all time. *The Purpose Driven Life* was also on the *New York Times* Bestseller List for over 90 weeks. According to both the author and publisher, Simon & Schuster, 50 million copies had been sold in more than 85 languages by 2020. (Wikipedia)

The Purpose Driven Life reached so many people simply because most of us would like to think we are on the planet for some purpose other than working, feeding our faces, and making babies to repeat the process. If we, after honestly assessing our capabilities, can get in touch with a potential purpose that fits our skills, education, talents, and personality, we are far more likely to pursue our involvement in that space with excellence and persistence. We will take more risks, delay gratification, and be willing to step outside our familiar boxes if we are on fire for a purpose greater than ourselves.

Elon Musk has been purpose driven since his youth. If we take him at his word (and his current actions seem to bear him out), he has long since believed that the key goal to his life would be leaving the world a better place for his having tread its surface and breathed its air.

Elon has epitomized the purpose driven life in so many ways, and the following few pages will take these apart one-by-one. We can all learn from these attributes:

- Clear, Customer-Centric Mission Statement
- Communicator
- Burn the boats mentality
- Relentless Pursuit of the Mission
- Fearless
- Tireless
- Sense of urgency
- Humble

Clear, Customer-Centric Mission Statement

Every business student and business owner has been harangued for at least the last half-century about the importance of creating a mission statement. I have had the opportunity to read many such mission statements, and almost all sadly lack any kind of clear plans that would motivate employees, investors, prospective customers, and suppliers. In fact, most are not even memorable. Even the owners often have forgotten what they said.

Now then, try this one: **Tesla's mission is to accelerate the world's transition to sustainable energy**

You don't have to be green, liberal, or an environmentalist to get excited about this idea. Sustainable energy is a good in itself. Unsustainable energy sources surely just sound wrong and give clarity to the problem. Of course, there is more to this idea than just sustainability. There is an assumption that this also means clean. You don't need to believe in climate change to want clean air, rivers, and oceans. But for those that do worry about a warming planet, the Tesla mission is an even more exciting prospect.

This mission statement could inspire people to participate in Tesla, even if the leader was not so charismatic. While every mission statement must be believable if it is to generate adherents, the Tesla mission statement will at least cause folks to pause and consider how they might be a part of the solution.

Maybe you will also like the SpaceX mission statement: **The SpaceX mission is to revolutionize space technology and to promote humankind to a multi-planetary life.** There are millions, maybe even billions, of folks who are interested or even tantalized by one of the remaining unexplored frontiers. The idea of participating in a company that has a vision that includes colonizing Mars is inspiring to a big percentage of the world's population.

More specifically, there are scientists, engineers, hobbyists, and others who love rocketry, satellite tech, or specific aspects of potential benefits of cheaper ways to get things into orbit. I don't think anyone has taken a poll, but I would suspect that there are hundreds of millions of potential astronauts who would love a trip into space if the price was right and the chances of returning to earth were reasonable.

Neuralink has a mission **to create ultra-high bandwidth brain-machine interfaces to connect humans and computers.** Elon has tweeted that the real mission statement is "If you can't beat them, join them," in reference to the idea that artificial intelligence will soon have robots doing everything better than humans, and that the linking of the human brain directly to computers will help us keep up.

We all know that Elon thinks in terms of solving some of the biggest problems facing humankind. Thus, his mission statements touch the hearts of billions. However, that doesn't mean that a local restaurant or clothing store can't devise a mission that is inspirational: Joe's Burgers Goal Is to "Become Known for the Best Bacon Burger in the US;" or Lydia's Fashion Stop has a mission to "Help Teen Girls Feel Great About Their Look."

Why does the mission statement help? Every business should be a leader that has many followers including employees, customers, suppliers, community leaders, and service providers. If the company has a great mission, it is easier to hire and motivate employees, reach, and sell customers, convince the best suppliers to provide their goods such as exclusive brands, and provide a general buzz within the community's support system in government, business groups, and service companies.

Communication

Elon Musk is on the spectrum. In fact, during his performance on Saturday Night Live, he announced that he has Asperger's syndrome. What exactly are the symptoms?

Signs and symptoms of Asperger's syndrome

- Lack of interpersonal relationship skills and instincts.
- Inability to express one's own feelings.
- Often verbalizes internal thoughts that most would keep private.
- Extreme focus.

- Flat tone / speaking style that lacks pitch.
- Appears to lack empathy.
- Has a difficult time interacting with peers.

While I think it is fair to say that Musk's Asperger's is not as debilitating for him as it is for many others, there can be no doubt that his speaking style is quirky at best. He has set the Internet on fire more than a few times that might be related to number three. There are certainly reports that he sometimes has a difficult time interacting with peers.

And yet, any honest judge would have to conclude he is one of the great communicators of all time. You could start with his communication of the mission statements above. What good is a mission statement if nobody knows you have one. But his 108M Twitter fans, 110,000 employees, and probably a huge percent of the global population know his company's mission statements.

Most might point to Twitter as the evidence of his ability to communicate. I would counter that it is his amazing willingness to sit down with pundits and podcasters and thought leaders on YouTube and other media. He not only sits down but will spend an hour or more transparently talking about his passions, quirks, and plans. There is no other business leader like this.

I started writing articles and books in my industry when I was in my twenties to generate communication with potential customers and suppliers. It worked. Musk has given us the perfect example of how to reach a mass audience by just being human. Any business owner can take a page from this example and build a following through communicating their vision to the audience they are seeking to lead.

Burn the Boats Mentality

Elon Musk needs no introduction on this one. He famously had to decide which baby to feed in 2008. Both SpaceX and Tesla were on the brink of bankruptcy. Finding adequate new capital from investors or loans was not happening. Here is how Elon describes this time:

"I could either pick SpaceX or Tesla or split the money I had left between them. That was a tough decision. If I split the money, maybe both of them would die. If I gave the money to just one company, the probability of it surviving was greater, but then it would mean certain death for the other company. I debated that over and over.

"And when you put your energy into building something, it's your baby, so I couldn't choose. I put the money into both and thank goodness they both came through."

SpaceX stayed alive by the skin of its teeth, and so did Tesla - if things had just gone a little differently, both companies would be dead.

This is just one example of many that could be cited. If you've ever run a business, you've probably had those moments. But success comes to those who go all in. Even if that particular fight turns out the wrong way, the character one builds will serve the owner well into the future.

Relentless Pursuit of the Mission

In a related, but distinct trait, Musk is also known for being relentless. This shows up in his 16/7 workday schedule, his insistence on setting what often seem like impossible goals, and his pressure on all employees and suppliers to meet exacting standards.

When there are tough times that demand over-the-top relentlessness, there has to be a source of motivation. A desire to enrich oneself is seldom enough motivation. Fear of failure, feelings of responsibility to staff, customers, or employees are better motivators. But getting up early and working until it hurts, day after day, week after week, in the face of doom, is most often made possible because the mission drives one to keep going.

Fearless

One of the major causes of business failure is fear. Owners fear to pick up the phone and call a needed supplier, a prospect, or even a customer who has a problem. Owners fear to walk into a room full of strangers in order to network. Owners fear to look at their financials, dreading the prospect of unexpected losses. The list of fears could fill a book: Success, failure, risk, loss, death, illness, abandonment, loneliness, speaking, spiders, and more.

Elon Musk wanted to buy a rocket. He picked up the phone and set an appointment with the Russian government official who was in charge of selling obsolete missiles. He flew to Russia, negotiated with this official, and didn't like the deal (The official literally spit on his shoe as evidence of his contempt for the entire meeting). On the way home, he did a back-of-the-napkin analysis of what it would cost to build a rocket. Then he called a friend from college and asked if the friend could help him learn to build rockets. Today we have SpaceX rockets blasting off almost weekly.

Fearlessness like that can make all the difference in success and failure.

Tireless

For over 20 years, Elon Musk has worked 80 hours a week or more. He almost never takes vacations. He is now the richest person in the world, yet he continues to work these kinds of hours. He isn't working to become a Trillionaire. There is almost no difference in his lifestyle between being worth $50m and multiple billions. He is working towards the mission.

Elon has stated that his work ethic makes him multiple times more valuable: "*Work* like hell. I mean you just have to put in 80-to-100-hour *weeks* every *week*. [This] improves the odds of success."

Work life balance matters. Understanding your purpose matters. Having time to spend with family, friends, avocations, and spiritual retreats matter. But the success of your business may require some very serious time sacrifices for months or even years.

Sense of Urgency

"If we operate with extreme urgency, we have a chance of making life multi-planetary. It's still just a chance, not for sure. If we don't act with extreme urgency, that chance is probably zero." Elon Musk

I must admit that my greatest frustrations often center on an employee's inability to understand the importance of urgency. But when an owner doesn't get it, they are asking to be outrun by their competition.

To be clear, this doesn't mean driving yourself to the point of mental or physical exhaustion resulting in some kind of emotional or physical illness. There is a way to pace your day, your project, or your goals that allows for that work life balance but doesn't allow for a slacker attitude when it comes to moving things along as if the wolf is at the door. Various wolves are always at the door. VW, GM, Ford, and other competitors are not just going to lie down and let Tesla take over the auto business. (Though sometimes it seems like it.)

There must be a sense that any competitor is working just as hard as you are, or harder, to produce a better battery, motor, or software setup. Tesla's sense of urgency is evident wherever you look. They are constantly improving, constantly inventing, always iterating.

Humble

I often ask myself, "How does anyone with massive success, especially if exposed to the public view, deal with the idea of their achievement and all that it represents? We know that some don't handle it well. Others, like Musk, seem to do okay. But why?

It appears to me that Musk remains humble. What exactly do we mean by humble? He does not fall prey to the idea that he is the center of the universe or that he knows everything. While sometimes it may seem otherwise as Elon interjects himself into issues like the Ukraine war, millions of folks do so with far less available information.

He has what psychologists call "openness." He has strong opinions but is open to having his mind changed. He is interested in your opinion on everything from philosophy to the way to engineer a wheel.

Openness is a necessary part of true creativity, and he has proven himself to be one of the most creative minds of all times. We can only hope that his massive wealth, incredible string of successes, and the growing mob of fans doesn't go to his head. According to many who have been interviewed on this exact subject, he is, in person, the same as he is on stage.

In my book, *The Elon Musk Method*, I have a much more detailed look at the ways that business owners can learn from Elon Musk. The chapters are:

Introduction

1. The Early Years
2. The Accomplishments
3. The Vision

The Principles Musk Lives By

4. Curiosity is Foundational
5. Observation – Seeing the Forest and the Trees
6. Expertise in Every Aspect of the Business
7. Analysis is an Acquired Skill
8. Asking Big Questions
9. Rule Breaking is Essential to Vision
10. Visionary
11. Leadership – Musk Style
12. Goal Setting
13. Networking Is a Core Value
14. Valuing all Human Resources
15. Executing on the Vision
16. Risk Taking – Of Course
17. Overcoming Obstacles
18. Creating Quality
19. Insists on Incremental Improvement
20. Relentlessness - Passion Plus Persistence

CHAPTER 4

Tesla, Inc. ($TSLA)

by Randy Kirk

Tesla is the 6th most valuable company in the world by market cap (share price times number of shares). It has reached this lofty perch in record time, a mere 16 years. The company is worth almost as much as the combined values of all other car makers. Many pundits believe that Tesla will be the largest company on earth in value, sales, and profits, and soon. Elon Musk said in the Q3 earnings call that Tesla has a path to a valuation of $4.5T, not counting Optimus. As we will later show, we agree, wholeheartedly.

This section of the book is designed to take a very deep dive at all things Tesla. There are at least 20 start-up companies or divisions. We will not look at all of them, but we will look at most. What we are really trying to accomplish here is to provide huge amounts of clarity in lay terms about the prospects for this company, and how its future will impact everyone's future.

To be complete in our description of these companies, their products, their future, and the impact on Elon's personal wealth, it will be necessary to start at the beginning and discuss some basics and fundamentals that might be well known to many readers. However, we will also attempt to offer as much material as possible that will speak to more advanced followers of Musk, Tesla, and SpaceX.

We promise that every reader will learn many new aspects of the story on almost every page. We will keep biographical information to a minimum, but I think it is very instructive to know some history about Musk.

Musk speaks often of two books that have been a source for his worldview, including Isaac Asimov's *Foundation* series. This collection tells the work of Hari Seldon, who invents a method of predicting the future based on crowd behavior. Seldon predicts a 30,000-year Dark Ages and creates a plan to save humanity by creating colonies of humans on other planets. Sound familiar?

"Asimov certainly was influential because he was seriously paralleling Gibbon's Decline and Fall of the Roman Empire, *but he applied that to a sort of modern galactic empire," Musk explains. "The lesson I drew from that is you should try to take the set of actions that are likely to prolong civilization, minimize the probability of a dark age and reduce the length of a dark age if there is one."* Rolling Stone Interview

The second book of influence was *The Hitchhiker's Guide to the Galaxy*, by Douglas Adams.

I guess when I was around 12 or 15 ... I had an existential crisis, and I was reading various books on trying to figure out the meaning of life and what does it all mean? It all seemed quite meaningless and then we happened to have some books by Nietzsche and Schopenhauer in the house, which you should not read at age 14 (laughter). It is bad, it's really negative. So, then I read Hitchhikers Guide to the Galaxy *which is quite positive I think, and it highlighted an important point which is that a lot of times the question is harder than the answer. And if you can properly phrase the question, then the answer is the easy part. So, to the degree that we can better understand the universe, then we can better know what questions to ask. Then whatever the question is that most*

Making The Future Awesome | 34

approximates: what's the meaning of life? That's the question we can ultimately get closer to understanding. And so, I thought to the degree that we can expand the scope and scale of consciousness and knowledge, then that would be a good thing." - FreshDialogues.com 2013

Elon Musk's interest in electric cars goes way back, well before he hooked up with two enthusiasts who had started an electric car company which would eventually be named Tesla. Musk believed that the future of cars would be electric and thought he'd like to be part of that transformation.

He often talks about the ways he hoped he would make a difference which he had first contemplated in University: Making life multi-planetary, accelerating the transmission to sustainable energy, the Internet broadly speaking, genetics, and artificial intelligence (AI.)

"In college, I sort of thought helping with electrification of cars was how it would start out. That's actually what I worked on as an intern, was advanced ultra-capacitors, to see if there would be a breakthrough relative to batteries for energy storage in cars. And then, when I came out to go to Stanford, that's what I was going to be doing my grad studies on, was working on advanced energy storage technologies for electric cars."

Inverse.com
https://www.inverse.com/article/21160-elon-musk-college-days-of-yore

But Musk got sidetracked by the more immediate opportunities he saw that were related to the Internet. This led to his outside the box idea to create an Internet application that became what we now know as Google Maps or Yelp. Musk believed that the Yellow Pages would be an historical oddity, and that you and I would use the internet to find a restaurant, bike shop, or dentist. This was Zip2.

Zip2 was sold to Compaq Computer less than five years after starting up. Elon's share of the sale was a measly $22,000,000.

Any thoughts of getting into electric cars were set aside again. Musk was fascinated by banking, and he believed that traditional banking was old-fashioned and clunky. He took his winnings and started X.com, which would, just three years later, merge with Confinity (aka PayPal). This time he cashed a check for $165,000,000.

How about a little math? For five years of work at Zip2, Elon earned $4.4m per year. For three years working at X.com, Elon's earnings accelerated to over $50m per year. You could do a bit of foreshadowing here, as his average earnings (from stock only) at Tesla would now be about $10b per year.

Recently Musk put the value of his time this way: Every minute is worth $1,000,000.

Cars would take a back seat again, however. Elon believes that the earth has a greater than zero chance that a catastrophic event will destroy human life or come very close. Among the possibilities would be: nuclear war, a really big asteroid, eruption of a super volcano, a pandemic, or simply the deterioration of the sun's energy which might result in the earth being too cold to sustain human life within the next 20,000,000 years.

Elon also believes in exploration, adventure, and, "**There have to be reasons that you get up in the morning and you want to live**."

He set his sights on colonizing Mars. His first idea was to merely pull off a stunt that would cause NASA to get back into the game.

He wanted to get a rocket to Mars that would automatically deposit some plant life, then automatically water and fertilize it to show it would be possible to sustain life on Mars. He hoped the publicity would inspire those in power to restart the US space exploration effort.

With this plan in mind, Musk approached Russia with an offer to buy some old rockets. When the Russians wouldn't sell him a rocket at a reasonable price, Elon decided to build the rocket himself.

Using $100,000,000 of the PayPal money, he started SpaceX. We will take a deeper dive into SpaceX after our section on Tesla. Some believe that SpaceX will ultimately be more valuable (Musk owns about 50% of SpaceX), but my personal analysis is that Tesla will be the primary driver of the trillion-dollar milestone. SpaceX could easily be responsible for the second $T, but I also think Tesla will also be a larger piece of the second $T.

But back to Tesla and electric cars.

J.B. Straubel should have his own biography. He'd been hanging out with Elon for a long time, and in 2003 he knew about Musk's interest in electric cars. JB suggested to Elon that they take a test drive in a hand-built sports car called the tZero, which, at a recommended $220,000, would take the driver from 0-60 in 3.6 seconds and had a range of 200 miles.

Elon was so taken with this concept car that he encouraged the company, AC Propulsion, to take the tZero to market. They demurred. Elon asked: *"If you're not going to commercialize the tZero, do you mind if I do it?"* They said they were fine with that, and that they knew another team that had similar ambitions. They sent Elon to visit Tesla Motors' team: Martin Eberhard, Marc Tarpenning, and Ian Wright. They were working on an electric powered roadster but needed venture capital money.

Back in 2001, Tarpenning, being a bit of a space nerd, had dragged Eberhard along to see a PayPal cofounder speak at a Mars Society conference held at Stanford. His name was Elon Musk, and his ideas about what to do in the space industry were strikingly clear. Tarpenning and Eberhard introduced themselves. – Business Insider

Eberhard sends Musk an email:
"We would love to talk to you about Tesla Motors," he wrote, *"particularly if you might be interested in investing in the company. I believe that you have driven AC Propulsion's tZero car. If so, you already know that a high-performance electric car can be made. We would like to convince you that we can do so profitably, creating a company with very high potential for growth, and at the same time breaking the compromise between driving performance and efficiency."*

Musk replied that evening.
"Sure," he said. *"Friday this week or Friday next week would work."*
Business Insider

Musk had been interested in saving the planet from global warming through the adoption of sustainable energy since college, so he sinks $10 million into this little company and helps out with engineering and design. He also becomes chairman of the board.

By 2007, Tesla Motors had a working product, had created quite a fuss, and had orders to build more. Unfortunately, the co-founders and CEO were in over their heads. Musk took over leadership just as the economy was tanking and the major auto companies were headed for bankruptcy due to the great recession.

But Musk was determined to create an electric car for a very specific purpose of proving his notion that it was possible to produce a compelling electric car for an affordable price. He stated that since he had already put $55 million into the company, he might as well take over the wheel. He became CEO.

Tesla history trivia: *"We didn't actually come up with the Tesla Motors name. Bought trademark off Brad Siewert for $75k in late 2004. He'd originally filed for it in 1994. Our alternative name was Faraday, which was used by a competitor several years later."*

Today Tesla has at least 21 current or planned income streams, has just completed construction of the 9th largest building in the world (by square feet of floor space) in Austin Texas, and is the 6th largest company in the world by market cap. Many believe that Tesla will pass Apple to become the largest company in the world within three years. There is also a chance that revenues, EBITA (Earnings before interest, taxes, and amortization), and cash flow will also be the largest of any company in about the same timeframe.

Who are the leaders now?

Rank	Name	Market Cap	Price	Today	Price (30 days)
1	Apple AAPL	$2.851 T	$174.72	0.37%	
^1 2	Microsoft MSFT	$2.276 T	$303.68	-0.14%	
v1 3	Saudi Aramco 2222.SR	$2.269 T	$11.36	0.00%	
4	Alphabet (Google) GOOG	$1.872 T	$2,830	0.15%	
5	Amazon AMZN	$1.676 T	$3,295	0.69%	
6	Tesla TSLA	$1.044 T	$1,011	-0.32%	
7	Berkshire Hathaway BRK-A	$793.70 B	$538,949	1.92%	

For market cap, Tesla only needs to be just more than triple the current share price to pass Apple. Some pundits think that Tesla's current share price is way beyond understanding. But others are already projecting Tesla to increase by another 100% by the end of 2023 from the bear market levels we are experiencing in October 2022.

Elon stated in their first quarter '22 earnings call that he estimates that sales will increase an average of 50% per year, although some years may be more, and others not quite reach 50%.

Tesla's revenues are currently under $100B, which keeps it out of the top 100 club in terms of revenues. However, with the opening of two huge new manufacturing facilities, a conservative estimate would put 2022 revenues at almost $100B, and 2023 at $150B

Rank	Name	Revenue	Price	Today	Price (30 days)	Country
1	Walmart	$572.75 B	$143.45	0.43%		USA
2	Amazon	$469.82 B	$3,295	0.89%		USA
3	Apple	$378.32 B	$174.72	0.37%		USA
4	PetroChina	$374.35 B	$52.54	4.09%		China
5	Berkshire Hathaway	$354.63 B	$538,949	1.32%		USA
6	Sinopec	$352.27 B	$48.28	2.34%		China
7	Saudi Aramco	$328.62 B	$11.36	0.02%		S. Arabia
8	CVS Health	$292.11 B	$108.56	0.41%		USA
9	UnitedHealth	$285.27 B	$513.03	-0.08%		USA
10	Volkswagen	$279.70 B	$166.53	-0.53%		Germany

While $150B in revenue would have Tesla only moving halfway up the top 100 companies for revenue, the measure of success is in earnings, and if you're Warren Buffet, free cash flow. How is Tesla faring on these two measures?

While estimates vary (a lot), Tesla is conservatively going to have $15B in earnings in 2022, which would put them around #50, and for 2023, earnings will likely hit $25B or approximately #25 on the list.

No large market cap company in history has ever grown to this size this quickly or been able to continue to increase revenues by such high percentages at these levels.

Please visit https://companiesmarketcap.com for much more detail on all of these charts.

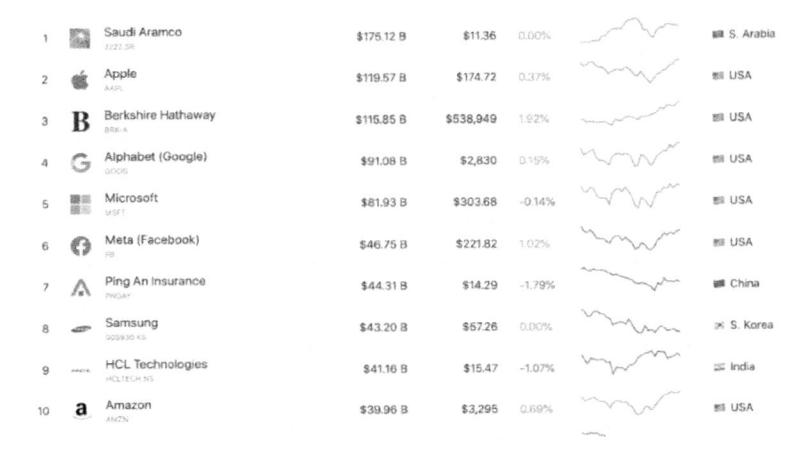

#		Company	Market Cap	Price	Change		Country
1		Saudi Aramco 2222.SR	$175.12 B	$11.36	0.00%		S. Arabia
2		Apple AAPL	$119.57 B	$174.72	0.37%		USA
3	B	Berkshire Hathaway BRK-A	$115.85 B	$538,949	1.92%		USA
4	G	Alphabet (Google) GOOG	$91.08 B	$2,830	0.15%		USA
5		Microsoft MSFT	$81.93 B	$303.68	-0.14%		USA
6		Meta (Facebook) FB	$46.75 B	$221.82	1.02%		USA
7	A	Ping An Insurance PNGAY	$44.31 B	$14.29	-1.79%		China
8		Samsung 005930.KS	$43.20 B	$57.26	0.00%		S. Korea
9		HCL Technologies HCLTECH.NS	$41.16 B	$15.47	-1.07%		India
10	a	Amazon AMZN	$39.96 B	$3,295	0.69%		USA

Now we come to free cash flow. Investopedia.com says:

"Free cash flow (FCF) represents the cash a company generates after accounting for cash outflows to support operations and maintain its capital assets. Unlike earnings or net income, free cash flow is a measure of profitability that excludes the non-cash expenses of the income statement and includes spending on equipment and assets as well as changes in working capital from the balance sheet."

Tesla's free cash flow in the 4th quarter of 2021 was over $4B, and over $2B for Q1 '22, which, if annualized, would provide $12-16B in free cash flow by year end 2022. This would place Tesla at about 10% of Apple's FCF and 25% of Microsoft. Tesla's prospects for increases in FCF will put them in the top 10 within a year or two, and they will be duking it out for top cash printing machine with Apple by 2025. At that point, the future run rate is almost beyond comprehension, if it weren't for the hard facts we will present showing the cash generation power to come.

Making The Future Awesome | 42

CHAPTER 5
Tesla Divisions

by Randy Kirk

From a nascent manufacturer of a hand-built roadster in 2007, Tesla has become the World's leader in battery electric vehicles (BEVs) by unit sales, revenues, and profits. While some, like Volkswagen, Ford, Stellantis, and General Motors are promising to pass Tesla by 2026 or so, the magnitude of merely catching Tesla at their current capacity is staggering to contemplate

Tesla's four auto plants are capable of producing at least three million cars per year now (Fremont 700K, Shanghai 1.2M, Berlin and Austin 500K each plus Semi and Cyber), with expectations that Austin and Berlin will be expanded, and that new gigafactory locations will be announced before the end of 2022. The closest current competitors in unit volume of BEVs are BYD and VW, who are each at roughly half Tesla's numbers.

Tesla has also shown that they can build a new plant in 12-18 months, depending on local regulations and other hurdles. No other company in the world has ever met these kinds of capabilities in creating huge scale manufacturing facilities for large products in such a short time. Other automakers typically take three years to build a plant.

Therefore, if any major company would strive to catch or pass Tesla in units produced or sold, they would need to build new plant capacity faster than Tesla. No current company CEO has made a public statement that offers any such detailed plan. Most only vaguely claim they will catch or pass Tesla in 2025 or beyond.

Tesla today is often characterized as a car manufacturer as the vast majority of their revenues are created by auto sales. However, the company has over 20 streams of income, some of which are poised to become significant, even by comparison with auto sales.

Following is a short synopsis of each revenue stream. By short, we only mean in comparison to what could be written. Almost every one of these "start-ups" could have a book devoted to their prospects, development, marketing, integration, competition, expected revenue and profits, and prospects of achieving success.

Many in the investment community still see Tesla as an auto manufacturer and are confused about the extreme multiples $TSLA stock is given compared to other automakers. Some get that Tesla is achieving much better margins on their vehicles and that their overhead is much lower as a percentage of revenue than legacy companies like General Motors, Ford, Volkswagen, Nissan, Toyota, and others. Most would also give Tesla some additional points for their explosive growth.

While the Tesla investment community and some analysts now understand that Tesla is way more than an automaker and deserves the multiple, the stock value (and thus Elon's stock equity) doesn't come close to pricing in the other 20+ income streams.

But, as of this writing, and probably until at least 2025, vehicles will be the largest producers of both top and bottom-line income, and thus are likely to provide the primary source of investor valuation strategies.

CHAPTER 6

The Valuation Story for Tesla Vehicles

by Randy Kirk

Tesla is currently the leader in BEV unit sales, dollar volume, and profit. BEV stands for battery electric vehicles and does not include hybrids.

It is important to be clear on the categories of competition. Tesla does not consider other BEV makers to be the competition. Rather, all those who make cars with internal combustion engines (ICE) are the competition. Market share comparisons by car model are interesting but are inconsequential to the Tesla plan. As long as Tesla's order books are backlogged by months, market share is not a very useful metric.

From a marketing perspective, Tesla is in a league of their own even more so than iPhone was 14 years ago. iPhone's margins were much higher than other makers. In fact, for many years, iPhone made more than 100% of all the profits in the smart phone business. This was because all of the other makers were losing money.

With Tesla's auto margins at around 30%, and net profits in the 15%+ range, they are currently making more than 100% of all BEV profits, since as of this writing, no other BEV product is profitable. Tesla has done this with no advertising, currently no US PR department, and without exploiting or even attempting to exploit a long list of possible markets.

Image supplied by Jim Ringold

If their sales were ever to slow down even a little bit, these are some of the marketing arrows still in the quiver:

1. Advertising - Tesla has yet to spend a single dollar on advertising. As a result, a large part of the population has no real idea about the benefits of owning a BEV, and specifically a Tesla. Assuming advertising works, Tesla could easily spend $1B per year without blinking an eye.
2. Public Relations (PR) - Tesla closed their PR department a few years ago. Most auto companies have huge PR staffs. These folks wine and dine the media, set up events, respond to interview requests, do fact checks regarding news related to their companies or products, and find ways to place articles about the cars or the company.
3. Sponsorships - Auto companies are one of the leading sources of sponsorships. They sponsor everything from racing cars to local car shows.

Making The Future Awesome | 46

4. Influencers - The world is full of influencers working YouTube and social media channels in an effort to persuade you to buy products and services. Tesla has dozens or even hundreds of such influencers, but they are not paid. They could pay influencers to expand their reach.
5. Product placement - Movies, TV shows, and other media are paid $millions to place products in their content. Teslas would be an ideal candidate due to their explosive acceleration and power.
6. Sales and discounts - Tesla's are only sold by Tesla. There is no dealer network, no middlemen, no third parties of any kind between the Tesla sales team and the consumer. This allows Tesla to maintain their one-price-fits-all, no-haggle, approach. It also means that they would be able to use pricing strategies to open new markets, respond to competitive challenges, and bump sales in any sales lull by offering contests, sales, promotional discounts, and other time-honored methods.
7. Rental cars - Famously, Hertz became the first major rental car company to buy huge numbers (at least 100,000) of Teslas for their fleet. Tesla made no effort to generate rental car sales, and Hertz received no discount for doing so. The potential for actively selling cars to rental car companies is untapped.
8. Corporate fleet sales - I don't actually know for certain that Tesla doesn't already have salespeople trying to sell cars to major corporations who supply cars for some of their employees. But I suspect we would know if they did.
9. Police cars - Tesla could make a car specifically designed for police work, as many car companies do. Because they are the quickest and fastest cars available today, and due to their low energy and maintenance costs, they would seem ideal for this largely untapped market. Many police

departments are already buying stock Teslas for their fleets and finding fantastic results in cost savings with lower down time for repairs and maintenance.
10. Government fleets - Once again, there doesn't appear to be a team at Tesla working to qualify Tesla's for government bids, or to lobby government buyers to change the requirements to be more prescriptive of BEVs or Tesla. It may not be public knowledge that many government buyers at all levels create bidding proposals that are designed to fit one product or a small group of products.
11. Government lobbying - Auto companies generally have large lobbying staffs that are attempting to pass legislation or stop legislation that affects their market. For example, Ford and GM have been lobbying for the new US rebate program for EVs (including hybrids.) Recently passed as the IRA (the ridiculously named, Inflation Reduction Act.)
12. Ride Sharing - While Musk has repeatedly shunned the idea of Tesla offering a ride sharing app with company owned cars, Hertz has offered a sweet deal for drivers in the Uber and Lift systems. Many are finding that they save enough money on gas to pay their entire monthly rental cost.
13. Other car and truck models –
    a. Most expect Tesla to eventually offer the model A, a smaller car that might also double as the robotaxi version with no steering wheel or pedals and a completely different interior layout. The consumer version would be in the $25,000 range. Elon has said this car will begin production in 2024. At the earnings call for 3rd quarter '22, he said this product is the entire focus of the automotive engineering team currently.

b. A second truck, possibly on the same chassis design as the Model A. This would be a small, two-seater truck.
c. At least one van designed for delivery and other work, which might also give a platform for an eight-passenger vehicle.
d. Boring Company is already using huge numbers of Tesla cars in the Las Vegas Loop. That loop is expanding, and other similar tunnels are likely to be built. There may eventually be many hundreds of such systems, many requiring autonomous cars to move folks in those systems.
e. Leasing - How could Tesla make their cars available to the masses while maintaining the current retail pricing. Extend the leases over more years, and still take possession at the end of the lease. Instead of 3-year leases, they could offer 5, 7, or even 10-year leases. They could even experiment with having the payments decrease each year. Maybe they start at $600 for two years, then drop to $500 for three. All kinds of unique approaches are possible when the cars' values are retained like Tesla's are.

Almost every other car company is using every one of the above to increase their exposure to consumers and bulk buyers of cars. Tesla currently saves the expense and sells every vehicle it can produce without needing these approaches.

CHAPTER 7

Competitive Moats

by Randy Kirk

"Patents are for the weak." - **Elon Musk**

Warren Buffett looks for three traits in corporations that determine if he is interested in an investment. He calls the combination a perpetual compounder: a wide moat, high return on capital employed, and customer loyalty. Tesla is a standout on all three. First the moats.

In a medieval castle, the moat was a defense to protect those inside the fortress from outsider attack. Likewise, a financial moat refers to any way in which a business can maintain competitive advantages over its competitors and protect its long-term profits and market share.

We will attempt to be comprehensive on each moat without going too deeply into the weeds. However, for several of these moats, we will risk being outside some of our reader's pay grade. (We have invited a couple of guest writers to help with these technical chapters that are outside my paygrade.)

We will identify and discuss 21 moats. Most companies would be happy to have one or two. I think you will see that these moats are all significant.

Investors love to see "edges" that one company owns that gives that company a moat. One of the most talked about moats in business today has been Apple's ecosystem. Buyers of one Apple product tend to also buy other compatible devices. Apple designs all their devices to work in a similar way, to be easily synced, and to be of impeccable style and quality.

Patents, other intellectual property rights, exclusive formulas, secret ingredients, designs, brands, unique materials, and exclusive contracts are just some of the kinds of moats that companies might have.

Moats can create an opportunity to completely dominate sales in a category. Moats allow for flexibility in pricing. Moats can be a source of very high profit margins and net, bottom line, profits. Apple is the poster child for moats providing them with immense profits.

The Tesla moats are very, very wide, and deep, and filled with crocodiles and piranhas. The following 21 chapters are all about the moats. If the Tesla community can get these 21 chapters into the hands of institutional investors, one can only wonder what might happen.

CHAPTER 8

Moat: The Blank Slate

by Randy Kirk

Tesla entered the BEV market with a blank slate in every way. They had no factories, reputation, employees, unions, attitudes, or culture. Elon was able to build the entire business according to his ways of doing things.

Other auto companies, called legacy automotive companies, have to build their BEV business on top of their existing businesses where their business concept and reputation are entrenched.

For instance, almost every legacy auto company has the following: massive debt; top heavy management; a buy and assemble approach; unions; factories full of ICE manufacturing equipment and molds; a consumer view of them as promoting ice vehicles that pollute and use gasoline; a dealer network that takes a percent of the profit; and a net profit built on maintenance and repairs rather than the initial sale.

Tesla has: almost no debt; a distributed management approach; vertical integration of manufacturing; no unions; no old useless molds or dies, equipment or factories; a consumer view that includes innovative, modern, and green; no dealer network; and a profit approach that relies on the car itself, since Teslas require almost no maintenance or repairs.

The task for legacy automakers in overcoming the blank slate benefit that Tesla owns is daunting at least, and potentially impossible.

Of course, some startups in the US and China also have blank slates. So, this moat is not as impressive when comparing Tesla to those firms. But each of those companies are still subject to the other 20 moats.

CHAPTER 9

Moat: The "Manufacturing Plant is the Product"

by Randy Kirk

Manufacturing - Elon Musk says that the factory is the product. By this he means that Tesla has reimagined everything about the factory itself, and the results are beyond stunning.

Tesla's first inclination is to build all the parts for the car. They do use outside suppliers for some finished parts, but they build most of the car, themselves. They are manufacturers, not assemblers. This single fact results in more profits, faster and more improvements, fewer barriers to change, and unique characteristics throughout the vehicle, from the frunk to the door handles.

The factories themselves are unlike any other factory. Starting from the speed of construction to the cost of the facility; to the methods of painting; receiving supplies, and assembly; to the speed of output and the square footage needed to produce a certain volume. All of these are revolutionary to the point that their competitors have even commented on their need to catch Tesla.

But, of course, Elon Musk will not stop improving. His entire approach is based on fail fast and fail forward, continuous and rapid improvement, and rewarding innovation.

While each new factory (and Tesla plans to create 6-10 more before 2030) will have improvements, by and large, the basic conceptual design is now baked in, thereby reducing the cost for future factories.

We will take a deeper dive into the stunning differences in manufacturing and factory approach in future chapters.

CHAPTER 10

Moat: He who makes the Best Battery, Wins

by Randy Kirk

We will address the battery moat regarding the energy storage part of the business under the energy section. Here we will merely address the shocking lead that Tesla has in BEV battery technology.

BEV batteries are judged on very few specs: Energy density, recharge speed, useful energy capacity, battery life (charge/discharge cycles), and cost. For the consumer it boils down to how far can I go on a charge, how long does it take to recharge, and how long the battery will last. Then throw in the bogie; are the raw materials available?

All of these specifications are fluid depending on which is of greater importance. Do you prefer longer life, even if you get fewer miles on a charge? Are you willing to pay more to get more miles per charge or to fill up the battery faster?

Tesla would lay claim to having battery tech right now that puts them at least a few years ahead of anyone in the BEV or storage business. The new 4680 battery takes advantage of many of the other moats in this list to provide Tesla with an unassailable lead.

The technology is ahead of its competitors. The ability to use various materials depending on application provides specs/price substantially below others. Tesla's vertical integration appears to be stretching even to some aspects of mining and refining. Their scope is unlike any other existing battery maker or car company, thus creating advantages of scale.

We will tackle a bit more of the battery tech in Chapter 40, **He who has the BIGGEST Battery, Wins**.

CHAPTER 11

Moats Abound all over the Factory

by Randy Kirk

You won't find a patents category in this list. Patents are commonly the most important moat. But Elon has open sourced all patents. Why would he do this? He says that patents are for the weak.

Moreover, the actual mission of the company is to accelerate the World's transition to sustainable energy. He wants his competitors to get better at making EVs, as he believes that all cars will be EVs by the end of this decade, and that Tesla can't make all of them. He'll be happy to make 25% or about 20,000,000 BEVs in 2030.

So, if there is no patent moat, why is Musk so certain he'll retain leadership? Simple. He believes that Tesla will innovate so fast that the patents will be old news. Companies that rely on Tesla patents will be years behind when they start attempting to replicate the patented items.

Tesla makes even small parts that are revolutionary and hard to copy. But at the other end of the spectrum, foremost among Tesla's innovation in tooling and parts is the gigapress technology for building the chassis of the car.

The typical (for even Tesla) method for building the major parts of the chassis has been to bolt and weld many dozens of parts together.

Tesla decided that there would be multiple benefits to make the entire back section and the entire front section of the chassis out of an aluminum casting, eliminating hundreds of parts and over 500 robots from the assembly line.

The gigacasting machine required utilization of state-of-the-art casting equipment, and the development of an entirely new type of aluminum. Some other makers may decide to copy this approach, but it will take years if they can do it at all.

Gigapress in Austin Gigafactory. Image supplied by Jim Ringold

For a detailed YouTube dive into the entire gigapress approach, see the fascinating videos on the Limiting Factor's YouTube Channel. https://www.youtube.com/channel/UCIFn7ONIJHyC-lMnb7Fm_jw

The octovalve heat pump is another breakthrough on a smaller level. Every automobile must use air, water, or oil as coolants or heaters for various processes, including cooling/heating the passenger cabin, cooling the battery pack (BEVs), cooling the oil for the motor and transmission, and cooling refrigerant for any radiators.

While Teslas don't have all of those functions (no cooling for transmission, for instance), there is still a big need for moving air and water. Using first principles approaches, Tesla started from scratch and developed a heat pump that used fewer parts and was substantially more efficient. So efficient that it added 10% to the vehicle range as it used less electricity to perform these functions.

I am unaware as of this writing of any other company attempting to duplicate these capabilities, though there may be.

For details and a clever video that shows the inner workings of the octovalve go to https://metrology.news/ct-scanning-looks-inside-tesla-model-y-octovalve/

Elon Musk says that he looked back at airplane wing innovations to realize that at one time the airplane carried the fuel as weight, thereby using fuel to carry fuel. The airline industry realized that it could replace structural elements of the wing with fuel storage that would turn the fuel into a zero or less than zero contributor to the weight of the airplane.

Elon then realized that he could do the same thing with the battery pack. Instead of carrying the batteries as weight, he could make them structural, reducing the overall weight of the vehicle, taking out the cost of the materials used to create that part of the structure, and eliminating complexity and steps in manufacturing.

These are just three examples of major changes in the auto manufacturing process, but it would be simple to write an entire book just on the unique approaches being used by Tesla to assemble the car and create the various parts. Next, we'll look at another breakthrough in the ways cars are made in the 21st century - vertical integration.

CHAPTER 12

Moat: Vertical Integration at Scale

by Randy Kirk

The world's auto makers are primarily just assemblers of parts made by OEMs (original equipment manufacturers). There are OEMs for motors and wheels and seats and axles and batteries and on and on it goes. The idea is that these specialists can make the products in quantity, and thereby at low cost, then sell it to the makers for less than they could make it themselves.

The various OEMs compete for the business of the car makers, and the lowest bid for a part which passes clearly defined specifications wins the bid. As in any such system there is plenty of room for dishonest behavior by company buyers, inspectors, and the supplier companies.

But the system has worked well for a very long time. What wasn't broke was unlikely to be changed.

Imagine for a minute, however, that every part is made up of raw materials that have to be mined and refined, then shipped to various stages of the manufacturing process. These parts and pieces would then be shipped to the final assembly of the motor or radiator, etc. This final part would then need to be shipped to the automakers various plants served by that supplier where they would be added to the final assembly line. The finished automobiles made at that plant would now be SHIPPED to dealers around the world.

Elon Musk saw things differently. Begin with the concept of a giant factory where every possible part would be manufactured in one building, though some parts, like tires, still need to be supplied by OEMs.

Now source the raw materials as close to that plant as possible to further cut shipping costs (and CO^2 into the environment.) Create one or more of these Gigafactories on each continent, so that the shipping of the final product goes only to that continent.

This is referred to as vertical integration, and besides saving on shipping costs, it has many other benefits.

Fast innovation and continuous improvement - All Tesla engineers are located in the Gigafactory. If there is an improvement, it is possible to test that improvement within days. No need to figure it out with a 3rd party, then try to integrate the possible change into the line where there might be unexpected issues.

Tesla doesn't have model years; they have model weeks. The cars are constantly being improved, and each improvement might only take a day or a week to finalize.

As noted above the assembly approach to auto making is intended to save money. When a car company has 100 models and some of the parts go into 10 or 20 or all 100, this approach might make sense.

After 16 years, Tesla produces four models with the Semi coming in December '22 and the Cybertruck due in mid '23. The Model 3 and Model Y share 70% of the same parts. The model S and X also share many parts with each other and with the other models.

With the scale that is created by making hundreds of thousands of four models, Tesla can make the parts far cheaper than would be possible if they were purchasing these from OEMs.

Vertical integration also reduces issues with quality control, as the control is now "in house." You are not depending on an OEM factory to inspect the parts, and then doing secondary inspections after arrival in the assembling factory. You don't have to worry about dishonest buyers or inspectors. And you can make the part any way you please. You don't have to worry about the limitations of the supplier or the supplier's potential priorities getting in the way of making your parts.

Will other legacy auto makers and even new companies follow Tesla regarding vertical integration? Maybe, but it would seem to be hard to get to scale, and currently, we are not seeing anyone truly take this direction.

CHAPTER 13

Moat: Software Technology in the Car and the Factory

by Lars Strandridder

There might be some Tesla or Elon haters (aka $TSLAQ) who would maintain that Tesla's software inside the vehicle is not by far the best of any automaker. However, the serious pundits and experts would disagree and have plenty of facts at their disposal.

Again, Tesla is also making its own software. This is compared to other OEMs that get their software from third party software companies. Herbert Diess, ex-CEO of VW, has said back in 2020 that not one single line of code comes from VW. It comes from many different software companies.

VW tried to invest 6 billion dollars in Cariad software, and has hired thousands of software engineers, to create VW's automotive operating system of the future. But so far, the future project is mainly producing trouble. The various programs are severely delayed and incompatible with each other and promised leaps in quality have failed to materialize.

The old car makers are having big trouble just making good reliable software, because they are not in the software business.

But software will become an increasing part of the whole car experience.

As Herbert Diess also said back in 2019 "Software will account for 90 percent of future innovations in the car". Tesla has been making their own software from the beginning. Tesla is as much a software company as they are a car company.

And Tesla has had the ability to make 'over the air' (OTA) updates since 2012. Most other automakers have yet to show they can do that.

My three-year-old Tesla Model 3 has many more features today than it did when I bought it. Even such improvements as 5% more peak power and 20% faster charging were added over the air. There have been so many new software features over the last three years that it would take up a whole chapter on its own just to list them.

Tesla's software is very fluent, responsive, and intuitive. It has many great built-in features that makes a road trip in a Tesla fun, easy and enjoyable.

One example would be the car's navigation software, it knows where all Tesla superchargers are located, so when you speak or type in your destination, the car will automatically tell you when you need to stop for charging, how long you need to charge, and then even notify you when you are ready to continue your journey. This will all show up on your screen, or if you leave the car for a bio-break, you'll see it on your app.

The computer will even tell you if you need to keep under a certain speed to reach your destination or the planned supercharger. It will preheat the battery as you come close to the charging station, so the battery is ready to take the maximum charge, speeding up the process.

Tesla has hundreds of unique software features that make it stand out. And Tesla has invented and created these in house. Everyone else really depends on other software companies and has to use software like Apple Carplay or Android Auto. They have not been able to make software that is able to do what Apple's Carplay can do.

While everyone else's software starts to look more like each other, Tesla stands out with its operating system which is constantly improving and getting new features like their entertainment systems, with Netflix, Disney+, YouTube, and a whole game center.

You see, Tesla stands out from everyone else, simply because they can make the software themselves. Tesla is a software company. That also shows in the factories. Every single software that is used in Tesla, is made by Tesla.

This also means that Tesla doesn't need to pay for a software license to Microsoft or anyone else, because it is all Tesla's own software running the company.

The factory itself is also running on software made by Tesla. Artificial Intelligence (AI) is pretty much running the whole factory. Tesla FSD software came from one of Tesla's AI systems in the factory that was running on the Tesla "Bamboo line." The Bamboo line is where the cars go through every test that is non-destructive, without human supervision. Tesla has eliminated most human approvals, which cuts out human bottlenecks. It is the AI in the factory that approves the car at each step of the process and sends the car to its next stage.

CHAPTER 14

Moat: The Amazing Tesla Fan Base by Lars Strandridder

One thing that is very difficult to place a value on is Tesla's fan base. How do you arrive at a value to Tesla of a customer who takes his new car home and then proceeds to take every neighbor, friend, relative, and workmate for a drive. Some say that every Tesla sold is a set up for the next sale due to simple word of mouth.

Tesla's fan base is a huge moat that is unmatched by any other company in history. Tesla does not spend any money on advertising, but still Tesla is the world's fastest growing brand. Tesla didn't ask people like me (Lars) to create hundreds of videos on our YouTube channels. Yet, there are thousands of people like me creating videos, podcasts, blog posts, Instagram content, Twitter activity, and more. Fans are making free advertising for Tesla.

If you search on YouTube, you see there are hundreds of videos about Tesla uploaded every single day, and it is not just about their cars. Tesla factories are probably some of the best documented construction in the history of humans building buildings. There are drone pilots out almost every single day at the Shanghai, Berlin, and Texas factories taking video about the progress of the construction of those facilities, counting the cars to estimate production, and contemplating the use of new buildings that are going up. Even Freemont has drone operators showing activity at the oldest and most built out location.

We have probably never seen a bigger fan base than what we see with Tesla. Apple might be the only one that is close, and they are the largest company in the world by value.

Tesla has a whole community helping one another out, sharing information, and making big events all over the world for Tesla fans, investors and EVs enthusiasts like the Tesla TakeOver in California. I can't think of any other car brand where we have ever seen anything on this magnitude from fans.

Elon Musk also has one of the world's largest number of followers on Twitter with 108.8M. Only Barack Obama, Justine Bieber, and Katy Perry, have more, with Elon taking 4th place. It is very likely that he will pass all of the others in the next few months to reign as number one here, too!

Former U.S. President Barack Obama (@BarackObama) is the most-followed person on Twitter, with over 133 million followers.

Canadian singer Justin Bieber (@justinbieber) is the most-followed musician on Twitter, with over 114 million followers.

American singer Katy Perry (@katyperry) is the most-followed woman on Twitter, with over 108 million followers.

Elon Musk (@elonmusk) is the most followed CEO on Twitter, with over 106 million followers.

Portuguese footballer Cristiano Ronaldo (@Cristiano) is the most-followed sports personality and European on Twitter, with over 103 million followers.

Prime minister of India Narendra Modi (@narendramodi) is the most followed Asian on Twitter, with over 82 million followers.

The result is that, when Elon Musk makes a tweet, the world reacts. Recently, he joked about buying Manchester United football club, and their stock price jumped up. Or when Elon Musk joked about buying Coca-Cola to put the cocaine back in, that is now the second most liked tweet in history.

> **Elon Musk** @elonmusk
>
> Next I'm buying Coca-Cola to put the cocaine back in
>
> Oversæt Tweet
> 02.56 · 28.04.2022 · Twitter for iPhone

We have not seen anything like this before from a CEO of a car company or any other company for that matter. It doesn't hurt that Elon has a wry sense of humor, has boyish charm, and has not become too big a deal for his fans. They appreciate that he is an active, almost daily presence, on Twitter.

Herbert Diess, VW former CEO, has about 50K followers on Twitter. GM's CEO Mary Barra has about 65K, Tim Cook CEO of Apple has about 13M. Even Joe Biden, the President of the United States, has only about 25M followers.

Here's the amazing part. Elon Musk can make updates or advertise for upcoming events or products on twitter, and within minutes, millions of people will be notified. On top of that, hundreds of thousands on Twitter will retweet, then YouTubers will make videos about it. Others will share the information on other platforms with their followers as well.

Twitter alone is a pretty powerful moat where Tesla has access to hundreds of millions of Tesla owners, prospective owners, investors, and just the curious that make up Elon Musk's fan base. Tesla, it might be noted, only has about 17 million followers on Twitter.

Amazingly, the Twitter community gives Tesla another advantage. Customers can get in touch with Elon Musk, if they are lucky, on twitter. We have seen many times where a fan comes up with an idea for a new feature for the car, and Elon Musk reacts to it on twitter, then implements the changes into the car. If it is a software feature, we have seen Tesla implement them with OTA updates a few days or months later.

One such idea that Elon didn't pick up on straight away was the waypoint in the navigation system. He heard customers ask for the feature over and over on Twitter. Then someone shouted it at him during the Model S Plaid event and he responded, "You really want a waypoint? Okay does everyone here want waypoints? (Crowd screaming) Okay, fine! We will do waypoints." Five months later Tesla's navigation system got waypoints with an OTA update. You will probably never see this with any other car company, where the CEO communicates directly with their customers almost every day. Then, more importantly, we see that the Techo King actually listens and implements ideas the fans propose. And fast!

Tesla has a decade of experience working closely with its fan base, and how to utilize it, which gives them a huge advantage over the competition. Tesla has an army of followers and fans that gladly help Tesla fight all the FUD that is being spread by short sellers and the companies that are being disrupted by Tesla.

The content makers and Twitter fans are saving Tesla billions of dollars on advertising. GM spends about 2.7 billion dollars on advertising in 2021, and Tesla zero. But Tesla is the company that is the fastest growing large manufacturer in history and has projected continued growth at the same levels year over year. GM needs to spend billions on advertising because they don't have this

Making The Future Awesome | 74

kind of fan base. Meanwhile GM has been shrinking in unit sales by an average of 8.6% since their peak back in 2016.

Any other company on earth can only dream of a moat like Tesla's fan base.

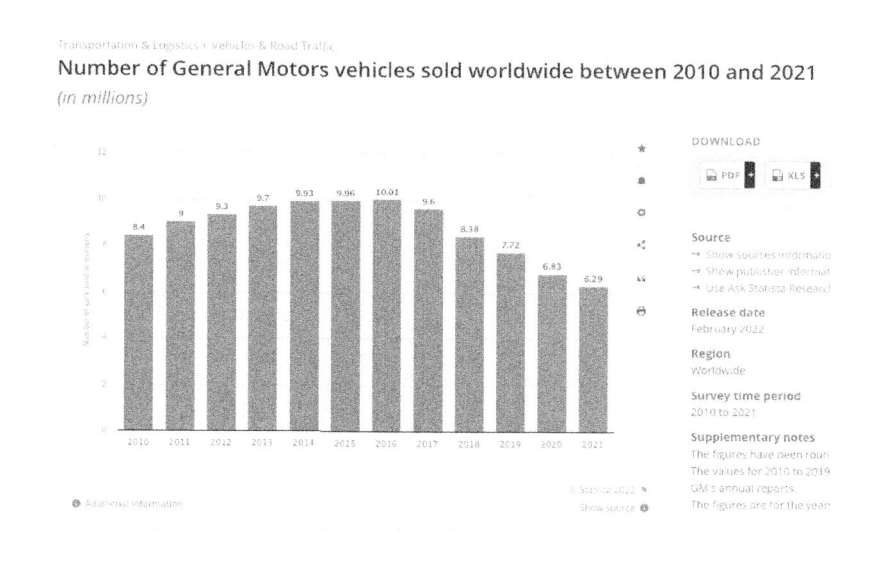

Number of General Motors vehicles sold worldwide between 2010 and 2021
(in millions)

Year	Vehicles sold (millions)
2010	8.4
2011	9
2012	9.3
2013	9.7
2014	9.93
2015	9.96
2016	10.01
2017	9.6
2018	8.38
2019	7.72
2020	6.83
2021	6.29

However, the problem is not limited to GM. Here are recent sales for several major automakers provided by James Stephenson. As you can see, Tesla's sales are increasing about 50% per year, while all the others are showing substantial decreases, regardless of advertising, promotion, and PR departments.

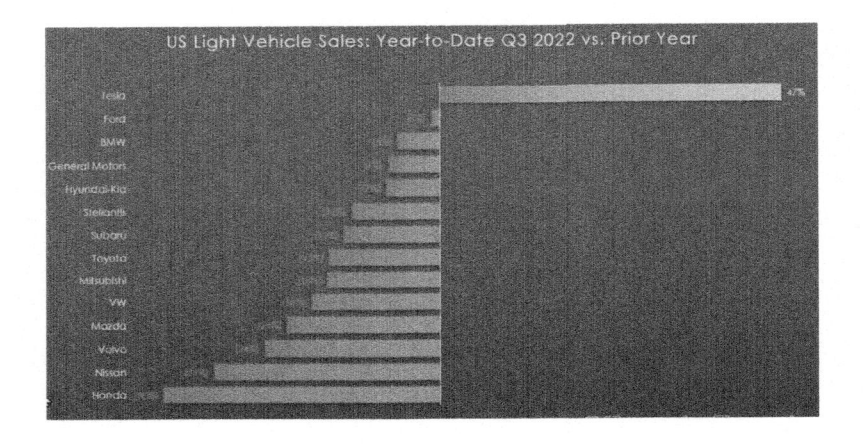

US Light Vehicle Sales: Year-to-Date Q3 2022 vs. Prior Year

Tesla	47%
Ford	
BMW	
General Motors	
Hyundai-Kia	
Stellantis	
Subaru	
Toyota	
Mitsubishi	
VW	
Mazda	
Volvo	
Nissan	
Honda	

CHAPTER 15

Moat: Data and Experience

by Lars Strandridder

In the information era, many, including the highly influential British weekly newspaper "The Economist," consider that data is the most important asset for a corporation. In the past, it might have been people, but arguably that day is now a part of history.
 https://www.economist.com/briefing/2017/05/06/data-is-giving-rise-to-a-new-economy

Tesla is a leader in collecting data in many ways, but in one way they are the clear leader. They are collecting massive amounts of data from their fleet of cars on the roads. They collect data from the eight onboard cameras and from the operating aspects of the car itself.

Among other things, Tesla uses the data to teach their Neural Network how to drive. It is not only the FSD beta testers (Full Self-Driving) who are collecting data for Tesla, but every single car is constantly collecting data. This information is fed into the most advance neural network training computer in the world (Dojo). Tesla ends up knowing more about human behavior in the car, human behavior of folks around the car, and interaction of the humans, dogs, and inanimate objects around the car than any other car company ...not by a little, but by orders of magnitude.

This is also why Tesla is able to show everything that happened in a crash where a Tesla was involved, because Tesla knows everything that happened in the Tesla before and during the crash. The guy who ran into you doesn't stand a chance.

Tesla can even show statistics about their cars and their crashes, as Tesla has the data. Tesla shows off their stats in an annual safety report. They show how many miles are driven in Teslas using Autopilot per crash. Tesla can then say that a Tesla on Autopilot on the highway is 10 times safer than a human driver. Other car companies don't even know if any of their cars have crashed. Tesla gets a notification of every incident immediately.

Tesla uses the data from every crash involving a Tesla to make the cars even safer. Even though Tesla is already the safest car ever tested by NHTSA (US National Highway Traffic Safety Administration) and already exceeds all the safety tests required, Tesla goes over and above to make the cars even safer. They make changes to the structure of the car, the way the seat belts react in an accident, and have changed the shape of the airbags. Recently they have put in a system that will cinch the seat belts ahead of an anticipated crash. All of this is thanks to all the "real world" data Tesla is collecting from the fleet.

And there's even more. Tesla knows everything about the car that was in the crash, from where the seat was, where the steering wheel was, how people were seated, and even how the airbag deployed down to the millisecond. Tesla's "real world" data showed them that the industry standard crash test that every car company goes through did not even come close to representing the real world.

Making The Future Awesome | 78

This resulted in Tesla creating some extra crash tests, other than what the industry standard demands, and only done by Tesla. For instance, Tesla could see that cars being hit from the side are hit in many places, but the industry standard crash test has the impact only on the door. Tesla came up with another test. They could see, from the fleet of over two million cars at that point equipped with sensors and cameras, that **this** was a more "normal" side crash.

REAR IMPACTS

INDUSTRY STANDARD CRASH TESTS

RIGHT HAND IMPACTS

LEFT HAND IMPACTS

FRONTAL IMPACTS

Tesla has used all this data to allow the car to detect what kind of crash it is in, in milliseconds, and react accordingly. A Tesla does not just deploy an airbag, it adjusts **how** to deploy the airbag, depending on what kind of crash it is in, what the passenger weighs, how he is seated on the seat, and many other data points. They even found that in some cases it is safer to **not** deploy the airbag at all. Tesla's cars are able to do this because of all the data they collect, and through the use of AI.

REAL WORLD CRASHES

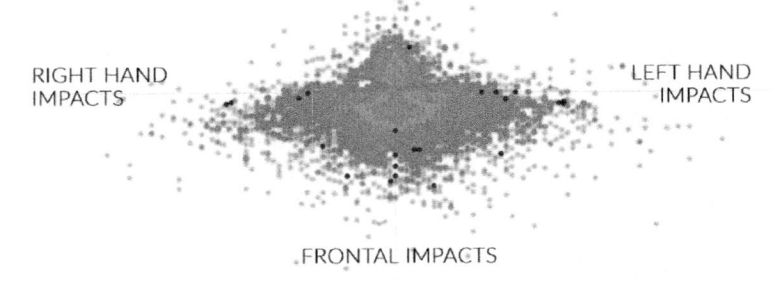

REAR IMPACTS

RIGHT HAND IMPACTS

LEFT HAND IMPACTS

FRONTAL IMPACTS

Conventional tests don't detect the kind of crashes that Tesla now tests for, as they are not part of the industry standard. So, Tesla is able to test things that no one else does, and teach its cars to react differently depending on the type of crash it is in. As a result, Tesla's safety system is substantially better than anything else on the market, and something that the safety regulators can't even measure.

I personally think this will become the way to do safety scores in the future. They will not rely on a few industry standard crash tests but learn from all the "real world" data collected by the world's fleet of cars.

This is also why, when NHTSA asks Tesla for data about a crash Tesla has been involved in, with or without autopilot, they can give them everything about this crash including videos from 360 degrees around the car. No other car company could provide this, even if NHTSA required it.

While some have tried to lie about a crash and to blame Tesla and their software for a suddenly accelerating car, no one has won. Tesla sits with all the data and knows all that has happened. They have been able to show that in the real world the truth is actually the other way around. Tesla prevents about 40 crashes every single day from people accidentally hitting the accelerator instead of the brake pedal. The car's software is designed to realize the error and correct in most cases.

Tesla knows everything about the cars they sell. Also, because, as we showed in the section about the factory in this book, every Tesla car has a digital twin in the cloud, Tesla knows how every car is made, down to what bolt and glue that was used.

Tesla also has all their chargers online and knows exactly what is going on at every charger and gets notified if one is going offline. Since Tesla gets all this data live, and knows exactly where your car is, if you turn on the navigation for a supercharger station, it will know if there are any charging stalls available at the stations and even redirect you to other stations if this one is getting busy.

The data helps them decide when they need to add more chargers to a location or add a new location.

This is also why Tesla Supercharging stations are the most reliable charging stations in the world. They have all the data about their charging stations. This data advantage is starting to become a problem for other BEV charging providers as more people switch to BEVs and rely on the chargers working.

A study of public electric-vehicle stations in California's Bay Area found that only 72.5% of chargers were operational. In other words, 27.5% of the charging stalls didn't work. Tesla on the other hand has an uptime of 99.96%. The chance of you coming to a Tesla charger that doesn't work, is about 0.04%. This makes a big difference for BEV owners, and Tesla is able to do this because they are constantly collecting data from every single stall in the Tesla network, which is closing in on 40,000 stalls worldwide.

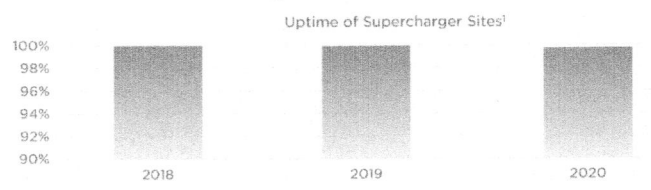

Uptime of Supercharger Sites[1]

Year	Uptime
2018	~98%
2019	~98%
2020	~98%

[1] Uptime of Supercharger Sites reflects the average percentage of sites globally that had at least 50% daily capacity fully functional for the year.

As Tesla opens up their charging stalls to other non-Tesla vehicles, the data advantage will create many advantages for Tesla and for Telsa owners. For instance, when the car knows it is going to a charging station, Tesla's batteries preheat. This cuts the time a Tesla takes to fill up at a charger by 25%. So even though the ID3 can now charge at Tesla chargers in 14 countries in Europe, and soon coming to the US, it will spend more time at the charger just by the simple fact that the ID3 doesn't know it is going to a Tesla charger and can't preheat the battery.

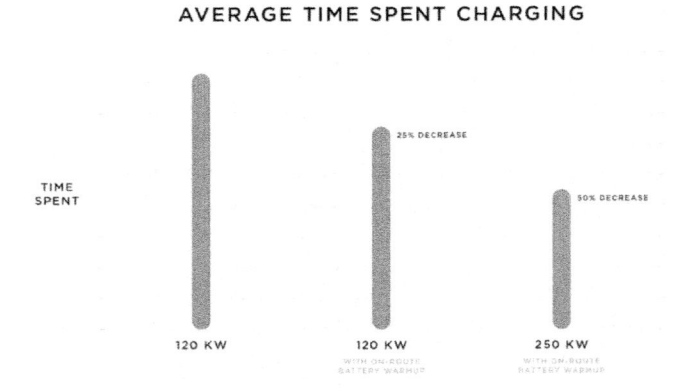

AVERAGE TIME SPENT CHARGING

Time Spent	120 KW	120 KW WITH ON-ROUTE BATTERY WARMUP	250 KW WITH ON-ROUTE BATTERY WARMUP
	(baseline)	25% DECREASE	50% DECREASE

Now imagine a future (next year) when non-Tesla EVs are charging at Tesla chargers because of all the benefits such as many more stations and stalls, better quality chargers, more stalls at each location, 99+% of the stalls working, and an app that gives them information about the status of charging stalls nearby. Meanwhile Tesla is gathering data on which types of cars are charging, how fast they charge, and more. No other car company will have this advantage.

But this was just a few examples of Tesla collecting data because Tesla is as much a software company as they are a car company; something not one of the legacy automakers can claim. Tesla has been collecting data for about a decade on everything from how the car drives to collecting data from the FSD beta testers teaching the Neural network how to drive. They have data on what is going on at their charging station, how their Megapack and Powerwalls are doing, and what kind of crashes their cars are in. They use data and AI to improve how their factories are being run, see where the bottlenecks are, and much more. This gives Tesla a huge insight into their business and gives the edge to Tesla over the competition on how to optimize their cars, the production, the charging station, their batteries, and the software. Everything!

Tesla's decade of experience in collecting data and writing software to extract and use that data is another huge moat. The old boys in the industry have barely even started on the data collection path yet as they don't have the data collection on the cars, they don't own their own superchargers, and most of their car parts are not made in their own factories.

CHAPTER 16

Moat: Already Scaled and Profitable - First Mover

by Randy Kirk

The fact that Tesla is now making electric cars at scale, replicating the factory capacity in regional settings, and making huge amounts of profit is a moat that should scare off every competitor.

Tesla, which has almost no debt and almost $20B in cash, is on a course to add to that cash pile by billions and even tens of billions per year. By 2025 Tesla could easily have $100B+ in the bank. This growing cash cushion is in addition to anticipated annual expenditures of $6-8B per year on capital investments like factories, tooling, and more.

Numerous major legacy competitors are wowing the world with their projections of spending $20-30B to move their companies' fleets to electrification over the next seven years. Tesla will spend at least $50B in that same time without touching their massive savings.

Stated another way, Tesla has plenty of free cash flow to build capacity of 20M vehicles per year by 2030, and still have tens of billions of dollars to play with. Every other legacy maker and startup will need to raise massive amounts of money through equity or debt or both in order to keep up. But the idea that any company could create that capacity in that time frame, even if they had the money to do so, is beyond reason.

Tesla admits that they are bandwidth constrained building three factories at once (Austin, Berlin, and expanding Shanghai.) But they can do it. If they break ground on two new factories in 2023 and two more every other year while continuing to expand Berlin and Austin, they will certainly be able to make 20M cars by 2030.

The largest car companies in the world currently produce about 10M cars per year. Let's say that Tesla only manages that capacity by 2028. In that year alone, their free cash flow from cars would be north of $100B. If you add energy storage, insurance, robotaxi, etc., the number would be substantially more.

Being in the lead is a fantastic moat, especially if that lead includes no debt, multiple profitable factories, and free cash flow that seems to be creating a cash pile last seen at Apple. It appears to cost Tesla about $2B to create a factory capable of building 500K cars.

Thus, there seems to be plenty of future cash flow to build out the projected capacity Musk refers to: 20M cars per year by 2030 and energy revenues equal to car revenues. Tesla should be able to reach their goals and more without borrowing money or raising capital in the market. In fact, Musk stated at the annual shareholders' meeting that there is future potential for share buybacks.

Compare this to every other car maker or energy storage company. They all have mountains of debt. They all have higher costs for building out production. None are making a profit on EV cars, and many are barely making a profit, period.

Is it possible for a company to be too financially well situated? Could it lead to reduced emphasis on hitting large goals or cutting costs. Yes, this is certainly a potential issue. The offset to that hurdle is keeping the company and its employees focused on the mission.

CHAPTER 17

Moat: The Tesla Culture - Dare We Say "Vibe?"

by Randy Kirk

Not many cars have fart mode or offer a video of a roaring fire with a soft warm breeze. Oh. Actually, no other cars have these. Add dog mode, camp mode, and cheetah mode. If you don't know what these are, they are the creative outpouring of engineers with a teenagers' sense of humor. Dog mode keeps the car at a perfect temperature when you leave the dog while shopping. Camp mode is for creating the perfect environment when you are sleeping in your car. Cheetah mode preps the plaid model to the most explosive acceleration off the line.

Tesla is developing its own games for the entertainment unit. They are now getting ready to let the cars talk to one another, (e.g., warn following cars about potholes.) Sentry mode takes video of vandals or thieves doing harm to the car. And the list goes on and on. Another car company that meets Tesla on specs will find it virtually impossible to create a personality that comes with being in the Tesla community.

CHAPTER 18

Moat: The Charging Station Network

by Randy Kirk

What if General Motors owned all the Chevron and Shell stations in the world 40 years ago? What if they could charge competitive cars more for gas than they charged GM products? What if they also owned the oil wells and crackers supplying the pumps? What if they could advertise their cars and other products to the competition while they filled up? Would that seem like a pretty good plan?

Elon Musk is an expert chess player. He plays the game multiple moves ahead of other players. Range anxiety was going to be a thing. Ability to get a charge on a long trip, not just in the home garage, was going to be necessary if volume sales were to happen. Some folks would not be able to charge from a home garage and would need a local charging station to fill up their batteries with electrons.

Other BEV and hybrid makers have known these things, even before Tesla was in business. But not one other car company has even a single charging station under their brand. (Lucid and Rivian appear to be the exception with a few stations.)

Other car companies ask their customers to rely on what are often second-rate charging facilities operated by third party suppliers.

Tesla only recently has come under pressure to open their branded chargers to other makes and models.

As of the end of 2021, there were nearly 3,500 Tesla Supercharger stations across the globe, with 31,498 charging points, which are often referred to as individual "stalls." 32,000 charging points times, let's say, one charge per hour or 24 per day = 768,000 charges per day. $20 per charge is conservative. So that equals about $15m per day in gross revenue. Musk says the stations currently make a 10% profit. So that would be $1.5m per day or over $500m per year profit on $5b in revenue.

In October of 2021, Tesla announced plans to triple their installations by the end of 2024 which would triple the financial results to $1.5B in net profit on energy alone on about $15b in revenue.

Will the revenue only come from charging? Not likely. Advertising, entertainment, plus food and drinks are all in the plans for the future. A restaurant/outdoor movie project has already been planned for Hollywood, CA.

One can imagine that Tesla will advertise their solar products, wall chargers, bots, and other products that are likely coming soon at these stations.

Tesla also has an amazing smartphone app for its cars. This allows owners to plug in, fill up, and leave without a credit card. The system takes care of everything. Other brands wanting to use Tesla's chargers will have to have the app. If the other brands want the same price as Tesla owners, they will have to have a subscription to Tesla, and here in Denmark where most of the charging stations are already open to other brands (in 14 other countries in Europe as of this writing) the subscription price is about $13 per month. So that will come on top of the charging session itself.

Why would other brands of cars use Tesla's chargers rather than other companies? Because the chargers are fast, have a reputation for working more often than others, and get this...Tesla owners have automation in their cars that plans their stops based on the navigation system. It is easy to see which local stations have available stalls, and other information right on the screen. One would suspect that those having the Tesla app subscription will also be privy to these helpful and exclusive services.

Getting the cost of energy down to close to zero will also increase net income. Tesla plans to have devoted solar supply and batteries for their charging stations in the future.

Ultimately the charging stations could produce enough income on their own to be one of the world's largest and most profitable businesses. We have a chapter on the potential value of the Charging Station network as an independent division.

CHAPTER 19

Moat: Materials Innovation

by Randy Kirk

Since legacy auto companies buy most of their components from 3rd parties, and since the amount of innovation in car components has been minimal for half a century, they have not had a need for their own materials science and engineering departments.

Tesla has some of the best materials engineers in the world. Elon knew that the kind of innovations that he had in mind would require sourcing and even creating specialized metals, plastics, glass, and even soft goods. The result is that everywhere you look on a Tesla, there are next generation materials unique to the brand.

The stainless-steel body of the Cybertruck, the special aluminum alloy of the gigacastings, the plant-based leather of the seats, and the chemistries in the batteries are just some of the more obvious material breakthroughs.

CHAPTER 20

Moat: The People

by Randy Kirk

Andrew Carnegie, one of the wealthiest individuals in all of history, is famous for having said:

"Take away my people but leave my factories and soon grass will grow on the factory floors ... Take away my factories but leave my people and soon we will have a new and better factory."

Elon Musk has the pick of the top talent in the US. According to Universum's rankings based on 51,000 students at 310 Universities. https://universumglobal.com/rankings/united-states-of-america/

Tesla and SpaceX trade back and forth between number one and number two choice, year after year, for where engineering graduates would like to work. Roughly 25% of all those surveyed said Tesla would be their top choice.

In 2021, Tesla had 3,000,000 applications to work at the company. Tesla regularly puts on major events at their factories designed to appeal to the top engineers in the US.

Most business experts would say that this ability to attract the top talent in the US would almost guarantee Tesla's very bright future. It also means that competitors are not getting the best and brightest. This is a moat of great consequence, indeed.

CHAPTER 21

Moat: Elon Musk

by Randy Kirk

Many pundits have tried to put a value on an hour of Elon Musk's time. The most common estimates have been $22,500 per minute, or $1,350,000 per hour. Others have been more conservative at $900,000 per hour. The exact amount is truly inconsequential, however, it is the sheer shock of the number, no matter which one you think is correct.

However, those estimates are not based on Elon's salary or income, they are based on the actual creation of his personal wealth of $220B+ in less than approximately 25 years. In round numbers, you could say $1B per year. This is what the market, not an employer, has said he is worth. And it is the average over the past 27 years.

So, I have my own fairly simple math here. Working a regular 2,000 hours per year would say his hourly income would have averaged $200B/54,000 hours or $3.7m per hour. Even if we assume he works double the average or 4000 hours per year, this will still make his time worth $1.85m average since he started his first company, Zip.2, 27 years ago. That is still higher than the highest online number being shown.

It is not unreasonable to think he will add $100B or maybe a lot more to this number in 2023 alone. If that were the case, his hourly rate for 2023 would be $100B/2000 hours or $50m per hour.

Elon's major achievements are listed here only because the description of this moat would be incomplete without doing so.

- Started first online company that today would be similar to Google Maps or Yelp.
- Started company that would disrupt banking which eventually became PayPal.
- Started the first successful privately owned spacecraft business. Has completely disrupted space payload business now having greater annual tonnage into space than the combination of all others, including sovereign nations.
- Started the first profitable car company in the US in over 100 years.
- Disrupted the entire auto industry with almost every company now acknowledging that all new cars will be electric by 2040, and many saying it will be 2030.
- Disrupted the entire energy industry with solar/wind/battery, now the cheapest method of providing new energy supplies. Conceived of the concept of distributed energy production and storage.

Just these achievements would make his presence in leadership at Tesla a huge moat against all others who would think about competing. But, of course, the projects on the drawing board are thought by many, including Elon, to be even more valuable than those already accomplished:

- Bipedal humanoid robots powered by general, real-world AI, that will eliminate repetitive, boring, dangerous jobs.
- Level 5 autonomous cars resulting in freeing up trillions of hours of time now used for driving.

- Robotaxi fleet eliminating driving and car ownership for most people, while lowering the overall cost of personal transportation.
- Complete conversion of energy production and storage to renewables while driving the cost of electricity to near $0.00.
- Creating the future of brain interfaces: building devices now that will help people with paralysis and inventing new technologies that will expand human abilities.
- Moving most transportation underground through multiple layers of tunnels made possible by major cost reductions in tunneling

CHAPTER 22

Moat: The Mission

by Randy Kirk

This critical element cannot be overstated. A mission to make money or maximize shareholder return or improve a product category are all fine and work for many companies. However, setting a mission that is consumer focused or even humanity focused, or galactically inspired obviously gets employees, investors, suppliers, and customers more "charged" up and motivated to accomplish the mission.

This is an actual moat, as the competition would need to find a mission equally inspiring in order to become #1 in recruiting or #1 in customer satisfaction or to build a huge fan base. There is no clear evidence that the competition has any mission other than to equal Tesla or pass Tesla. Inspiring? Not!

CHAPTER 23

Moat: Cash and the Ability to Raise WAY More Cash

by Randy Kirk

Tesla currently holds $20B+ in cash and cash equivalents with most analysts expecting this number to continue to grow by very large amounts into the future. The company also has almost no debt, which is a unique position for a company as large as Tesla.

Due to the huge fan base for Tesla and Elon Musk, raising additional capital through sales of shares is not likely to ever be an issue. At the same time, since there is no debt and clear expectations of major future income, raising billions through debt would also be as easy as making a phone call or two. Entire countries have already shown a willingness to loan money to Elon's ventures, not to mention banking institutions.

When you have this kind of cash on hand and availability to raise more, you are able to move faster, weather setbacks, take larger risks, increase advertising and marketing spend, reduce selling prices (pricing power could be a moat all unto itself), and accelerate growth through acquisition of strategically interesting businesses, innovative early-stage companies, and competition. These acquisitions are also sometimes made to acquire talent.

This particular moat does have some potential competitors with the power to bridge the moat and attack the gates. Apple, Alphabet, and others have very powerful balance sheets and capital generation engines. But the list is few and dwindling as Tesla's free cash flow increases.

CHAPTER 24

Moat: Capital Allocation and ROI

by Randy Kirk

If you give ten of your employees $100,000 to do with as they please, some might bury the money in the ground, some might put it in the bank at 2% interest, some might invest in stocks, with the risk of good gains or losing it all, and some might employ the money in an enterprise that would return lots of money in the future. (You might be contemplating the Biblical story of the Talents, here.)

The ability to take capital and put it to work for a future stream of income is called capital allocation. The gain is called return on investment or ROI. Sophisticated investors are interested in the amount and timing of the return on allocated capital. Tesla may be as good as any company in this space, and certainly better than other manufacturers.

Startup companies often take years or even decades to reach profitability. There is no ROI until there is a profit. This was true for Tesla who only began making a consistent profit in 2020. Even when a company isn't profitable it is possible to assess the ability of the company's management to allocate capital. For example, if you buy a robot for $100,000 to do the job of two employees who each cost the company $50,000 per year, the return on that capital would be one year. Of course, if the robot only replaces one such employee, the return would be after two years.

Bankers and investors are happy if manufacturers can show a plan to pay for equipment through savings or production within two or three years, depending on the type of investment.

Tesla has shown that they can consistently pay back these investments within a year. Tesla's new factories such as Austin and Berlin cost about $2B each to build. This capital is allocated over the 1.5 - 2.5 years it takes to build and ramp the factories. Approximately two years after groundbreaking, each factory should have a run rate of 1,000 cars/wk. If the profit is close to $20,000 for each car, the annual profit on that factory would be $1B. Of course, the run rate will increase to 10,000 per week within another year, meaning that a $1B investment will now be returning 10X per year.

Elon refers to this process often. He says that the product is the factory. That the factory is the hard part. Once you have created the factory, the product can make the product, cars. Now you can iterate on that factory to make it better and better, but you can also cookie cutter that factory next door or halfway around the world, including all the improvements you've made along the way.

No other manufacturing company has this kind of thinking, and this moat would be at least a 10-year protection against all competition

Tesla Return On Capital Employed Benchmarks

Name	Ticker	Return On Capital Employed
Workhorse Group Inc.	NASDAQCM:WKHS	-43.7%
Virgin Galactic Holdings, Inc.	NYSE:SPCE	-39.3%
Rivian Automotive, Inc.	NASDAQGS:RIVN	-33.8%
Ford Motor Company	NYSE:F	6.3%
Elio Motors, Inc.	OTCPK:ELIO	6.5%
General Motors Company	NYSE:GM	7.0%
Consumer Discretionary	SECTOR:DSCY.US	9.8%
Amazon.com, Inc.	NASDAQGS:AMZN	10.5%
Tesla, Inc.	NASDAQGS:TSLA	16.2%
Netflix, Inc.	NASDAQGS:NFLX	18.3%
Meta Platforms, Inc.	NASDAQGS:FB	32.3%
Apple Inc.	NASDAQGS:AAPL	51.4%

https://finbox.com/NASDAQGS:TSLA/explorer/roce

CHAPTER 25

Moat: Supply Chain Expertise

by Randy Kirk

Prior to 2021, the supply chain issue was something only nerds paid much attention to. Now we have all seen the headlines that explain why there is no bleach or clothing on the shelf. But for the zipper on the fly, the entire jacket can't be shipped. If the ships can't leave the harbor or enter the destination harbor, it doesn't matter if the fly was delivered to the zipper company on time.

Walmart is the largest retailer in the world today largely because of their incredible supply chain innovations. Tim Cook of Apple was selected for CEO by Steve Jobs because of his expertise in managing supply chains. Any manufacturer, wholesaler, importer, or retailer can completely alter their profit picture by improving the efficiency of getting parts, products, and services from supplier to warehouse or factory floor which improve on-hand percentages, turns per year, and dollars per square foot generated.

Even in service industries or the service side of product businesses, supply chain matters. You can't run a business today without product liability insurance, transportation expertise, or automated computer systems and programs.

There are many ways to be top-of-game in supply chain management, but the more complex the product, the more uncertain the market, and the shorter the list of available suppliers, the harder things become.

Tesla has shown itself to be at least the equal of Walmart or Apple when it comes to managing worldwide, highly complex, supply chains. Often the materials and services required have never been produced before, produced in the way Tesla needs them, or produced at the scale required.

How do you convince a battery cell manufacturer in 2019 to ramp up production of auto battery cells for future production of millions of cars when current production is under 500,000 per year? Why will a lithium mine make plans 5-10 years in advance to increase capacity by many times current levels on the word of a new entry into the market?

But, over and over again, Tesla shows it has the chops to get the necessary products and services in place needed to increase production by over 50% per year. Here are two specific examples where Tesla has shown dramatic power over competitors: semiconductors and batteries.

Semiconductors were the most reported-on example during the pandemic. Almost every major car company was reporting huge reductions in production due to their supply chain issue, especially computer chips. Even at the end of 2022, several major automakers are cutting shipment expectations due to semiconductor and other shortages.

Tesla was able to take chips that were still available, reprogram their systems to accept those chips, and keep production humming along. Their supply chain superiority resulted in increased sales and production in 2021 of 77% while worldwide auto sales were up just 4%. Comparing sales results to 2019, total auto sales fell 11% while Tesla increased by 93% over those two years.

Making The Future Awesome | 110

To add another layer of proof to this amazing story, Tesla was still hampered by some supply chain issues, but primarily saw setbacks due to government related COVID-19 manufacturing plant shutdowns in California and China.

Going forward, these supply chain issues have the potential to be even more of a moat. For example, staying with the battery supply issue, Musk says that the primary limiting factor on production is now, and will be, batteries, with lithium and nickel as the major raw material problems. Tesla has contracts with almost every battery manufacturer in the world, multiple contracts with mining companies, and is ramping in Austin and Berlin what will be the largest battery manufacturing plants in the world.

Each of these plants is slated to make 100 GWh of batteries at minimum, with a small 10GWh facility in California. This capacity would be enough for 3.5m cars with 60KWh drive trains, just from Tesla's own factories and only the already announced plants. Currently there appears to be serious talk of another battery plant in Indonesia.

These three existing plants are all subject to increasing beyond their current planned production through increases in productivity of existing lines, reduced use of floor space allowing for more lines, or the addition of adjacent capacity. All three of these approaches seem very likely, based on both the statements of Tesla leadership and rumors.

Of course, those battery facilities are only the Tesla owned capacity. Panasonic has a plant on Tesla's property in Nevada that is now producing 39GWh. They are building a second factory in Reno, NV, and are looking for property in middle America for another US plant. Both plants are slated to make batteries for Tesla.

Total worldwide capacity for EV batteries at the end of 2021 was about 300GWh. CATL was closing in on 100GWh of that total with major plans for expansion. In late 2021, Tesla placed an order for 45GWh with CATL. It was not immediately apparent if this was for one year or an extension of current contracts that are still to be fulfilled. Clearly, Tesla's relationship with CATL will be important in future years when competitors are looking for resources.

But Tesla's reach goes far beyond Panasonic and CATL. In fact, Elon has told all factories that Tesla will buy as much output as they are willing to produce. The question has to be asked. Where will other car makers and storage suppliers, large and small, go for batteries when Tesla is buying up massive amounts of a product that is in such short supply? What will they have to pay for their smaller requirements compared to Tesla? And how will their product compare to the batteries made by and for Tesla that include advances not available to anyone but Tesla?

CHAPTER 26

Moat: Raw Materials Sourcing

by Randy Kirk

Now move one step further along the supply chain. The massive battery requirements will require a lot of REMs (raw earth materials). The mining and refining of these REMs will need to increase 40-fold to meet demand, according to Musk. He says that this will be the largest human undertaking ever attempted: Moving the world to electricity in one generation will require moving many mountains, literal mountains, of dirt.

For the most part, the necessary raw materials are abundant. Even those items that are hardest to mine or refine or either accessible in required amounts or can be replaced by other materials. Even the most talked about metal, cobalt, is being phased out of all but a few batteries.

But even the 40-fold increase in extraction and refining would not be so challenging were it not for the reasonable and unreasonable hurdles placed in the way by governments and lawyers. Depending on the material, it might take 4-10 years or longer to go from land acquisition to scaling output. At the Q3 earnings call, Elon said that they are having productive talks with the US congress and administration about ways to speed up permitting. He also said that Tesla will mine if necessary and seemed to imply that the lithium refining facility in Corpus Christi, TX, is going to be built by Tesla.

As of this writing, one lithium mining company, Piedmont Lithium, is changing plans for early increases in capacity. Their expansion plans in North Carolina are being hampered by approval processes that may not be as difficult in Canada. Therefore, they have started a new effort in Canada.

Tesla's basic principles are founded in environmental and human improvement; thus, they understand about doing mining as sustainably as possible. However, as with so many things, good intentions of well-meaning citizens and bureaucrats can thwart good outcomes with unnecessary limits and rules.

But back to the business of materials sourcing as a moat. Tesla is active all over the world lining up extraction sites, contracting for raw materials, and even helping with technological advancements in mining and refining. Elon says that Tesla will do their own mining or refining when necessary and has already leased some land to test theories regarding extracting lithium directly from clay.

As this book is being finished, Tesla is in the first stages of getting into the lithium refining business, with a proposed plant somewhere along the Gulf Coast.

I don't think it is open to dispute that any car company or mining company is anywhere close to resourcing battery raw materials on the scale that Tesla is.

Because Tesla has teams of experts working at sourcing needed raw materials, companies, and methods for processing those materials, and companies and company-owned factories for producing the final batteries, they have a moat that by itself could keep them with double digit market share for years to come, as both EVs and energy storage ramp up exponentially.

CHAPTER 27

Moat: Pace of Innovation

by Randy Kirk

Sandy Munro has become something of an automotive legend over the past few years. Prior to his interest in Tesla's technology, Sandy was primarily known in the inner circles of the ICE vehicle business. He had worked as an engineer/inventor or consultant for many top automakers worldwide.

His company, Munro and Associates, now consults with many of those same companies, helping with lean design. Munro tears down automotive products to study and suggest improvement and/or help his clients to reverse engineer competitive products.

More recently, Sandy has become a YouTube star, and fans of Tesla have become his biggest fans. He is known for cracking open various aspects of Tesla autos and exclaiming loudly that they "blow his mind."

Sandy Munro would be among the first to agree that most of the moats we have pointed to place Tesla years ahead of competitors. But one thing Munro harps about often is the incredible speed of innovation at Tesla.

> "We made recommendations to Tesla, and they implemented them and implemented them really fast. Now that's not one of our customers. That's an OEM.

"I am giving a speech, and one of the things I'm going to talk about is change at the speed of thought. That's not quite the speed of light, but it's pretty damn fast, and it certainly is faster than anything I've ever seen from anybody; from Bentley to GM, to Ford, to Chrysler...whoever! Nobody moves as fast as Tesla does.

"A good example would be the comments we made on what we're calling the super manifolds, the octovalve. We tore it apart and we made some comments, and also talked about the compressor...anyway, we made some comments, and I'll be damned if they didn't implement them already on this casting right here...they've made 13 changes since we tore our car apart...Our car was built in March. This car was built in July. How the heck?!

"I don't know of anybody that makes changes like that...

"Now I know that you would expect other companies want to do the same, but let's see what actions they are taking. None. That's the point. Tesla is listening to feedback from everyone.

"They're watching random teardowns on the Internet...I mean I know for a fact that there are countless people who work at Tesla, specifically engineers, who watch this Munro Live channel."

It is hard to say it any better than that. Many companies are struggling to make a car anywhere close to the quality of the current S3XY lineup. But while they are aiming at equaling current specs, safety, customer experience and satisfaction, and price, Tesla is making changes at the speed of thought. The competition needs to be aiming at where Tesla will be in 3-5 years, not where they are today.

CHAPTER 28

Moat: Flexibility

by Randy Kirk

We will use just a single story to explain the flexibility moat. In 2020-22, the entire world was beset by supply chain issues. From toilet paper to diesel, from masks to baby formula, and from shipping containers to human labor, the headlines constantly screamed about important products being gone from the shelves, with any potential relief months or years away.

In the auto industry, the biggest supply issue among many was semiconductors. Elon often talks about the fact that an automobile line can be fully stopped due to a missing part that might cost less than a $1.00. While the major auto companies closed factories and lowered production expectations by 30% or more due to the semiconductor shortage, Tesla grew sales by 50% or more.

They used their own engineers to rapidly change the specific use cases so that semiconductors that were available would work for Tesla's production. So, while Tesla didn't ship as many cars as they hoped in 2021 or the first half of 2022, the disruption was much less than for the competition.

This flexibility doesn't just affect shortages of parts, it affects the entire enterprise. All employees are trained to go where the issue is, rather than waste time doing meaningless tasks.

We will devote an entire chapter to "Agile" management later in this book, but the basic idea is that Tesla employees assign themselves to tasks based on a list of available needs. When they complete that job, they look on the Tesla company app to find another opportunity to use their specific skill set on a team that may have just been formed that day.

This type of efficiency and flexibility gives Tesla another edge that most company cultures will NEVER duplicate. This moat is so significant and important that we will devote a full chapter to it further on.

CHAPTER 29

Current Moats in So Many Categories

by Randy Kirk

Most companies would be happy to have a few significant moats and maybe a handful of smaller advantages that would challenge their competition to meet them in quality, service, or price.

But, when you start adding up the moats, many of which are deep, wide, and filled with crocs, Tesla's prospects for dominating the BEV, battery storage, autonomous driving, real-world AI, automation, and robotics businesses is something that is way beyond anything Warren Buffet likely has ever seen before or will see again.

Look at the situation this way. Let's say that a competitor comes up with a better battery. In a perfect world it would take that company five years to first production, and potentially much longer than that to get economies of scale. As they ramp, they will need scarce raw materials, and they may or may not be as flexible in their choices as Tesla.

Because they are late to the game, it may be hard to raise capital. The battery would need to be A LOT better for investors to be interested, as the lead is so large. Moreover, Tesla might have an even better battery that is a mere iteration of their current product almost ready to test or deploy.

Then the question becomes who buys the new battery? Will they be able to sell it for a low enough cost to take out the competition? Will Tesla merely lower their margins to keep the new player out of the market?

The above example is the reason that startups in major industries are often just hoping to get bought out by the majors.

21 moats and counting. Maybe you saw some that we didn't include. Love to hear from you. These moats are not just an interesting list that might be fodder for an MBA classroom, though many feel Tesla will be the major focus of many MBA programs in the future. They are massive impediments to all competitors and represent a major reason why Tesla deserves a much higher multiple than the legacy ICE car makers.

CHAPTER 30

Tesla Cars and Trucks

by Lars Strandridder and Randy Kirk

S3XY They Are

Currently, Tesla offers four cars in their lineup. Models S, 3, X, and Y. Each of these is available in multiple trims that provide differences in color, interior, wheels, tires, range, and performance.

The model Y is a crossover SUV which is, as you are reading this, probably the number one car in the world by dollar sales volume. It is almost certainly going to be number one in unit volume sometime in 2023. Increased production in Shanghai, Berlin, and Austin should increase total model Y sales by 700,000 units or more in 2023.

Legacy automakers have had a decade to learn how Tesla makes electric cars, and even had access to Tesla's patents for the original Model S from 2012 and all other patents since. Tesla made all of their patents publicly available as of June 12, 2014.

All Our Patent Are Belong To You

Elon Musk, CEO • June 12, 2014

Yesterday, there was a wall of Tesla patents in the lobby of our Palo Alto headquarters. That is no longer the case. They have been removed, in the spirit of the open source movement, for the advancement of electric vehicle technology.

Tesla Motors was created to accelerate the advent of sustainable transport. If we clear a path to the creation of compelling electric vehicles, but then lay intellectual property landmines behind us to inhibit others, we are acting in a manner contrary to that goal. Tesla will not initiate patent lawsuits against anyone who, in good faith, wants to use our technology.

But even though legacy makers have enjoyed the advantage of using Tesla's patents, Tesla's vehicles are still unique and years ahead in technology. These advantages are why Tesla is on its way to becoming the largest vehicle maker in the world, the largest company in the world, and the most profitable company ever in history.

New electric cars can't even keep up with Tesla's Model S 85D from 2013, which clocked a 0-60mph in 4.4 seconds, had a top speed of 130mph, a range of 265 miles according to the EPA, and could charge with 120kW (speed of charging the car.) Tesla's competitors are barely equaling some of these specs today, almost a decade later.

Tesla raised the bar to new heights last year (2021) with the Plaid Model S. This 4-door family sedan turned a 0-60 in just 1.99 seconds, reached a top speed of 200mph, provided a range of 348 miles EPA, and a charging speed of 250kW. All in the same car! The Model S Plaid beats every other internal combustion engine supercar on the dragstrip, but costs only a fraction of most supercars.

Many might think that these performance cars are irrelevant, and it is only the mass market cars that really matter. But Tesla is creating these amazing vehicles to show the world that the best car is the electric car, and the ICE (internal combustion engine) car has become obsolete.

Moreover, Tesla has the best performing electric car in the world, which will give Tesla what is called the halo effect. People want to buy Tesla's more affordable cars like the Model 3 and Model Y, in part because of the fun acceleration that Tesla has become known for in the Plaid Model.

Of course, all Teslas enjoy the benefit of instant acceleration. Cars priced well under $80,000 can take you from 0-60 mph in under 4 seconds.

But it is much more than the insane performance that makes Tesla's cars unique and highly desired.

Safety Is Job One

Tesla states that their most important consideration is safety. They have built the car from the ground up, with safety being the number one priority. Due to this emphasis and their outstanding execution of the goal, Tesla's cars are probably the safest cars on the road today. The Model 3 has the lowest probability of injury of any car ever tested by NHTSA, and Tesla's safety features are not optional, they are included in every car they make.

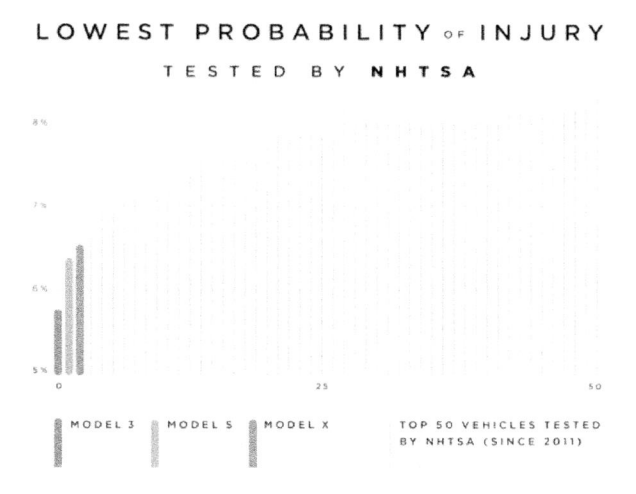

LOWEST PROBABILITY OF INJURY
TESTED BY **NHTSA**

MODEL 3 | MODEL S | MODEL X | TOP 50 VEHICLES TESTED BY NHTSA (SINCE 2011)

Tesla is able to stand out as the safest car maker because they don't stop at what is legally required for a car. They go over and beyond what is needed and make frequent changes and updates to the cars to make them even safer. Tesla is able to make changes to the production of the car on a weekly basis in their "agile" factories. We will discuss the "agile" idea later in the book.

Tesla has multiple layers of driver assist features, which allow their cars to correct errant behavior on the part of their all-to-human drivers. We'll detail those later in the book.

In the 4th quarter of 2021 Tesla recorded only one crash for every 4.31 million miles driven in which drivers were using Autopilot technology (Autosteer and active safety features). For drivers in Tesla vehicles who were not using Autopilot technology, Tesla recorded one crash for every 1.59 million miles driven. By comparison, NHTSA's most recent data shows that, in the United States, there is an automobile crash every 484,000 miles. So, Tesla's Autopilot is already about 10 times safer than a human driver. All of this makes Tesla's cars highly desirable for people who care about safety.

The Mission is about Elimination Carbon and Creating Sustainable Energy Resources

Performance and safety are great motivations for a car purchase, but others might choose Tesla because of the low carbon footprint. Tesla is known for its electric cars and their mission to accelerate the world's transition to renewable energy. Tesla is synonymous with the green transition which makes Tesla's brand very popular with people who want zero emission electric cars.

Thanks to Tesla's more efficient electric motor and battery pack, their cars are the most efficient electric cars on the market, thus making them even better for the environment. For example, a

Model Y will use less energy than a Ford Mustang Mach E that has similar specs.

The Mach E needs a much bigger battery to get the same performance or less. This Tesla technology advantage also makes the Mach E more expensive to "fill up" than a Model Y, partially because there is more kWh needed to fully charge the Mach E.

Total Cost of Ownership

In general, an electric car is much cheaper to operate than an equivalent ICE car. For those who do the math, the lower overall cost of ownership over a five-year period makes Teslas highly desirable. With an electric car, you end the hassle of going to the filling station and the service checks to tune the car, change the oil, and do other standard maintenance that require time and expense.

There are far fewer moving parts in an electric car, so fewer things to go wrong over the life of the car. No engine, transmission, fuel system, or radiator.

I personally save about $4K a year driving my Tesla Model 3 compared to my previous car, a diesel Mazda 3. And with the rising gas prices we see now, the real savings are even higher today. I love that I have a much better, safer and fun car with my Tesla for a lower overall cost compared to my old polluting Mazda 3.

Coming Price Parity

EVs, especially Tesla's, are getting very close to price parity with an equivalent ICE car. Most pundits predict that electric vehicles will reach price parity by 2024 at the latest. Once that happens, combined with the monthly costs being much lower than ICE, the electric car choice will be a no-brainer-better performance, lower long-term costs, greater safety, fewer trips to the repair shop, and no more gas stations...all for the same price or less! Who wouldn't take that deal?

Range and Charge Speed Not a Tesla Issue

When it comes to making the switch to an EV from an ICE car there are still two main things people are concerned about - range and charging speeds. Superior range and charging speeds are two big reasons why people choose Tesla's over the competition. You will get the safety and fun performance of the Tesla, but you will also get a range of between 260 and 400 miles EPA.

Added to the longer range, Tesla's cars can charge up to 250kw, which not many other electric cars are able to copy. The faster charge speed means you spend less time at the charging station.

It is one thing to have a car that can handle 250kW charging speed, and another to find a charger that can deliver that charging speed. Here again Tesla stands out in the crowd. They have now installed over 35,000 supercharger stalls around the world as of this writing. And all their stalls offer 150-250kW of charging speed. They are also adding over 10,000 new stalls per year and continuing to improve their capabilities.

Then there is the icing on the cake when it comes to refueling. Tesla makes the cars, and they also make the chargers, and they make the computer software in the cars. This integration results in Tesla's onboard computer telling the driver where all the nearby Tesla superchargers are located, how many stalls are at the station, and if there are any available. The car will even plan a desired route in the navigation system, telling you where you need to stop for charging, and for how long. Combined with the long range of the car, and fast charging speed, this completely removes range anxiety, making road trips in a Tesla a breeze.

Tesla Software Provides Dozens, Maybe Hundreds of Unique Benefits

One more thing that sets Tesla apart from all their competition is all their proprietary software. First, all the software Tesla has in their cars is made by Tesla, not by a third party. They can control the whole car with their software system. Where legacy automakers like VW are having huge problems with the software in their cars, Tesla has almost none.

Tesla can change many aspects of the car with OTA updates, just like your phone or computer. They can add new features, increase the range of your car, improve the braking, or unlock things like rear seat heating. Your car never seems old because the latest features get added years after you buy it.

Like any other car company, sometimes Tesla has a defect or issue that needs to be addressed. You may have had your ICE car recalled for anything from a faulty suspension to airbag problems. When you need these fixed, you have to go to the dealer. 95% of Tesla's "recalls" have been fixed using OTA.

Unfortunately, legacy automakers don't make their own software, or the computer hardware, or most of the electronics in the car, or even most of the parts. They have many different software companies that are making different software that controls different parts of the car. This makes an OTA update a very complex issue. They have to make sure that the software changes from one software company don't mess up the software from all the other software companies.

The result is that legacy automakers are having huge trouble with just being able to make an over the air software update. And if they are able to make an over the air software update, it is usually for minor things. Most of the time when legacy automakers have software issues, they still need to recall the car into the service center to fix them.

Tesla's software has done more than just make a great user interface providing many useful tools and allowing updates and fixes by OTA; Tesla has become world famous because of all the entertainment and fun things the car can do.

It starts with the famous fart mode to the more useful dog mode or camp mode. Then there is just the fact that you can play video games in the car, and see Netflix, Disney+ and YouTube. But maybe you don't even know what these features are: Here are just a few:

- Each seat in a Tesla comes equipped with an electronic whoopee cushion. You can control the time and the type of flatulence your guest will experience.
- Your car has a speaker in the grill that allows you to make a wide array of noises instead of your regular horn. These include flugel horns, old fashioned horns, farts, or even your own voice, asking the person in front of you to please move over.
- Last Christmas, an OTA included the ability to turn your car into a Christmas light show with music and the entire car "dancing" to the beat. Lights flashing, windows rolling up and down, doors opening, side mirrors jiggling, and more.

- There is a dog mode that keeps your beloved pet comfortable by keeping the temperature cool in the car while you step away.
- You can have a video of a lovely fire and a soft warmth from the fire at your feet. So romantic!
- The cars have sentry mode which activates the eight cameras on the outside of your vehicle to take video of any attempts to steal or harm your vehicle.
- The car can be set to have the interior temperature never go over a set number. You can also turn on the A/C or heat using your app, so that the car is comfortable when you get in.
- You can look at your app and see where the car is at any time, whether it is charging, driving, the current energy available, and much more.
- If you do need any kind of service, you just go to the app and press service. You go through a few steps and you'll either have a mobile repair vehicle come make the repair or you'll be set up with an appointment at the service center.

The list goes on and on and is constantly being updated with new fun things. Some of these are Easter eggs. They are not included in the information about the update. It is up to the owner to find them or learn about them in the Tesla community. (You will find the Tesla community mostly on Twitter or YouTube.)

Many of these features were not available in my Tesla when I bought it, but it now has all of these features. For free! My car has become a much better car over the last three years since I bought it. This is a unique thing for Tesla, and one of the reasons why they have such a good resale value.

No wonder when we put all of this together that Tesla is the most popular electric car in the world. You will get the full package. Safety, Autopilot, performance, range, efficiency, charging speed, charging network, great software, OTA update, and fun. All for the true cost of ownership that matches inferior ICE cars whose sticker price is maybe $5-$10K less.

Tesla sales have been growing more than 50% a year since 2014, and even as much as 87% in 2021. Elon Musk says he expects a minimum of 50% growth going forward through 2030, at which point he projects unit sales to be 20,000,000 per year, twice what industry leaders Toyota and VW produce today.

One of the most impressive things about all this for me is that unlike the legacy automakers that spend billions of dollars on advertising, Tesla has become the fastest growing brand in the world while they have spent $0 on advertising. Tesla has spent every single dollar on trying to make their product better.

This is also why they score high on all owner satisfaction lists. Check below of one such list from Zutobi. They released a report tracking four different car owner rating reports from Parkers, Honest John, Autotrader, and Edmunds in order to put together a global owner happiness tracker. The Tesla Model 3 tops the list, and the Tesla lineup also had the most satisfied customers as a brand.

THE BRANDS WITH THE HIGHEST AND LOWEST OWNER RATINGS

Brand	Average rating	Brand	Average rating
Tesla	4.53	SEAT	4.07
Land Rover	4.30	Toyota	4.06
Mazda	4.30	Hyundai	4.04
Peugeot	4.27	Jeep	4.04
BMW	4.25	Fiat	3.99
Volvo	4.21	Citroen	3.93
Kia	4.20	Honda	3.84
Renault	4.20	Subaru	3.81
Volkswagen	4.20	Vauxhall	3.77
Ford	4.14	Nissan	3.76
Dacia	4.13	Mercedes-Benz	3.75
Mini	4.13	Perodua	2.80
Mercedes	4.10		

C?RS - The Other Vehicles

Tesla is set to start shipping the Cybertruck in 2023 (the C in the above acronym.) Their first car was the Roadster, and a new Roadster is promised for late '23 or '24. The Semi-truck is still semi in production at this writing but is supposed to be delivering units shortly. That leaves the ? in our acronym.

I think the next model will be the model A or use A in the name. Now the eight vehicles together would spell out S3XY CARS. This just seems like the way Elon would do it.

Cybertruck Rocks

Someday someone will write an entire book on Cybertruck. There is a story to tell from the business and marketing perspective. There is another story dealing with consumer psychology. More stories are yet to come when the truck actually hits the road and consumers get to try out all the futuristic aspects of this vehicle.

What kind of potential does this crazy machine represent? There is no public statement from Tesla, but various reporters say over 1.5M are reserved. Some believe the number is over 2M. If Tesla were able to make 500K units between mid-2023 and the end of 2024, then 500K per year after that, the backlog wouldn't be filled until the end of 2026 or '27.

Since consumers were only required to place a $100 deposit, some of the 1.5-2M reservations might not take delivery. I have an order, but I would only take delivery if I decided to use it for renting it out on Turo.

What is it about this truck that has folks lined up for years to buy it?

Exoskeleton - The outside of the car is made of a similar stainless steel to that used in the Starship. It requires no paint, you can't scratch it or ding it, and you'll never need to detail it. Plus, it just looks…futuristic, wild, masculine, ugly, amazing…or you can add your own adjectives.

Power and range - Most folks who buy a truck aren't that interested in how fast it goes from 0-60mph. But in case you are the exception, the Cybertruck will make that dash in just 2.9 seconds while providing up to 500 miles of range.

Towing and payload capacity - If you want the truck for work, not for show, then these stats are the ones you care about. It carries up to 3,500 pounds and can tow up to 14,000 pounds.

Then there is a list of additional benefits as long as your arm, such as multiple power outlets for your electric tools, an air compressor, 100 cu ft of external storage, a built-in cover for the bed, a built-in ramp, and much more.

Of course, you still get all of the amazing safety and software advantages mentioned above.

Currently, Tesla says they will only build 250,000 per year. Some rumors say that this number will almost immediately expand to 500,000 per year when they have finished the initial ramp. I suspect that more lines will be added if a high percentage of the reservation holders actually take delivery.

Model A or Model Aardvark or Fill in the Blank

Elon has stated that the robotaxi will ramp by 2024. By this, he can only mean a design which has a fully operational FSD and therefore, will not necessarily need a steering wheel. It may also mean a very different interior configuration allowing for chairs to face each other, at least as an option.

At the Q3 '22 earnings call Elon confirmed that the number one issue for the auto design and engineering teams is the development of a new model that will cost half of the 3/Y models. This seems to acknowledge that at least for a few years, Tesla may feel the need to supply a $25-30k model that still allows for an optional driver. This may depend heavily on just how good FSD (full self-driving) is working by the end of 2023.

I make the argument that some people will still want to own their own car in the age of robotaxis, and that the robotaxi roll out will take at least five years. Therefore, it may be that the robotaxi skateboard and underbody will be a standard structure upon which you can add a robotaxi, a small car or truck, or even a small van.

The vehicles that sit on the Model A platform will clearly be the additional 10M+ needed vehicles that will get Tesla to 20M total. At that same earnings call, Elon predicted that the new model would outsell the combined sales of both Model 3 and Model Y.

Here is the critical part of the story if robotaxis are not yet happening in 2024-26. Tesla will be the only car company capable of making a truly compelling smaller car at prices that will be equal to or lower than any competition, while still maintaining crazy margins above 30%. Why? If you haven't yet read the moat chapters, you will find the answer there.

The Roadster

Elon says that the Roadster is really just the icing on the cake. There is no good business reason to make it, other than the halo effect. However, now that Tesla is maintaining that batteries are not a limiting factor, maybe the Roadster will see the light of day, again.

The car is designed for those among us who love the art of a car, want to be the center of attention wherever they go, and who love speed. Here are the specs:

- 0-60 - 1.9 seconds
- 0-100 - 4.2 seconds
- Quarter mile - 8.8 seconds
- Top speed - 250 mph
- Range - 620 miles, but not at 250 mph or when going 0-60 in 1.9 seconds away from every stop light.

The car is said to fit four, but it is unclear whether the back seat is designed for full-sized adults.

While the website doesn't speak to the possibility of a rocket thruster being employed for an extra boost, Elon has suggested this option. He says that this will provide a 0-60 time of 1.1 seconds. He has also spoken of side thrusters that would allow for help in handling turns under pavement ripping speeds. There is even talk that the Roadster will be able to hover.

Semi-Truck

Converting the Semi-truck fleet to electric would have a substantial impact on particulates and CO^2 emissions. Specifically, replacing any Class 8 truck that doesn't have an advanced filtration device with an electric equivalent would be like replacing 21 cars. Approximately 3M of the 4M Class 8 trucks on the road today do not have this filtration system.

Tesla has thousands of reservations for their new Semi, but each Semi uses a huge number of batteries. Tesla felt it was wiser to use limited batteries for passenger vehicles. Now Tesla says the company has enough batteries for all purposes, so we should begin to see a roll out of the Semis.

Total average US sales of Class 8 trucks are between 250,000 and 300,000 per year. Tesla's initial plan is to ship just less than one per day or about 250 per year. There is good reason to think that eventually Tesla would ramp to as many as 100,000 per year. At the Q3 '22 earnings call, Tesla said they plan to ship 50,000 in 2024.

The Tesla Semi was introduced with 300-mile and 500-mile range options for $150,000 and $180,000, respectively. It is very likely that this pricing structure will change. It dates to 2017, and inflation plus commodity price issues have almost certainly impacted the costs of the Semi, as it has all the other vehicles. On the other hand, the IRA subsidy for electric semi-trucks is $40,000 per truck.

The Semi will be disruptive on many levels. The total cost to operate is much lower than the equivalent diesel truck. Down time on trucks is a major issue. There are far fewer moving parts and things to go wrong on an electric vehicle, so down time will be much less of an issue. Companies are looking for green alternatives that make sense. Another huge factor in the Semi business is that Tesla will be offering an autonomous capability on the trucks which will be a complete game changer.

Just announced that Tesla will begin shipping Semi-trucks to PepsiCo in December 2022.

CHAPTER 31

The Competition Is Coming

by Randy Kirk

"There is no competition," say the Tesla bulls and fanboys. "The competition is coming," say the haters, short sellers, and $TSLAQ (a loose, international collective of largely anonymous short-sellers, skeptics, and researchers who openly criticize *Tesla)* community. "We will pass Tesla by 2025," shouts GM, VW, and Stellantis. The street and the press love a duel, so they call every new BEV a Tesla killer. Meanwhile, the landscape is already littered with the could-have-beens.

It would take at least 100 pages to really dig into the details of the competition. We won't bore you with that. Instead, we'll look at the broad strokes. The big questions every investor should be asking are:

- Who is the competition?
- Does the competition even matter?
- What is the right way to think about market share?
- Does being #1 matter: Units, revenue, profit, performance, customer satisfaction, safety?
- Who is the "next" Tesla?

Who Is the Competition

Most of the pundits on Wall Street and in the mainstream press believe that the competition to Tesla is other clean or cleaner autos.

This would include other plug-in BEVs, plug-in hybrids, and even Toyota's planned hydrogen cars.

The companies who make these cars are divided into two categories, legacy, and startups. Legacy car companies have been making ICE cars for decades, but are now transitioning into EVs or hydrogen. Start-ups are companies who have only entered the business to make a BEV and have no history of making other cars. To my knowledge, none of these start-ups are offering hydrogen or hybrids with the possible exception of BYD.

If you agree with the pundit's definition of competition, then you will be gauging Tesla's success on the various leaderboards showing worldwide or regional sales of Teslas compared to other companies' sales of their clean cars. You might look at unit sales, dollar sales, or profits as a better indicator of relative success.

Allow me to take a short sidebar. Many pundits and stock analysts made a huge mistake when Apple introduced the smartphone. They looked at the competition and saw that Apple was not leading in unit sales or market share. Others were sweeping in with much less expensive models, and often those models had specs that were very, very good by comparison to iPhones.

What the smart investors noticed is that for many years Apple had more than 100% of the profits. How is that possible? Every competitor was losing money, and Apple was making huge amounts of profit. So, for the industry, Apple was making more than 100% of all profits.

While there are other profitable smartphone companies now, the reality is that Apple still makes the lion's share of the money, which is one reason they are the most valuable company on the planet.

Making The Future Awesome | 140

There is a lesson here. Right now, Tesla makes more than 100% of the profit in BEVs. I'll let you finish the story.

The moral, however, is this. Which leaderboard do you want to watch? It's fun to see who is selling more cars. It is interesting to see who is generating the most revenue. But the only number that really matters to investors is the bottom line. I can safely say that Tesla will make more than 100% of the BEV profits through at least 2026, and probably beyond that. Remember, it took Tesla 18 years to consistently turn a profit. Every company has to go through that same ramp.

Does the Competition Even Matter? - How Elon Sees the Competition

Elon Musk doesn't see the competition in the same way. The goal of the company is to accelerate the switch to sustainable energy. BEVs are a huge part of that vision, but there are much more important competitors than other BEV makers. Tesla's competition according to Elon:

> "When Tesla's market cap, making sustainable energy products, exceeds that of Saudi Aramco, producing fossil fuels, you know the future will be good for Earth."

So, every producer of fossil-based energy, oil, coal, natural gas, gasoline, and charcoal are the competition. Utilities who buy these resources in order to generate power are both competitors and prospective customers.

What Is the Best Way to Look at Market Share? - Tesla's Metric for Success

In the auto sector specifically - ICE cars are the competitors, not BEVs. This is not just some happy slogan at Tesla. Tesla makes their patents available open source for other makers. They have offered to license their unique products and services to the other BEV makers. They are opening up their charging stations to all comers. Elon compliments other products when they arrive on the market.

For Tesla, the KPIs (key performance indicators) that matter:

- What is Tesla's share of all auto sales, and what percent of all autos sold are BEV?
- Is Tesla maximizing its assets in building and selling cars, solar cells, batteries, and related software that will get us closer to an almost 100% electric world?

Part of maximizing or optimizing assets is making a profit. Profits are necessary if there are to be new factories built, new innovations added, the best employees hired, and investors made happy. As of this writing, the future prospects for growth of both profits and free cash flow would appear to be well more than enough to satisfy all of the above.

Does being #1 matter: Units, revenue, profit, performance, customer satisfaction, safety?

In business, you can't completely ignore the competition, even when you have a very long lead. But great companies concentrate on improving existing products/services and developing new ones primarily from in-house innovation. Tesla is so far ahead of the pack on so many levels that almost all of their improvements have to come from the inside team. The competition is not showing much that isn't already known to Tesla.

There are exceptions. The Rivian truck had a few bells and whistles that undoubtedly got the attention of Tesla's designers. In fact, it appears that one or two of those innovations may have already been added to the Cybertruck. So, too, some of the engineering approaches in the Lucid drivetrain and battery pack were probably good fodder for water cooler conversations at Tesla.

However, for those who take a hard look at each new BEV that is announced or actually makes it to production, it is rare to see features or benefits that actually make the overall product superior to the similar class of car in the Tesla line.

Of all the products in production now, most are not even competing in the niche of any Tesla EV. This is good for all makers. If everyone can develop specific body types or performance criteria that meet the needs of disparate customer groups, better for everyone.

The real competition is more likely to come from China or other low-cost Asian manufacturers. Many pundits currently see BYD as the likely runner up to Tesla in the BEV space, long term. They have a good product, a lower selling price, a huge local market, and the blessing of both the Chinese government and Berkshire Hathaway, thus unlimited financing.

But BYD is a traditional Asian company, meaning that there is little innovation in their cars. Chinese manufacturers are experts at quickly copying others. BYD fits that tradition.

In terms of beating Tesla in units sold, there are probably only a handful or two who have any chance of achieving anywhere close to Tesla's volume. To win the dollar sales contest would be even harder. And, as noted earlier, getting to Tesla-size profits, impossible. I think you won't find any serious pundit who thinks another company will beat Tesla on profits in this millennium. Here is my list of the BEV makers, top down, with a couple of paragraphs on each.

I'll start with large legacy auto companies. Rather than repeat the harsh reality facing these companies for each, here is a set of general problems they all face.

Built in legacy costs:

- Buildings, molds, equipment need to be retrofitted or just written off. Electric cars are not anything like ICE cars, so existing facilities are not easily changed over.
- The Dealer network adds extra costs. The new companies are not using dealers. Legacy companies will need to pay off their dealers or continue to be at a disadvantage.
- Employee overhead due to pensions and other benefits is a serious issue. Legacy companies are faced with millions of retired employees and add more every year who receive ongoing benefits.
- Unions create all kinds of headwinds. While the new companies will point to better pay packages and stock offerings than union shops, unions are resistant to the kinds of changes that will need to be made.
- Management culture is often a roadblock to progress, and top managers and engineers are not drawn to legacy companies. Not my job, we tried that before, it ain't broke, 9-5, and other mentalities that interfere with progress are not present at Tesla. Unclear whether other start-ups are

going toward this old-style managerial route or will have more agile-type approaches.
- Cash issues from massive debt. Every one of the legacy companies have crippling amounts of debt, and only limited ability to raise cash through the markets.

Who Is the Next Tesla - Late to the Party

It is always harder to catch the leader than to lead in a new direction. This is especially true if the leader has a decade more experience, and huge moats that are filled with alligators and worse.

There are limited amounts of resources, and Tesla is hoarding them all. Great engineers top the list. Every other BEV maker is going to need great engineers, but the very best want to work at Tesla or SpaceX. In addition, there is now and will continue to be shortages of batteries and raw materials for batteries.

Branding is already established. Like Apple, it will be hard for any company to unseat a brand that has such a strong positive appeal. Tesla is equated with innovation, green energy, safety, performance, and fun.

All competitors will need to scale each model to a profitable level. Some will make it. Most won't. While they are scaling, the cars will be sold at a loss, eating up mounds of cash. No one knows if there are enough winners, and soon enough, to offset the losses before the money runs out.

ICE cars are losing share now. Sales are dropping and will continue to drop as the companies cannibalize their own best brands. Who will want a Ford 150 when the cost of a Ford 150 Lightning is the same sticker price and overall cost of ownership is less? And that is before taking into consideration competition from the Cybertruck or Rivian. In other words, ICE vehicles will soon become albatrosses that lose money on each one sold.

How do you make a profit if you are ramping new vehicles that lose money while also losing money on the cars you've sold for decades? Meanwhile the cash burn is even higher than the paper loss due to R & D (research and development) plus capital expense needed to build new plants and lines.

Overall sales are very likely to drop. For every car sold by Tesla, BYD, Lucid, or Rivian, there is one less sold by legacy makers.

General Motors sold 6.3M units in 2021

Many pundits pick General Motors as most likely to go bankrupt first, though it has a lot of potential competition from Toyota and BMW for that distinction. GM is currently the fourth largest car company in the world by unit sales with 6.3M in 2021.

GM has every problem noted above in spades. It isn't clear that Millennials, much less GenZ have any interest in the Hummer or Cadillac brands. The Silverado should do well, but what will be its unique selling proposition vs Rivian and Tesla?

GM has announced plans to introduce a total of 30 EV products by 2025. Their goal is to sell 1 million cars in that year. This would say that the average new offering will only sell 30,000 units per year. This is about how many Model X's Tesla sells per year at over $100,000 each. It is hard to imagine that 2025 will be a profitable year for the GM EV division. Assuming that they sell 1M fewer ICE cars due to their own cannibalization, not taking into account lost units from other BEV companies, can the ICE division still make money?

In 2025, Tesla will almost certainly produce and sell 5M cars, so it is unclear why GM has pronounced that they will catch Tesla even this decade. Possibly they don't believe Tesla's projections.

Tesla and the authors of this book wish GM, and all others in the BEV space, well. The goal of our analysis is to see what is likely to happen, not what we'd prefer to happen.

Ford Seems Confused

Just weeks before publication of this book, I was surprised to hear this - Ford CEO Jim Farley said that Ford will continue to spend on future ICE models: "We're investing in ICE segments where we're dominant and where we think, as competitors leave the segments, we can actually grow. I find it intriguing that we're portraying the future of our industry as monolithic. That's not how it goes. That's not how it's going to manifest itself."

Many pundits pick Ford to be a survivor. I think Ford is seen as nimbler than many other car companies. Their decision to launch BEVs that have prospects for quickly selling at scale, seems slightly better than the GM approach. It is surprising to see no 100% new brand offerings but are relying on established brands like Mustang and F-150.

While it is hard to find any specifics, Ford also seems bent on offering a wide range of models under Ford and Lincoln.

Ford is shooting for 2M BEVs in 2026 and state that they have the contracts for batteries and raw materials lined up to support that plan. From almost zero in 2021 to 2M in 2026 seems like an aggressive goal. I think they might achieve that run number by the end of 2026 or into 2027, but it would be a stretch.

Stellantis - Who? - 8.9M units

Even car buffs often look at me quizzically when I bring up Stellantis. Stellantis is the company formed by the 2021 merger between the Italian American conglomerate Fiat Chrysler Automobiles (FCA) and the French Peugeot Société Anonyme (PSA) Group. Stellantis Groupe PSA includes the brands Peugeot, Citroen, DS Automobiles, Opel, and Vauxhall Groupe. Stellantis FCA includes Fiat, Chrysler, Dodge, Ram, Jeep, Abarth, Alfa Romeo, Lancia, and Maserati. Overall sales of 8-9M make Stellantis the fourth largest in the world in unit sales.

They have been the least public about their plans but are bringing out several Jeep models.

Toyota 9.5 million units in 2021

Toyota is the largest carmaker by unit sales, with over 9.51M in 2021, wrestling away the crown from VW in 2020. They are far behind in the BEV space, though starting to sound like they will join the race. They are planning to offer various ICE models, 10 brands of hybrids, 15 brands of BEVs, and a potential offering of hydrogen cars into the '30's, with the statement that they will offer a full range of options. Any serious roll out of BEVs is slated in 2025, which puts them in last place among the larger legacy companies.

VW Group – 8.8M units

VW is the 2nd largest automaker. Brands include Volkswagen, Volkswagen Commercial Vehicles, ŠKODA, SEAT, CUPRA, Audi, Lamborghini, Bentley, and Porsche. Together they produced 8.8M cars in 2021.

There is so much to say about VW. They have several decent offerings on the market and are a factor in Europe. Their previous CEO seemed very fired up about entering the BEV era. But then he was fired. The new leadership has not been very clear, thus far, on how aggressively they will pursue the BEV game. I expect them to be consequential, but they could be a major loser if they have now taken their eye off the ball.

Hyundai Kia includes Genesis - 6.6M units

With 6.6M total units sold in 2021, Hyundai Kia is the world's third largest maker as they have been growing while GM has been shrinking.

Quietly, Hyundai and Kia have planted 4 BEV models in the US market. With inexpensive and attractive offerings, they now have sales placing them in the top 20 US BEVs.

Hyundai's first U.S. electric car was the limited-availability Ioniq hatchback in 2017, followed by the Kona EV in 2019. Kia introduced the Soul EV in 2014 and the Niro EV, which came into the U.S. market in 2019. Both companies now offer the Ioniq 5 (Hyundai) and EV6 (Kia), two, all-new, fully dedicated electric cars, each with over 300 miles of range and starting prices around $42,000. They are planning to roll out a $60,000 electric Genesis.

This early start could easily provide Hyundai/Kia with a serious potential for success. They plan to build a new factory in the US with production beginning in 2025. Their goal is to make 3M BEVs by 2030.

Where Is Honda?

Honda includes Acura. Honda comes very late to the party with no significant entry into BEVs until at least 2024. Their goal is to produce 2M units by 2030, putting them far behind the other major makers. Their unique selling proposition is their solid-state battery which they hope to test in 2024.

Nissan

Nissan plans to launch 23 new electrified models by 2030, but only half of these will be BEV. The other half? Some kind of hybrid. Nissan plans to sell 1M electrified vehicles annually by 2023 and about 2M by 2030. This unambitious goal is not likely to be the best strategy for success.

Aggressive Renault

Offsetting Nissan, where they are a 40% owner, Renault has one of the most aggressive BEV plans in the auto market. Renault intends to be 90% BEV in 2030. While many pundits expect 90% of all auto sales to be BEV well before 2030, most legacy makers are nowhere near Renault's projections. Their 43% stake in Nissan could push Nissan to drop their reliance on so many hybrids in favor of full BEV. With 6.7M cars produced in 2021 between the two companies,

Renault/Nissan might be one of the winners in this race.

Recent reporting shows Renault reducing their ownership in Nissan from 43% to 12% over the next months.

BMW - Lost

BMW says it will have 13 BEV models on sale in 2023, from compact cars to the biggest, most luxurious cars to wear the blue-and-white propeller. BMW has been an early adopter, but their sales results have not been stunning. With this ramp to 13 models, they will definitely have more styles than any other maker. Is this approach going to be a winning strategy? Many pundits see BMW as one of the first legacy companies to go bankrupt.

Changan - Nio - No Guess

Chongqing Changan Automobile, the state-owned Chinese partner of Ford and Mazda, has renamed its EV unit, Changan NIO New Energy Automotive Technology, to Avatar Technology Corporation. The brand-new EV unit of Changan will partner with telecom giant Huawei and Contemporary Amperex Technology (CATL) to develop smart vehicle solutions.

Nio has been much in the news as offering a battery swap/subscription approach. The jury is still out on whether this method can work even in China.

Changan plans to roll out as many as 26 smart EV models over the next five years, with the first two scheduled to be released in 2022.

Mercedes Offers Big Talk

No legacy maker is talking a bigger game than Mercedes. They have already launched their EQS, an electric version of its opulent flagship S-Class sedan, and it has unveiled the EQS SUV, which goes on sale in late 2022.

By 2022, Mercedes-Benz will have battery electric vehicles in all segments the company serves, but many of these will be hybrids. From 2025 onwards, all newly launched vehicle architectures will be BEV and customers will be able to choose an all-electric alternative for every model the company makes.

Mercedes is working with partners to ramp 200 GWh of battery production, enough to supply a 2M BEV run rate. While others, like GM, also plan to have a major production capacity in batteries, Mercedes appears to have bigger goals than most.

Geely Lotus · Proton · Volvo Car Group · Polestar

Geely sells about 2.2M cars under various local Chinese brands, plus they fully own Volvo, which contributes another 600K units. Polestar was recently taken public through a SPAC, but Volvo, who is 100% owned by Geely, owns just under 50% of the stock in Polestar.

Volvo has been an early adopter of intentions to go all in on BEV, but they have definitely done so with fits and stops. Geely itself is planning to offer 10 hybrids and 15 BEVs with a goal to sell more EVs than it currently sells ICE cars. Polestar is all BEV.

Mazda

Mazda doesn't currently offer a compelling entry in the BEV space, and there is no clear strategy announced from Mazda about their future in this sector.

Revisiting the Market Share Question

We have already noted above that the market share that really matters is worldwide sales as a percentage of all cars sold.

There are also tons of headlines about market share losses by geographic area. Since Tesla is supply constrained and is never going to use market share headlines to decide where to ship cars each month, there are going to be months and quarters where Tesla doesn't have the leading market share in one or another country or region. In other words, these headlines are nonsense unless they include nuances about likely ebbs and flows due to shipping.

Tesla typically does most exporting in the first month to six weeks of each quarter, then almost none during the final six weeks. Due to the fact that the market watchers are all attuned to quarterly performance, this strategy allows Tesla to maximize their overall sales within a quarter. Vehicles shipped in January don't typically get officially sold until February or March. Product delivered locally will end up "sold" within a week or so of being produced.

As of early November 2022, Tesla will attempt to smooth these export issues to concentrate on the customer experience and the costs of transportation. However, since Shanghai supplies all of Asia and Asia Pacific, Berlin will export to all of Europe, and some Mediterranean countries, and the US based factories will be exporting to North American countries (with S & X exported from CA worldwide), local market share comparisons will still be hard to use for competitive analysis.

Number One in Safety is the KPI Tesla Cares About

As a fan or investor in Tesla, what are the headlines that really matter? Tesla says consistently that their number one concern is safety. Therefore, I would assume that any comparison of competitors (ICE or BEV) around the subject of safety would and should be important to everyone in the Tesla community. As of this writing, no other car can hold a candle to Tesla in safety.

Tesla has set the standard for safety. Not only does Tesla ace all the tests required by government agencies and insurance companies, their own record keeping shows that Tesla's are less likely to be in accidents than other similar cars.

Now that Tesla vehicles offer a safety score and insurance rates based on safety scores (explained in detail later), Tesla is already seeing a change in driving behavior that results in better overall driving. So even the safety score idea has helped make Teslas safer.

Finally, the driver assist features, even without full self-driving (FSD), result in fewer crashes. Tesla has the data that clearly shows fewer accidents with each ratcheting up of the driver assist options.

The "enhanced" features for greater safety are as follows:

Traffic aware cruise control comes standard with every Tesla. I like to call this feature point and drive. You set the speed, the distance you prefer between you and a car you are following, and you are ready to go. When you are in traffic, merely push the right-side stalk down once, release and take your foot off the accelerator. From this point, your main job is to point the car, it will take care of the rest.

Of course, you still have to be alert to every possible issue. But it will warn you about many issues such as drifting into another lane or onto the shoulder, or a car in the lane you are trying to merge into. It does not warn you about speed limits, help you with navigation, or respond to stop lights.

Autopilot also comes standard with a Tesla. If you push down twice on the right-side stalk, you will engage Autopilot. The Tesla owner's manual lists these features to reduce driver workload:

> *Traffic*-Aware Cruise Control
>
> *Autosteer* - keeps you in your lane, takes you around corners, slows for various difficult driving conditions or objects.
>
> *Auto Lane Change* - Changes lanes automatically when you need to exit a road or freeway and offers you the option to change lanes based on slow traffic or other issues.
>
> *Stop Light and Stop Sign Warning* - Sometimes stops for stop signs. Starts again automatically. Works very well if there is a car in front of you.
>
> *Navigate on Autopilot* - Set your destination and the car will do almost all the driving on freeways and major roads. Can do some city driving. Automatically disconnects with a warning when it is not able to drive in certain conditions. The car also sees the speed limit and will adjust accordingly. You can set the car to go faster than the limit

Traffic Light and Stop Sign Control - Sometimes stops for stop lights. Starts again automatically. Works very well if there is a car in front of you.

All of these enhanced driving features are subject to automatic upgrades over the air and may work differently by the time you read this.

Autopilot is also designed with an accident-avoidance system that helps alert you and provides braking or steering assistance to avoid an accident.

The car is designed to minimize impact if it knows the accident can't be avoided by using positioning that will do the least injury to passengers. The seat belts will also cinch prior to impact. No other car has these features as of this writing.

If you use Cruise Control, your safety is better than if you don't. If you use autopilot your safety improves compared to Cruise Control. For the safest system, you need to purchase FSD, which is not automatically included when you buy the car.

While there is almost no difference between Autopilot and FSD on the freeway, there is a huge difference in the city. FSD will stop for all required stops. It will turn right or left without assistance from you. It will navigate door-to-door with no help from you. Traffic circles are not an issue. Work zones are just part of a day's work for FSD.

FSD sees all cars, people, animals, road work cones and horses, curbs, and anything else necessary to take you safely from place to place.

When you use FSD, you are significantly safer than when using autopilot.

Unit Sales, Revenues, Profits

If you are a fan or an investor, these three performance indicators are likely what you are checking out. Are they important?

While Tesla has a backlog of months, these numbers are inconsequential compared to production numbers. When production outstrips unit sales, then the game becomes more interesting. If every market has immediate availability or even less than one month, all three of these KPIs are the ones you'll want to follow closely.

Customer Satisfaction

There have been studies that have shown that profit is directly linked to overall customer satisfaction. If most of your customers are recommending your product or service, you are likely to be more profitable than the company who gets fewer recommendations.

So, this is a big stat to follow. Apple has, once again, shown how critical this business skill can be. They are always right at the top of all companies in customer satisfaction. As shown elsewhere in the book, Tesla is also at the top of the charts over all other automakers.

CHAPTER 32

The World Needs a Lot More EVs

by Randy Kirk

Elon Musk just projected that 50% or more of all new cars sold in 2030 will be BEVs. He further estimated that less than 20% of new cars sold in 2035 will be ICE.

YouTuber, Steven Mark Ryan, and financial analysts at ARKK Investments have both estimated that just under 60M BEVs will be shipped in 2027. That would be at least 75% of all cars shipped that year.

California recently passed rules that require 100% of all new vehicles sold starting in 2035 to be BEV. Many European countries have similar laws on the books.

Geely has announced that they intend to be 50% BEV by the end of 2023. Other car makers have various goals to reach zero ICE by 2030, while very few project any ICE vehicles after 2035.

But Geely isn't alone. Ford and Toyota have announced much faster increases in their BEV production than just a few months ago. Expect other manufacturers to increase their projections.

Tony Seba and others, including me, believe that consumers will be completely over ICE cars by 2026, and most car makers will find they have no market for any ICE vehicles. It won't be government edicts or marketing mavens who will determine the end of the ICE age. It will be consumers who aren't willing to pay the same or more for cars that pollute, need regular expensive trips to a dwindling number of gas stations, and require oil changes and other maintenance.

One could say that there is no issue as to whether the time of ICE is over, but rather the question is only focused on when. We'll start with the most conservative estimate. What will it take to get to zero ICE car production in 2035? We'll assume a steady ramp.

Let's start with an estimated 10% BEVs sold worldwide in 2022. If we continue with 70% growth each year, we will hit 100% in early 2027. With a drop to 60% average growth, 100% will come in early 2028. If we see a huge drop to 50% growth, the final ICE year would be 2029. 40% equals 2030. 30% takes us to 2032. 20% is finally slow enough that we might slip into 2036.

I would be shocked if even the most anti-EV pundit would honestly estimate that BEVs will increase at less than 30% per year. Almost every car company has agreed that the ICE age is over. When do you think ICE production will stop?

What will it take to get 70% annual growth? Is this a pipe dream? Will the law of large numbers finally take over? Or is it more likely that folks will be willing to wait for BEVs rather than buy a flip phone version of a car in 2026?

And then there is this wild card. What effect will the new US incentives have on production and sales?

Tesla has clearly stated their plans and is building the infrastructure and supply chain to add 50% to their production each year. Since they currently make up about 25% of all BEVs and that is likely to continue, where will the other 75% come from? On the one hand, this seems like a huge get, but we have been warned repeatedly that the competition is coming. Can the competition make 60M BEV cars in 2027 or will it take until 2030? Longer?

Pickup trucks account for about 4M vehicles or 5% of vehicle sales, worldwide. Ford, GM, Chrysler, and Tesla are all pushing hard on this segment, not to mention Rivian. Having enough manufacturing capacity for 4M BEV trucks in 2027 seems a no brainer.

SUVs are the elephant in the room, representing about 45% of all vehicles produced each year. Where will all those SUV's come from? Unsurprisingly, the smartest of the automakers are very busy building SUV's and factories to produce many, many more. Tesla alone will make about 2M SUVs in 2023 and should be able to maintain their 25% of the market with 8M in 2027. Tesla is planning a small vehicle or vehicles by 2024, which could help them reach that number or even exceed it.

There are dozens of reasonably good BEV SUVs on the market already. China has a solid lead with BYD, but Ford, VW, Kia, and others are certainly capable of hitting 2-5M each by 2027. Maybe the top 10 makers will average 4M, the next 10 makers at 1M, and the rest make up the difference. Many of these will come from new companies like BYD.

Similar to Tesla, when Ford hits scale on their Mach-E, it will not be difficult to copy and paste factories to produce more. Other major makers should be able to increase capacity quickly once they have one or two production lines fully scaled. The limiting factor is much more likely to be raw materials and battery cells than creating facilities, tools, etc.

Here is a possible 2027 BEV sales projection by company:

Tesla - 12M
BYD - 8M
VW - 4M
Hyundai-Kia 4M
GM - 3M
Ford - 3M
Stellantis - 3M
Toyota - 3M
Mercedes - 2M
Honda - 2M
BMW - 2M
Porsche - 1M
Nissan - 1M
Renault - 1M
Other - 10M
TOTAL – 59M

Therefore, contrary to almost all the pundits, it is possible we'll see the end of the ICE age by 2027 or very shortly thereafter, and Elon will have underestimated the change for once. It is possible that each legacy maker might be able to find six models each where they can be competitive. GM can talk about 30 BEV models, but it is much more likely they will end up with half-a-dozen that have significant scale and make them money.

If all the Tesla competitors are able to make this ramp and produce good enough BEVs to satisfy a growing demand, Tesla will still be able to sell all they can make for years into the future. They will grab 20%+ market share and keep their lead in the categories where they choose to compete.

All the above assumes that the robotaxi revolution is only slowly ramping by 2027, and that there is still a huge demand for cars you drive yourself. Once robotaxis are a serious item, the entire landscape changes. Who is going to want to own a car if they can be driven by a "chauffeur" anywhere, anytime, for half the cost of ownership?

What about the effect of the Inflation Reduction Act (IRA) on increasing production of BEVs in the US? It is hard to see how the IRA will increase overall worldwide sales when production seems a bigger issue than demand. The IRA will very likely increase the production of vehicles, battery cells, battery material mining and processing, and assembled battery products such as energy storage and BEV packs in the US. Europe is calling these incentives unfair. Changes may be in the works.

The reason worldwide production may not be affected is that there are many limiting factors that will keep overall sales growth to the numbers above, such as material and battery supply.

The IRA might also cause a shift in some sales plans. The overall savings per vehicle may be well over $10,000. This will make a bigger difference to the buyer interested in a $40,000 car they can purchase for $30,000 than it would for the buyer of a $60,000 vehicle that now gets the car for $50,000.

I also look for the IRA to help legacy automakers with the transition. Generally, there is a long lag time from the first sample off the line to the first profitable unit off the line. The IRA bill is likely to reduce that time lag and increase profits on each car after reaching break even.

What about the effect on Tesla, specifically? Assuming Tesla gets any kind of a fair shake from those who are now working out the details of the bill, Tesla could be increasing profits by many, many billions of dollars per year.

Tesla is planning to make at least 110 GWh of batteries per year. Tesla is supposed to receive the benefit of the subsidy from all of the batteries made at the factory shared with Panasonic in Reno. That is another 40 or so GWh. The bill provides $45 per KWh or about $3,000 per car. If Tesla keeps the entire amount as profit, this alone will bring in almost $7B each year.

Elon has already stated that these incentives will cause Tesla to ramp US production "pedal to the metal". It could easily mean additional lines in Reno, although Panasonic has announced other new US plants where at least the $45 portion would probably go to Panasonic, not Tesla. Tesla would still make $10 per KWh for assembling the US produced battery into an energy storage unit or an auto pack.

Tesla seems to be ready to start refining lithium in Texas. This would be additional potential subsidy money.

Finally, while the $7,500 per car and $40,000 per semi-truck is a subsidy to the purchaser, most suspect that all makers will increase their prices to some degree in order to get some of that benefit. Then the market will decide if those price hikes can hold.

CHAPTER 33

The Robotaxi Revolution

by Lars Strandridder

Elon has made some big comments on FSD lately, including at AI Day2 on Sept 30, 2022 (where Tesla highlighted their successes and plans for all things artificial intelligence) and is still confident that Tesla will solve Full Self Driving in 2022. Tesla's leadership, in general, seems more confident than ever before. Even other experts in the field are getting excited about Tesla FSD progress.

James Douma is cofounder and Chief Software Architect of Nitobi Software. He is an experienced software and Internet application developer with a background in information system design. He also has experience in artificial intelligence and information science. He has a computer science and applied mathematics background from York University where he began his career in software development. So, he knows a thing or two about this subject. James' mind was blown when he recently took his Tesla with Tesla's full self-driving beta software out for a drive in the mountains. This test trip was complete with hairpin turns, soft shoulders, and non-existent lane markings. The car handled it all perfectly.

If you follow Tesla and their many beta testers, you may have seen thousands of such videos. But just remember, no one else can do what Tesla's FSD can do. Sure, Waymo could spend a year mapping out the exact road that James tested, and then they would be able to navigate it. But then if James takes the Tesla car for a drive on a different route, the Waymo car can't follow. They have to map that route as well to keep up. What companies like Waymo and Cruise are doing is simply not scalable and will never become a general solution.

So even comparing Waymo and Cruise to Tesla is not really the right thing to do, because they can all have success in their own specific field. Waymo and Cruise have some cars today providing robotaxis in a few cities and will expand the service to many other cities when they have more experience, and when they get more cities mapped out.

Tesla will still be able to offer their robotaxi, as well. But Tesla will not be stuck in geofenced mapped areas. Teslas will be able to go anywhere they choose.

Additionally, Tesla is not relying on various expensive systems like lidar and radar to "see" the environment around the car. Tesla believes in vision only. If humans can drive with two eyes fixed in one direction, Tesla vehicles can get all the visual information they need with eight cameras strategically positioned around the car.

Tesla doesn't need lidar, as Andrew Karpathy, past Sr. Director of AI at Tesla, has already shown. Tesla is able to make a map of its surroundings with only vision, and this virtual map looks exactly like the lidar system. As Elon also talked about in the interview with the Silicon Valley Owners Club, radar and lidar are not helping make a great Neural Network. Quite the opposite.

Radar was like biking with training wheels. The kid with the training wheels thinks he is actually very good at riding a bike, but as soon as you take the training wheels off, he will fall, and he will find out that he can't actually ride a bike yet. When Tesla removed radar, aka their training wheels, they also found out that their Neural Network was not as good as they thought it was. Radar was helping the Neural Network too much, even at times confusing the computer with too much contradictory information.

Now Tesla no longer runs into the "local maximum." While using lidar, radar, and vision previously, they would get really close to a certain goal, and they would think they were just about to solve a certain level of the FSD puzzle. But then, the learning curve would start to taper off. That's why Elon has been wrong before about the timing. They thought they were just about to get it, and then the learning tapered off.

Tesla is no longer seeing any local maximum. Elon has been confident for more than a year that they will reach or exceed the ability of an excellent driver in 2022. We have been close for a long time now, as so many times before, but Elon is not seeing a slowdown. The learning curve is not tapering off. Quite the opposite. That is why Elon is still confident it will happen soon.

The big breakthrough came when Elon realized the scope of the problem. Elon concluded that Tesla needed to solve real world Artificial Intelligence (AI) Vision to realize the goal of having the car drive better than a human. Tesla is not trying to get to level 3 or level 4 driver assistance capabilities, they are shooting straight for full autonomy. This is also why some think Tesla is behind. They don't have a good level 3, or any level 4 driver assist package. Tesla is not trying to solve that problem. Tesla is not making a driver assist system. They are making a car that will be able to drive itself everywhere.

When Elon says that everyone else is about five years behind Tesla in full self-driving, many agree that this is true and probably an understatement. Because even if Waymo or Cruise hit their goal at the same time as Tesla, they are still at a huge disadvantage.

Waymo does not make any cars, and Cruise would have to start ramping up production of their EV vehicles with the needed hardware. We have seen just how fast GM has been able to ramp up their EV production through the last five years. From Q4 of 2021 to Q2 of 2022 they produced about 2,300 EVs. So, companies like Waymo and even Cruise will suddenly have to ramp up EV production like crazy just to get any meaningful number of robotaxis deployed. And they are not ready for it.

Even if they had a great robotaxi solution at the same time as Tesla, they would still be years behind since Tesla can already produce close to 2M EVs per year as of today's production run rate. Tesla can also make an OTA update today and have 2M robotaxis immediately.

If Waymo and/or Cruise decided they wanted to try and copy Tesla's general approach, they would have to dramatically increase the fleet and the data collection and auto labelling of the data.

If you have the data, now you need an advanced neural net training system with massive amounts of storage and compute speed. Tesla has that kind of computer capacity, and is now adding Dojo, the world's best AI training computer, which they have built themselves. No one is even close to starting to build any such capacity.

Tesla only being five years ahead of the competition in robotaxi is probably conservative. I think they are more like eight years ahead, because the other guys don't even understand the scope of the problem. They are currently in the same place as Elon was over two years ago, when he didn't understand that to have a car that is autonomous anywhere, you need to solve general AI.

It appears that Tesla will have the vast majority of the robotaxi business to themselves for the rest of this decade, with Waymo and Cruise and others doing a little work in some cities which they have mapped.

Let's take a look at that. We see right now that EV demand is pretty much endless. The same will be true for the robotaxi service. Everyone who has some kind of FSD can just jump on board until the whole fleet of 2B cars on the road is switched out with FSD cars. So that will take at least a decade.

When Tesla has solved FSD and passes any regulatory hurdles necessary to allow driverless vehicles, they will be able to turn it on for all of their cars. This includes expected new entries: The Semi truck (which will take some additional learning), Cybertruck, little robotaxi, Roadster, and the van they no doubt will produce later on.

Tesla will be able to just spit out as many FSD vehicles as possible in all categories for decades to come. They will have a huge first-mover advantage, and therefore also become the biggest player by far. In 10, 20, or 30 years the world may only have robotaxi cars on the road.

Those who laugh at the idea of an all robotaxi world in 10 years should consider this. If robotaxis only cost the consumer 25¢ a mile, and if they are just 10 times safer than a regular car, and if most folks won't even need to own a car, the transition could be extremely rapid. Much like going from landline phones to smartphones.

But let's do some numbers here. If we say Tesla will have solved FSD by the end of 2022 or early in 2023, then by the end of 2023, they will start to receive approvals in some cities, states, and countries to drive the cars as robotaxis. They will get these approvals because their data will show how incredibly safe they are. Much safer than human drivers.

I do expect Tesla to be able to produce at least 2.3M cars in 2023, all of which can be turned on as FSD cars. Elon says Tesla will continue to increase production by 50% per year until reaching 20M cars in 2030

This suggests a total output of

3.45M in 2024
5.17M in 2025
7.76M in 2026
11.64M in 2027
17.40M in 2028
20.00M in 2029

And all these cars Tesla produces in just these seven years from 2023 until 2029 will add up to just under 70M vehicles. All will be capable of being robotaxis or being driven autonomously.

Elon thinks the competition might be measurable in 2028 or '29. Or maybe some of the other automakers are getting their hardware and software from Tesla. As noted with EVs, Elon knows he can't make enough to satisfy the demand. Because even if we take this example out a couple of more years to 2030 or 2031, Tesla will be well over 100M robotaxis. Therefore Tesla, all on their own, has already turned about five percent of all vehicles on the road to robotaxis. That's quite amazing, but who will supply the other 95%?

Making The Future Awesome | 170

Indeed, Tesla will be the Apple of the FSD car industry. Everyone will know Tesla has FSD cars and was the first to do it. The public will know that Tesla has the best robotaxis, and that other robotaxis have "Tesla Inside."

Everyone will have a Tesla app to summon a robotaxi or to use at a Tesla charging station if you are still driving your own vehicle. You can just press summon robotaxi in the Tesla app and it will come to you.

The value of a robotaxi network is off the charts. Elon estimates that a Tesla robotaxi will earn either Tesla, the fleet owner (like Uber or Lyft), or you, $30K per year after all expenses. In 2030 Tesla might theoretically have a fleet of 100M robotaxis, each earning Tesla $30K per year, each and every single year. That will be $3T dollars in profit. The cars will likely cost Tesla less than $20K, so the amount of depreciation is minimal.

The $30K per year is a very rough estimate. How many hours per day will the car be used? What will the charge be per mile? There will only be a little spend on maintenance, cleaning, and charging. Tesla would be using their own charging stations and those would be generating their electricity from Tesla solar panels and battery storage. So that cost should be very small as well for Tesla.

Maybe we should be a bit more conservative. Possibly Tesla only keeps ⅓ of the cars it produces for the Tesla fleet. We'll keep it simple and say 30M cars. If those cars create $30K per year income, that is still $900B. Apple, the largest company in the world, ONLY earned $153B in 2021.

Of course, if Tesla only uses ⅓ for the fleet, they will sell all the others with FSD, and Elon says that FSD will cost $100K or more when the robotaxi is possible. If Tesla averages 10M cars per year at $100K each for just FSD, that would be $1T per year in profits.

Yeah, good luck catching up to Tesla at this point. When Tesla has such a big lead with maybe 30M to 100M robotaxis on the road by 2030 or 2031. And in late 2022, Toyota, Ford, and BMW still think they will be making a lot of ICE cars by then. Well, good luck with that my friends.

Tony Seba from the think tank Rethink, believes that most of the public will want to just have a subscription to a robotaxi service. TaaS, Transport as a Service, might cost $200 a month, as compared to paying 20¢ per mile for a robotaxi ride. The average person drives about 35 miles a day. That still only adds up to about $210 a month if you simply just summon a robotaxi when you need one. This is why I speculate a subscription might be as low as $200.

A new study has shown that in the US it now costs an average of $712 a month to own a car, everything included. A robotaxi subscription of $200 will be 2-3 times cheaper than owning the average car. I think many people in the cities and suburbs are going to want TaaS instead of the hassle of owning a car.

It is astounding how fast Tesla can be a dominating taxi service in every single big city on the planet. If we take cities of 1 million people or greater, there are only about 512 of these in the entire world. In a city like Copenhagen, here in Denmark, that has a population of 1M, the biggest taxi companies have about 1,000 taxis. Even in a big city like New York, they only have about 13,500 taxis in total.

If we say that in 2030 Tesla will actually be able to produce only the 20M cars that they have as their target, that is enough cars to replace all the taxis in 1,481 cities the size of New York. We don't have anywhere close to that many such cities.

We have about 10,000 cities in the whole world, according to the World Urban Forum. So, 20 million cars would be enough to put about 2,000 robotaxis in every single city on the planet, just from the production from that year. Some of the cities will need 5 taxis and some might need 60,000 taxis in a place like Tokyo, the world's largest city by population. In fact, it is theoretically possible for Tesla to easily take over the entire world taxi service by 2030, since Tesla will have produced about 70 million FSD cars from 2023-2030. So, by then, Tesla could already have taken half of those 70 million and put an average of 3,500 robotaxis in all cities on the planet.

When we hit 2030!

After 2030 Tesla will just continue to put 20 million robotaxis or more on the road every single year as others might start ramping up their robotaxis services. Yes, it is already all over with the lead Tesla has today. No one will be able to compete, because Tesla will be a worldwide established name as a robotaxi service long before the other even gets started.

How much of the world do you think someone like Waymo will have mapped in 2030. This is not comparable, as Waymo's solution is hardly scalable.

Tesla is going to win this one, as Windows won 75% of the market for computer operating systems. If any legacy automakers want to be a part of this game, I think they might have to license software and hardware from Tesla. Some maybe will, others would probably rather die before they license anything from Tesla. But that's their funeral.

Since Elon now understands the scope of the problem, and doesn't see any local maximum anymore, I think Elon is right this time. He might, of course, be off by six months or so, but that doesn't really matter in the big picture.

I know when the kid has yelled "wolf" too many times people stopped believing him. But eventually the wolf does come, and I do think the wolf is coming this time around.

And this wolf is going to swallow the whole transportation industry.

When will Robotaxi Income Ramp?

Conservative pundits in the Tesla community and among the Wall Street analysts believe that Tesla will be able to start rolling out robotaxi service in late 2024. So, what might that do for Tesla's bottom line in 2025?

The difficult part of the ramp will be the cart and horse problem. You don't want to put 1,000 robotaxis in a city where only 100 people know the service exists. You don't want to have 100,000 people expecting to hail a robotaxi if there are only 25 working in that region.

Fortunately, Tesla can go to school on Uber and Lyft's experience with their roll out. In fact, I believe that Uber and Lyft will be only too happy to buy Tesla's to replace their own drivers. Maybe some of the drivers will become Tesla robotaxi fleet operators.

Conservatively, Tesla might start ramping a few cities at first. This way they could saturate the market with available cars, and then let the public know about the Tesla App. Maybe in 2025, there will only be 100,000 robotaxis operating at $30,000 profit for Tesla. But, if Tesla continues to sell cars, Tesla will charge $100,000 for FSD. Additionally, folks who already have FSD, and want to make their cars available on the App, will be paying a service fee to Tesla.

CHAPTER 34

The Factory IS the Product

by Lars Strandridder

"...About five or six years ago, we said we wanted to become the *best manufacturer* in the world, and **that**..., somewhat counterintuitively to some people, will actually be...*our strongest competitive advantage*." Elon Musk Q2, 2022 earnings call.

It doesn't matter what the product is, if you have the ability, through manufacturing, to make it more suited to its purpose and/or less expensively than your competitor, you have an advantage that should be unassailable. You can still lose out to a lesser manufacturer due to poor marketing, lack of capital, bad luck, etc., but generally the advantage is huge.

To make the best cars in the world, Tesla designs vehicles and factories from the ground up. But the car is not the real product. Elon has always said the factory is the product. This is one of the single most important things to understand about Tesla. The factory and the production are what set Tesla apart from everyone else, now, and especially in the long term.

Elon talked about the factory as product back at 'Battery Day' in 2020. He noted that there were more innovations to be had in the manufacturing process itself than the electric car. Moreover, Tesla's goal is to be head and shoulders above everyone else in manufacturing by increasing the volumetric efficiency of the factory.

Because Tesla is building the new factories from the ground up, Tesla has the opportunity to change everything about the factory, from how it is built to how cars are produced. Tesla had nothing holding them back, like culture or ingrained ways of doing things. They were able to go back to 1st principles and figure out what is actually the most efficient way of producing a car with the available technology, and just make one big machine that makes cars…the factory.

Toyota is famous in business school classes as the company that perfected the production line with its agile approach. But Tesla has now changed almost everything about the way a car factory manufactures cars.

They don't have a traditional production line but divide the factory up into small hexagonal cells that can be operated independently. Tesla doesn't have a production line, but production cells.

In a traditional production line, if one section breaks down, the whole production line stops. This is not the case with Tesla production cells. Tesla can stop one cell, while all the others' cells are still producing. This is also one of the reasons Tesla is able to make so many improvements and innovation to their cars and production cells on a weekly basis.

Now, if Tesla wants to make a change in a part or a process, they only have to stop one production cell and try to make the change they want. Once the process has been changed or the new part inserted, the AI of the factory calculates if the new idea makes the car more efficient, the production faster, or whatever it is they want to test out. If the computer says, "Go,"' they can then ramp up that production cell with the new feature, and when it is 100% ramped up, they start implementing it into all the other cells, all without ever stopping production.

Image supplied by Jim Ringold

This makes Tesla's pace of innovation almost impossible to keep up with, because they can make changes and implement new ideas every single day.

When legacy automakers have an idea or a new design change to a car, it takes years for them to implement those ideas into actual production. One of the world's most agile car companies is Toyota, yet to implement a new idea takes between 2.5-4 years. It is truly shocking that Tesla can implement new ideas daily.

Legacy automakers and even startups commonly take the catalog approach to manufacturing. They are merely glorified assemblers. Engineering attempts to fit existing parts and approaches into a new car, so as to avoid the R & D, testing, molds, and tooling cost associated with a new product. Even when buying products off the shelf, these companies rely on third parties to provide consistent quality in materials and final products built to close tolerances. After all of that, the product may still have issues fitting with other 3rd party products.

Tesla attempts to build as many of these parts as possible, themselves. They rarely buy off-the-shelf products. Even those items provided by third parties are often created and produced specifically for Tesla to Tesla's specs.

Sandy Munro, CEO of Munro & Associates, is a car expert who has worked for both Ford and GM. For the past 35 years, his company has been reverse engineering cars and selling the reports to other original equipment manufacturers (OEMs) such as major automakers and helping them get better at manufacturing. So, we will probably not find anyone that knows as much about how a car is built and how legacy automakers work than Sandy Munro.

He was very critical about Tesla's cars in the beginning because he didn't think their build quality was good enough. But that changed.

The more he learned, the more often he exclaimed that he was "blown away." He was blown away when he first ripped apart the Model Y and saw the octovalve, the innovative pump that heats and cools everything in the car. He was blown away the second time he ripped apart a Tesla. He was astonished to find that Tesla had made 13 design changes to the octovalve in only four months. Like Sandy said, "No one does that". No one but Tesla, that is. "They work with the speed of thought," as Sandy put it. He noted that it would have taken some legacy automakers five years to implement that many changes into a system like that.

Making The Future Awesome | 180

Another factory approach that Tesla has taken to a whole new level is the artificial intelligence that is running the whole factory. Because Tesla has the best engineers in the world working for them, they write the AI software themselves. One example is the AI that is checking the car's paint job to see if the paint is good enough before it goes on to the next step in the process.

At the other end of the line, the software checks every critical function in the car, making sure that the specific car meets every government requirement (plus Tesla's own requirements that are more critical than any government) before it is driven out of the factory. Then that car receives a virtual copy in the cloud. As it is driven for the next 30 years or so, data from the car is matched to the digital twin. No other car company has anything that can compare.

Tesla is trying to remove all human bottlenecks that will slow down production and scale. Everywhere in the factory where you would normally wait for a human 'okay,' Tesla has AI that will check if the car is 'okay' and ready for the next step.

This approach to manufacturing is what some experts, such as Joe Justice, call "Digital Self-Management." Joe was head of Agile at Tesla in Fremont and has worked for both Microsoft and Amazon. He has also helped car companies like BMW, VW, and Toyota to become more agile. He also holds four world records for fastest production of a car with his company Wikispeed. You can see why Joe is the go-to guy about production of cars and agile production.

Joe says this about Tesla's factory, "There is agile, and then there is Tesla." So even though he has taught BMW how to run an agile company, and BMW hopes to become more agile in three years' time, it is not like they will become as agile as Tesla. Tesla is on a whole other level when it comes to the pace of innovation.

Digital self-management (DSM) is a huge advantage for Tesla. Every single step of building the car Tesla has a DSM system that will determine if a car is ready to go to the next process. Everything within the factory has a definition of 'ready' and a definition of 'done,' as Joe Justice has explained. A DSM AI system can determine if it is ready or done, and Tesla doesn't need humans to approve any step along the way. That is all controlled by AI.

When you start working at Tesla you will also get a special app from Tesla, they have made themselves. The app shows you everything about the company. So, you know how the company is doing and what needs attention.

This leads to a philosophy of applying **The Gemba Walk to Its Absolute Maximum**

The following is taken from a LinkedIn article by Hao Li that gives a summation of Joe Justice's thinking about Tesla. You can find the complete article here.
https://www.linkedin.com/pulse/insights-agile-tesla-joe-justice-hào-lǐ

Gemba (現場) is a Japanese term meaning "**the actual place**". In lean practices, the Gemba refers to **"the place where value is created"** such as the shop floor in manufacturing, the operating room in a hospital, the job site on a construction project, the kitchen of a restaurant, and the workstation of a software programmer. The Gemba Walk, much like Management by Walking Around (MBWA), is an activity that takes management to the front lines to look for waste and opportunities to practice Gemba for improvement.

現場
GEMBA

OBSERVE
RECOGNIZE
COMMUNICATE
COOPERATE
SOLVE THE PROBLEM

WALK

The goal is to be able to **walk up and, in less than 5-7 minutes,** completely grasp how you can contribute. You can see the board that has been wiped hundreds of times; you can imagine how many people are solving problems. Using definition of done (DoD) and definition of ready (DoR): "we are done when xxx happens", when you walk there, you can see the DoD and DoR pillar, where wishes are coming in and wishes are going out, then you look in the middle and can ask yourself with "the law of two feet", is it the most valuable spot if I am standing here right now? If yes, stay, if not, "the law of two feet" says walk somewhere else where you can add value. The idea is to get each employee to another great opportunity quickly.

All of the above approaches to manufacturing are next level, and it is unlikely that the legacy manufacturers or even the new start-ups will ever employ these approaches, as they either have a very old culture or they have learned from these old cultures and methods. To be honest, the old ways are actually easier to manage, as they don't require placing so much power and trust in the employees. Employees with the other firms will never get the power to just go spend money or make other critical decisions on their own, even if it makes something better or a production faster. They all have a budget and layers of management required to spend any money or make any changes.

The problem for someone like VW that really wants to move fast is they have made a nine-year budget. So, for the next nine years they have already made the plan of what to do, and how much it will cost. So, for the next nine years, they will make very few changes to that plan, and very few new ideas will see the light of day until they are nine years out in the future, because it does not fit within the budget.

This is why Tesla does not have a budget. They want to be able to make changes every single day if those changes make the production or the product better - even if it costs more money.

So, because of this management system, and the fact that all employees are empowered to make changes, Tesla has made certain that changes or innovations are something that is almost free and can happen on a daily basis. According to ex-employees, like Joe Justice, changes do happen almost every single day.

As Elon has said, "The pace of innovation is the only thing that matters," and Tesla has made sure that their factories are the most flexible and the fastest innovating places on the face of the earth.

This advantage will ensure that no one else will be able to keep up with Tesla, even if they try to copy Tesla. Because, by the time they have a copy ready, Tesla will have made thousands of changes to both the product and the production of the product. As Joe Justice has told us, and Elon has confirmed, Tesla sometimes makes more than 20 changes to a production line in a week. Changes that would probably take the other guys years to implement.

This makes Tesla absolutely impossible to catch.

CHAPTER 35

Beyond Agile – The Speed of Thought

by Lars Strandridder

"Pace of innovation is all that matters" - Elon Musk

Elon has repeated the above quote many times, but most people don't really understand what this actually means. How fast is Tesla's pace of innovation?

What is Agile Manufacturing? There are four key elements for agile manufacturing:

Modular Product Design: designing products in a modular fashion that enables them to serve as platforms for fast and easy variation.

Information Technology: automating the rapid dissemination of information throughout the company to enable lightning-fast response to orders.

Corporate Partners: creating virtual short-term alliances with other companies that enable improved time-to-market for selected product segments.

Knowledge Culture: investing in employee training to achieve a culture that supports rapid change and ongoing adaptation.

https://www.leanproduction.com/agile-manufacturing/

Some companies are using SCRUM project management approaches or other tools to become more agile. With SCRUM you are working with weekly or monthly sprints to make one or more changes.

But these tools do not work for Tesla. Tesla is working much faster. They don't wait until the end of the week or the month or the year to make a change. They make changes on a daily basis. Multiple times a day.

When Elon says the **pace** of innovation is all that matters, he means it, and his companies are hardwired to work this way. Not many know how all of this works inside Tesla's factories in comparison with other car companies. But one man does.

Joe Justice is known for his extreme manufacturing techniques which he invented at Wikispeed.

Joe not only knows how Tesla actually works inside their factories, but also knows how other OEMs are working, and has built a car from the ground up from start to finish. Joe has also written the book *SCRUM Master and* is teaching companies to become more agile.

I interviewed him for this book to get the secret of what it is that makes Tesla so agile, and what is needed for other companies that want to get to that "Tesla Speed".

Here are some of the things other companies will have to change or do in order to get to Tesla's insane **pace** of innovation.

- Agile supply chain
- No Budget
- Autonomous testing
- Digital twin of every car
- Flat organization
- Empowering Employees
- Production cells

Agile Supply Chain

Contracts between Tesla and their suppliers are just one page long and written in plain English. You don't need a legal review. Everyone can read and understand the contract and make changes to it. So, it becomes fast and easy to make changes in any contract with any supplier. Everyone can do this within Tesla. They can make changes to these contracts every single day in order to get new versions of the parts.

Tesla is arguably the most successful company working with suppliers. For example, when Tesla and every other car manufacturer was faced with chip shortages or shortages of other materials (Ford recently shut down shipments of finished vehicles over not having Ford badges), many were forced to shut down production because of the missing chips.

Tesla responded on the very day they first learned about the shortage of chips from one of their suppliers. They started ordering other chips from other suppliers and started immediately figuring out how to rewrite software that would accommodate these new chips coming from many different suppliers. Within two weeks Tesla had 18 new chips with new software in production. No one else on planet earth operates at those speeds.

Many are still struggling with the chip shortage even in late 2022 and announcing reduced production due to these shortages.

Budget

Another roadblock keeping other companies from reacting to challenges and opportunities as quickly as Tesla is the complexity of dealing with "It isn't in the budget."

You may have experienced this issue at the companies you have worked for. I know I have. You come up with an idea that can possibly make your company more efficient, save money, or increase sales or margins…something that improves the company. But implementing the change requires you to spend some money. You ask your manager for permission, and he/she might even get excited about the great idea you have, and goes to ask the boss who says, "no, of course not. It's not in the budget!"

So, you have to wait until next year, when you can TRY to get the idea into the budget.

In the last few years companies have been faced with many emergencies including COVID and the Ukraine war. The average consumer had never heard of a supply chain before, but now it was front-and-center in their life, from toilet paper to Diet Pepsi.

When most companies are forced to find another supplier, it takes a long time to figure out a solution. The first step is to shut down production, because they don't have the part anymore. If there is no backup supplier already involved, the company has to find a supplier who has the needed part or is capable of creating it, then have the part approved for production. The new part may need to be modified, or the product may need to be modified to accept the new part. If a company gets all hands on deck to accomplish this task, but every step in the process requires moving the issue through budgets, days or weeks might be added to the time needed to solve the problem.

For a company like GM or VW, some of these issues can't even be solved at the division level but need board level approval. Because the change will cost money to fix, and the disruption in the supply chain was not a line item in the budget, the COO or even the board may need to be involved. Getting even small changes implemented can be a very frustrating challenge that may take weeks or months to get done.

This is never an issue at Tesla because Tesla does not have a budget, and there are no goals or targets. There is only the mission, and an ethos of constantly improving the product.

When you don't have a budget, you don't have to wait for approval to make a change that costs money. If it is the right thing to do, you just do it, no matter who you are.

Empowering employees

Every employee at Tesla is empowered to make changes and spend the company's money, if necessary. Joe Justice had this experience all the time. A great example Joe has talked about many times was when someone came up with an idea to make the charging speed of the car faster. The idea was that charging speed could be improved by making some changes to the tube that connected the charging port with the battery pack. Joe joined the people working on this, and within about three hours from when the idea was proposed, it was tested, approved, and included in the production of all future cars! Three hours!

The employees didn't have to ask a manager for permission. There was not a budget holding them back. Rather, they were empowered to make the change. All Tesla employees do self-management, and because of that, these changes, big or little, are implemented into the car and the production line immediately. Such a big change would probably have taken between 5-7 years for any other car manufacturer, as Joe pointed out.

Who, you might ask, actually decides whether a change makes sense?

Autonomous Testing

This leads us to the Automated Testing of a car that Tesla has invented. The unique testing approach empowers employees through instant feedback, letting them know if the new idea they have attempted actually works and has made the product better or the production faster. That is all automated.

A huge bottleneck to fast change is approvals and certification. Even if management agrees that a new idea is worthwhile and should be immediately implemented, most governments take as long as a year to review a new variation. So how do you get that review to be immediate?

You negotiate in advance with all appropriate government entities and ask, "What do you need." The goal is to give them everything they wished they had, instantly! In fact, the Tesla approach is to go beyond their wildest dreams and give them what they need and want.

When the agencies are getting all they need, they can approve new approaches in 10 minutes instead of one year. So, Tesla automated their process such that every car is put through all the tests needed to be approved to be a road legal car.

Tesla has something called 'Factory Mode.' From the moment it is assembled, the car puts itself through every required road legal test. Every single car does this autonomously. This is very important to understand. Because, if you only test one of every 1,000 or every 10,000 cars, the way many car manufacturers do, you can't introduce change until 10,000 cars from now. That is the cadence of your company's ability to make small changes.

Tesla does not work with this kind of cadence, they implement immediately, and Tesla is able to do that because they test every single car. Every car Tesla makes has what is called a digital twin in the cloud. Tesla knows everything about every single car…what glue is used, what chips are in it, what wires are used and so on.

Tesla's service employees also know what is in this specific Tesla when they have to repair one. But Tesla doesn't have huge warehouses with thousands of old spare parts. If something is wrong with the wire in your car, you will not get a replacement of the old version in your car. Tesla will just put in the new improved version and switch out the whole thing.

Joe Justice told me that there are 60 changes introduced in a Tesla factory every single day. Let that sink in for a moment.

Most other car companies have a 2.5-year cycle that introduces a number of small changes. Depending on the model, they have a 5–10-year model cycle where most of the parts of the car are changed.

This might give you an idea of just how fast Tesla works compared to other car companies. Small changes take about 2.5 years, whereas Tesla makes about 60 small product changes every single day! Keep in mind that these are hardware changes, not software changes. This rate of iteration is simply unheard of by any other company on the planet, except Elon Musk's other companies like SpaceX. But no other automaker makes 60 hardware changes a day. Not even close!

Of course, Tesla also makes software changes every single day. Owners of Tesla vehicles might only see software updates being pushed to the fleet every 2-4 weeks OTA, but internally Tesla makes changes to its software every single day.

Even if the competition was inclined to iterate their software this frequently, they would not be able to do so. None of the other car companies create their own software. They use third party developers.

Moreover, they don't have one company doing all their software, but multiple companies specializing in providing software for various aspects of the vehicle. The result is that they have to get multiple software companies to talk together and make sure the change they want them to make does not cause issues in the software from the other software companies.

Maybe the other car companies will move towards in-house software development. However, you simply don't overnight become a great software company that can make world leading and compelling software for electric vehicles. Some experts believe it could take automakers a decade to reach Tesla's level of software sophistication as it is today. But, of course, Tesla will have moved to new levels by then.

There are many reasons Tesla can make all these changes every day and still keep production going. For instance, Tesla has invented a whole new way of producing cars. Tesla no longer uses a simple production line, they use production cells, as we talk about in the chapter on Tesla factories. Because if you introduce changes to a production line, you have to stop the production line all the time. A production line is very efficient in making the same thing over and over again, but it is very inefficient in handling changes. Production cells provide a way to allow multiple changes while not slowing the line.

When Tesla wants to make a change, they just shut down the production cell or cells relevant to the change, while all the other cells are still producing cars. When the change is ramped up to 100%, they start implementing it into all the other cells.

Tesla was impressed with the agile approach Joe Justice introduced to the company. But Joe says agile is too slow for Tesla. Tesla has taken every part of the factory process back to first principles:

- Empowering your employees to make those changes. To do that you need no budget and a very flat organization.
- In order to keep track of all those different versions of the car with different parts you need a digital twin of the cars

The Elon Musk MISSION | 195

- To constantly make innovations you need productions cells, so you don't constantly stop the production line
- To constantly get new products you need very agile partnerships with suppliers who can also make changes to contracts in minutes
- You need to be able to get road legal approval for the cars in minutes using an autonomous testing system

A factory based on these principles will reduce the cost of making changes to almost zero, which is the goal, but without the automated testing you will never get there.

So how do other companies become as agile as Tesla? They have to change everything about their company. They would need to start with the structure of the company:

- Hire the very best people and turn them loose to manage themselves
- Change their production lines
- Completely change how to work with suppliers,
- Eliminate the use of budgets,
- Eliminate managers and trust every employee to make changes
- Learn how to write artificial intelligence software to run the whole factory, so the cars themselves can go through every single test needed to satisfy the Governments around the world.

Oh, is that all! Actually, no. They would also need to become as vertical as possible in the supply chain.

Will other companies catch Tesla? We all know that changing the culture of a company is close to impossible, especially if that company is 100+ years old, still beholden to families of the founders, and limited at every turn by unions.

But every step on this list underlies Tesla's ability to make the pace of innovation so unbelievably fast. It may simply not be feasible for an old legacy automaker to keep up with Tesla.

Think about this. The VW ID3 has been on the road for about two years as of this writing, but production of the car started back in Nov. 2019, about 3 years ago. The ID3 that comes off the assembly line today is 100% identical to the ID3 that came off the assembly line three years ago.

Then you have the Tesla Model Y, which has also been produced for a little over two years. New production coming out of Fremont or Shanghai is a completely different car underneath than what it was two years ago. In fact, the model Y in each factory is slightly different. Some cars now have a single Giga casting, others now have two. Even the brand-new Giga casting has changed, and it lost about 4kg in weight since they made the first ones. This is according to Sandy Munro who has ripped them apart.

The newest Model Ys have a structural battery pack, not the separate pack used in the "old" Model Y. Even the way Tesla assembles the car is completely changed because of the Giga castings. There is no longer a separate floor in the bottom of the car. That is where the battery pack, including seats, carpet and middle consoles are assembled to the top of the battery pack before sliding the entire bottom of the car into the top portion. The production is completely different from how Tesla did it two years ago. The ID3 and the way it is being produced is completely the same as it was three years ago, save minor cosmetic changes.

We also see this lag of pace of innovation in real time right now. We have heard about VW's new Trinity platform, which is their next version of the electric car platform. But even though we have known about this for a couple of years now, it leaked in 2019 and VW revealed it in 2020, it will still take another four years before they can implement this into their production. It won't come out before 2026 at the earliest.

Tesla would implement it today.

So that is why I am very confident that Tesla will not only keep their lead but will rapidly extend their lead in their electric cars, and in the way they produce the cars, and the factories themselves.

Tesla is even inventing new tools and processes to make the changes they know will improve their cars. They rarely have the convenience of buying parts or tools from a catalog. An example would be the Plaid motors that are wrapped in a carbon fiber sleeve to be able to produce much higher revolutions per minute. The machine to make those carbon fiber sleeves didn't exist, so they had to make that in house. Like Elon has said:

"Every production line and new production system was invented. Instead of playing chess with the same pieces as everyone else, create new pieces" - Elon Musk

CHAPTER 36

Charging Network as a Stand-Alone Business

by Lars Strandridder

Setting up a charging network was essential for Tesla if they were to become successful. If a long-distance road trip in an EV was to be more than a pipe dream, Tesla had to set up enough of a charging infrastructure to support cross country trips.

Unfortunately, no one wanted to help. Elon said Tesla was very much open to letting others use their charging network, but only if they wanted to help pay for getting the charging network up and running. Unfortunately, or maybe fortunately, no one wanted to help. Neither Ford nor GM would chip in to get access to the network and help build it out.

Tesla knew that, without the network, their cars would be nothing but a city car, so they believed there was no choice but to go it alone without any outside support. Tesla took the burden upon itself to start building a network of Supercharging stations 10 years ago.

However, and Elon Musk undoubtedly knew this would be the case, the Tesla charging network is definitely one of the biggest advantages for Tesla today. Long term, even when they open it up to other EV users, this division will not only make Tesla billions of dollars, but with Tesla's other technologies, help turn Tesla into one of the biggest utility companies on the planet.

No one else is even close. There are other charging companies like Electrify America (EA). I just interviewed EA at The Fully Charged live show in San Diego (Sep. 2022). After hearing about their plans, I realized that Tesla is now, and will continue to be, in the lead with their charging network. In fact, Tesla is in a league of their own. No one comes close. And Tesla is about to take their charging network to whole new levels never seen before.

When the story about the EV revolution ends, Tesla will not only be the leader, and the winner of the greatest underdog story ever, their charging network will make sure they will also be seen as the hero of the story.

Because, when we look at Tesla competition in charging infrastructure, we have someone like EA in the US, and Ionity in Europe. Both companies do nothing but build charging stations, and both were founded by the VW Dieselgate scandal. Today, they are two independent businesses and have been making charging stations for six years starting in 2016.

You might expect them to have a huge charging network by now and try to outpace Tesla. Since Tesla has many other projects to manage, not just building charging stations, the opportunity was certainly there. But once again, Tesla's plans far outshine the competition, as we have also seen with EV production.

EA operates just over 800 stations with an average of 6 stalls per station, which gives them about 4,800 stalls worldwide. So that is about 800 stalls per year they have put into operation. That is about what Tesla puts up in a month. In June 2022 Tesla put up 842 stalls worldwide.

The target for EA is to double their total installations over the next two years. By the end of 2024, or the beginning of 2025 EA should have about 1,600 stations and close to 10,000 stalls.

Ionity, the EA European twin, has a little less ambitious plan. As of this writing, Ionity has 1,879 charging stalls at 430 stations. They expect to have 7,000 stalls by 2025.

It all sounds great with their expansion plans, but when we look at what Tesla has done, and what their plan is, EA and Ionity suddenly look like half-hearted attempts.

Tesla currently has about 850 Stations and about 9000 stalls in Europe, alone. This is almost five times as big as Ionity in Europe, and Ionity will still be about 2,000 stalls smaller than Tesla is today in 2025.

EA will also be far behind Tesla. Tesla already has more than 1,600 stations in the US, so again EA will have as many stations in 2025 as Tesla has today.

Tesla said back in Oct 2021 that they expect to triple their charging network in the next three years, and they already have the installed manufacturing capacity to do so. Therefore, by the end of 2024 or beginning of 2025 Tesla should have 90-100,000 supercharger stalls worldwide, almost 6 times as big as both EA and Ionity combined.

One very important difference between Tesla charging stations and all the others - Tesla superchargers have an uptime of about 99.96%. A study done in California showed that, on average, other charging stalls only had an uptime of about 72%. So, the stalls were not working 28% of the time. That is not good enough. This is a big reason why other EV owners will probably choose Tesla's charging network when they open it up to non-Tesla EVs. They can count on them working.

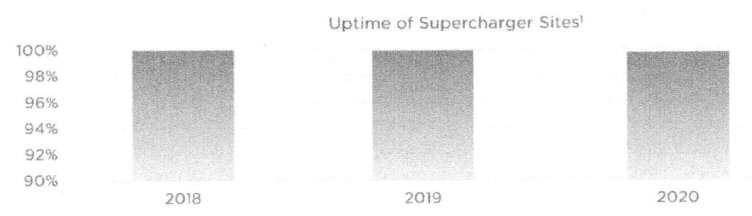

Uptime of Supercharger Sites[1]

2018	2019	2020

(Y-axis: 90%–100%)

[1] Uptime of Supercharger Sites reflects the average percentage of sites globally that had at least 50% daily capacity fully functional for the year.

Another big moat for Tesla's charging network compared to everyone else, and a big reason why Tesla can build so many compared to the rest, is the price of building the charger itself.

Texas has a program which gives grants to install fast EV chargers, as long as they support non-Tesla cars. They received applications from Tesla and others back in April 2022. The grants can cover 70% of the cost of the stall to a maximum of $150,000 per charger. Tesla's applications ask for as little as $30,000 per charger, while most other applications are claiming the maximum $150,000, and perhaps these cost even more as that was the maximum they could get.

It would mean that Tesla's Superchargers cost no more than $43,000 per stall versus over $200,000 for the competition based on the documents in these applications to the program. As you can see, Tesla chargers are probably about ⅕ of the price of the competition.

One of reasons why Tesla can build them so much cheaper is they have simplified them over the last decade. Because they build so many in a factory specifically created for the chargers, Tesla also

Making The Future Awesome | 202

realizes economies of scale as they produce a lot more chargers than the competition.

The simple fact is that Tesla's charging stalls are very simple since everything is controlled through the car if you drive a Tesla, or through the app if you drive a non-Tesla. So, there is no payment equipment in the stalls or big touch screens to control the charging and see the price. Everything is controlled through the car itself or the app. Others have to build all of those other features into the charging stall itself, adding a lot of complexity and cost to the chargers, not to mention adding things that can go wrong.

Tesla is now trying out various different opportunities at the charging stations. You might have heard about Tesla's upcoming Supercharger station with dinner and drive-in-movie. Here in Europe, we also saw Tesla building a really cool station like the one my family visited on our trip this year in Endsee in Germany. This version had a nice aircon room, with very nice bathrooms, PlayStation games, food, drinks, and other items you could buy, including a pizza that would be ready in just four minutes. This is the first of 300 expected BK World climate-positive lounges to be built together with Tesla. A very cool concept.

Tesla is testing these methods of earning even more money on their charging station by selling goods and services at the stations. Therefore, it would be a good idea to make them big, so it can host many guests, rather than just 4 or 6 guests like EA and Ionity are aiming for. Tesla has stations in California with over 100 stalls. Tesla is really seeing the grand vision here, and is building the future of the fueling stations, just better.

Tesla has also created a system that preheats the battery as you approach the station. Preheating provides a 25% boost to charging speeds. This is a big moat for buying a Tesla. As Tesla opens chargers to other brands, some brands will already be charging more slowly because they are only capable of charging at 125kW compared to 250kW possible on Tesla and some others. Regardless of the charging speed, if the battery is not preheated, the Teslas will have a 25% advantage.

AVERAGE TIME SPENT CHARGING

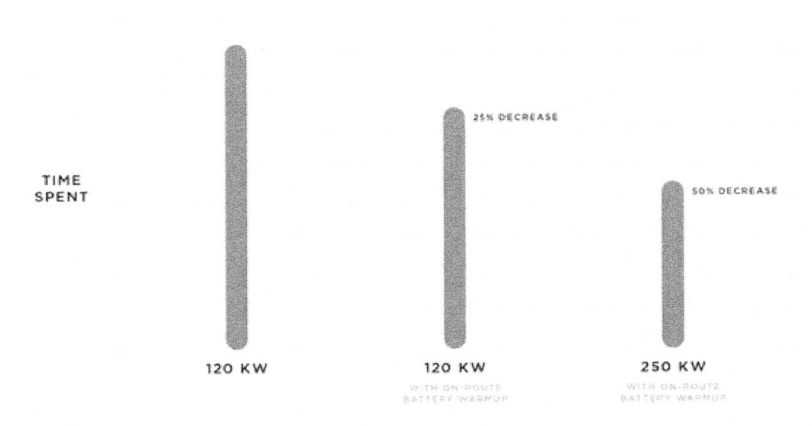

TIME SPENT

120 KW	120 KW WITH ON-ROUTE BATTERY WARMUP	250 KW WITH ON-ROUTE BATTERY WARMUP
	25% DECREASE	50% DECREASE

Some still think that Tesla's plan to open up their charging network is a disadvantage for Tesla owners. The worry is that they might find the stalls full and have to wait more often.

But I still think this is going to be a brilliant move from Tesla. They will become one of the biggest providers of energy to the new transportation sector, earning Tesla billions of dollars worldwide. And at the same time Tesla will get a HUGE advertising benefit, as every other EV owner will have to download the **Tesla** app and create a **Tesla** account. Then select 'Charge your **non-Tesla'**. So that is how the world will see this. There are Teslas and there are non-Teslas.

Making The Future Awesome | 204

It doesn't really matter if you drive a Dacia or a Mercedes, they are all just non-Teslas. I think this is brilliant marketing and will be paid for by the non-Tesla customers. They can soon even buy a new Tesla through the app on their phone.

On top of all of this, Tesla is also going to put up battery storage and solar panels at their charging stations. EA is also doing that but needs to buy these batteries from someone. Tesla already makes their own. Tesla can just slam down a Megapack at each location and be done with it. And because Tesla also has a little software program called Autobidder. If Tesla doesn't don't get enough free energy from the sun, they can use these batteries to buy energy from the grid when prices are low during the night, and then sell it to its charging customers for a much higher price doing the day. And even if the station is not being used as much as it can handle during one day. Tesla can just sell the energy back to the grid during peak hours and still earn a lot of money…even with no car charging at the site.

Tesla's charging stations will literally become small power stations, for Tesla. And as I said, they do expect to already be at 90,000 stalls by 2024, so Tesla will probably have something like 8,000 charging stations at that point.

Tesla is also really ramping up Megapack production now; the new Megapack factory in the US has a capacity of 40 GWh of Megapacks in annual production. That is enough for 13,300 Megapacks. Tesla is sold out of their Megapacks through 2023 but could start setting them up at their charging stations after 2023 and build out the world's biggest energy storage system. This can earn Tesla a lot of money, no matter if cars are charging at the stations or not. What a money printer.

Tesla is really setting itself up to become the world's biggest utility company, with the biggest charging network, and the biggest energy storage system, especially if we also count in all the 6,500 Powerwalls per week Tesla is producing right now.

Yeah! Tesla is just a car company. No, GM is just a car company that did not want to help Tesla 10 years ago with building out a charging network. And now they pay the price. Their customers will get a Tesla app, make a Tesla account, and take their non-Tesla car and go charge at Tesla's charging station, as they are the most reliable and widely available charging stations worldwide.

And all of this will earn Tesla billions of dollars, and Tesla will not only be the leader of the EV race, but also the winner of the best underdog story ever told. Tesla will also become the hero of this story, as they build out the very much needed reliable infrastructure needed for the world to embrace the EV.

How to value the charging network
by Randy Kirk

Various estimates suggest that while Tesla is still buying energy from 3rd parties to power their stations, Elon only plans to make a 10% profit. I (Randy) suspect that he will want to at least double that with non-Tesla vehicles.

Tesla is not providing any data, so our estimate will be that each stall averages 1 customer per hour between 6 a.m. and 10 p.m. and none the rest of the day. I estimate that each car purchases about $30 worth of energy. So, a stall should produce $30 X 5,840 hours per year in gross revenue. That equals $175k per year per stall.

As of the end of 2022, Tesla should have about 40,000 stalls worldwide. 40,000 X $175k would be $7B in revenue. At 10% net profit, this would equal $700M in profits for 2022.

Tesla plans to triple the number of stalls by the end of 2024, so the total might be $21B in revenue and $2.1B profit by then. This assumes no extra profit from non-Tesla vehicles, no income from other products, services, or advertising at the sites.

What would Wall Street pay for a company that has virtually certain profits of $1.4B in profits next year? What multiple do they give for companies that will continue to ramp profits at the rate of at least 50% per year? 50X earnings? Does it seem unreasonable that a massive network of "energy" stations would be worth $70B? Is anyone including that value in the $900B valuation of Tesla at the end of Sept 2022?

CHAPTER 37

Disrupting the Car Insurance Business

by Randy Kirk

I have many favorite quotes, ideas, products, business principles, and foundational ideas created or manifested by Elon. But a little noticed, little talked about idea may be one of the most ingenious of all. Was this insurance industry disruption Elon's idea? Did he just happily run with an idea proposed by one of his fans, employees, suppliers, or investors? I can't find any reporting on this.

To be sure, other auto companies have tight relationships with insurance companies and offer products that are tied to data supplied by the cars, cameras, and other monitoring equipment. However, there are multiple differences in the Tesla approach as you'll soon see.

The Safety Score

The cost of insurance is totally determined by the safety score. The car's various monitoring equipment gives Tesla a read on likely future accidents based on five driving factors. The score is reported on the computer screen and the app, allowing the driver to take steps to correct practices that harm the score.

The score is also reported to Tesla for the purposes of determining the insurance rate, instead of using age, location, tickets, accidents, and other factors generally employed by traditional insurance companies.

The components of the score follow:

1: Forward Collision Warnings per 1,000 Miles

When your Tesla senses a likelihood of a forward collision, the system notifies you with both a visual and auditory signal from the computer screen, and sometimes activates automatic braking, too. Whether you have any contribution to the potential problem, the system still records and counts a forward collision warning. This might be due to a car cutting you off, a cyclist running a light, or your own negligent failure to slow fast enough when approaching an object that might result in an accident.

2: Hard Braking

Hard Braking (in excess of 0.3g) is defined by Tesla as "backward acceleration." Anyone with experience driving a Tesla knows that the driver brakes using regenerative braking almost 100% of the time. By lifting the foot off the "accelerator," the motor is very effective at slowing the speed of the car.

From time to time, you may need the actual brake pedal. For instance, you might be accelerating as you approach an intersection with a green light. Then it turns yellow, and you decide to stop rather than run the light. Regenerative braking won't generally be enough for that situation. So, you help things with your brake.

It doesn't really matter how hard you hit the brake for the purposes of deciding whether to ding your safety score, but rather how many g's are exerted by the braking. Maybe you have looked down at your phone, and when you look up, you need to go from 30 mph to zero in a very short distance. That is going to cost you.

3: Aggressive Turning

Whether in a hurry, frustrated, or just having fun, some drivers will take a turn much faster than they would have done on a lovely family outing. If this results in "left/right acceleration in excess of 0.4g," you are going to get points off. While Teslas have a fantastic center of gravity which keeps the car stable and almost impossible to flip in a turn, you might still feel the car lean, the gravel busting loose, or the tires squealing. These signals would clue you to a possible lowered score for that outing.

4: Unsafe Following

If you are traveling over 50 mph, the unsafe following scoreboard lights up (metaphorically.) The car calculates how far you need to be away from the car in front of you in order to avoid a collision if that car were to hit a stopped object.

You won't lose points for being too close for a second or two, and then backing off. This part of the safety score is attempting to dissuade you from habitually following to close. Don't count on the one car per 10 mph idea. If you are getting points off for this, you'll know you can improve your score by backing off.

5: Forced Autopilot Disengagement

This is not about you disengaging autopilot. This is about the computer determining that you can no longer be trusted to use autopilot due to inattention. You will know when you lose points, as the autopilot will switch off, and you will need to drive manually.

Of course, Tesla has reached the conclusion that these are the five material issues that determine accident potential vs safe driving because they have more real-world data than anyone. They don't need driver, passenger, or witness accounts. The eight cameras will tell Tesla everything they need to know about the cause of the accident, and they can compare the driving habits of those who have accidents to those who don't.

So, if you can predict accidents, and you have exacting information about the cause of accidents that do happen, you have a massive edge in computing insurance rates. Tesla isn't concerned about what city you are in, how old you are, or how many tickets or accidents you have in your recent history.

Most people might think that speeding, fast acceleration from stop lights, "unsafe" lane changes, and rolling through stop signs are predictive of accidents, but that is not what the data tells Tesla.

Since Tesla only ensures Teslas, they know exactly what it will cost to fix them and can do the fixing themselves.

Tesla is the insurance company

In a major departure from existing car company insurance plans, Tesla is the actual insurance company. All other programs work with insurance companies as the actual underwriters and claims adjusters. The result for Tesla is a vertical integration that cuts out the middleman, and therefore cuts out costs.

Tesla has no advertising cost for its insurance

In case you haven't noticed, Farmers, Geico, State Farm, and other auto insurance companies are some of the largest advertisers on TV and in other media. Tesla has no need for advertising. A new Tesla owner gets a quote and can then compare that quote to other insurance companies. That's it.

Tesla is rolling out their insurance program worldwide. They are hoping to be approved in 80% of the US by the end of 2022. They are active in China and parts of Europe. They are looking at other markets as of this writing.

Tesla may have had a second theory in mind when they entered this business. When autonomous cars and robotaxis are finally a thing, there are all kinds of issues around who is liable in an accident that is caused by the robot. If Tesla is already an insurer, the complication becomes far more manageable.

The Bottom Line

The Tesla community on Twitter has reported that Tesla Insurance in everywhere but California (which is not allowing Tesla to use the safety score to set rates), is much, much cheaper than other carriers. I couldn't find any comprehensive reporting. Tesla says their rates are 20-30% less than others.

If even 20% of Tesla owners sign up for insurance at say $2,000 per year, that would be about 300,000 by the end of 2022. This is $600M in revenue. Starting in 2023, Tesla will sell 2.5M cars, so they would now add 500,000 insurance customers or another $1B in revenue. If Tesla insurance really is 20-30% cheaper, the take rate will not be 20%. It will be much larger. Doesn't take a math genius to see this as another money printing machine. Elon said at the Tesla Q3 21' earnings call "Obviously, insurance is substantial.

So insurance could very well be, I don't know, 30% or 40% of the value of the automotive business, frankly."

CHAPTER 38

Royalties and OEM Sales

by Randy Kirk

Tesla, as noted earlier, open sources their patents. So why is there any thought or discussion on the potential that Tesla might have for generating royalties? While most royalties are made from intellectual rights such as patents, copyrights, and trademarks, Tesla's royalties would come from providing tools, methods, services, and/or combinations of hardware with related software.

Autonomous cars - If you have any doubt that autonomous cars represent an historic income opportunity, look no further than the resources being devoted to helping humans legally Tweet or text while driving. Apple, Samsung, Alphabet, and most of the major auto companies are all in the hunt to lead in this technology.

The stakes are huge. We cover the market size and potential income elsewhere in the book. But just to quickly summarize, top analysts believe that net profits from autonomous taxi (robotaxi) fleets could easily reach $1T per year in this decade. And the number might be multiples higher than that, including estimates as high as $5T and more.

Tesla uses a vision only system (cameras), and they appear to be the only company approaching autonomous driving from the view that vision plus data from miles driven and subsequent training of a neural net will allow the car to drive itself better than a human in virtually any situation.

Other automakers, both legacy and startups, are exploring the use of lidar, radar, vision plus lidar and geofenced mapping to equip their cars to traverse a specific set of roads. The theory here seems to be that if they map many, many roads, at some point the computer may be able to extrapolate the data to apply to all roads with the help of maps, lidar or other systems, and vision.

These systems might eventually compete for the autonomous business, but it seems unlikely that every auto company will be able to create their own version. Therefore, some car companies will need to buy some or all of the hardware, software, and data management from one of the leaders in this space.

If Tesla were one of those leaders, then some companies would almost be forced to buy from Tesla in order to have any chance of competing in the auto business, much less the robotaxi business.

In a best-case scenario, Tesla's system might be so much better than any other system that every other maker would of necessity need to get a license and/or buy hardware, chips, etc. from Tesla. In a world where there are 2B cars on the road and only a fraction of those would be Teslas, even in 10 years, the addressable market might be 1B+ cars paying royalties. At $10 a month…you get the picture.

In a much, much more conservative scenario, maybe Tesla is only supplying 10% of all vehicles made after 2025, or around 10M per year. But maybe the fee per month is more like $100. In this modest case, the income would still be $1B per month…the first year, $2B per month the second year, and so on.

Batteries or battery technology - It seems evident that all new cars in the future will be electric. Whether that happens in 2026 or 2035, only Toyota seems to believe there is a future that still includes some other form of propulsion for vehicles. Toyota might be right, but it seems unclear where they are seeing the signals.

In addition, the future of home and building heating, lights, energy to run factories, and even energy for planes, trains, and ships will likely be electric. A huge percentage of that electricity will come from solar/wind which requires batteries to operate efficiently. There is a growing chorus of voices suggesting nuclear may be in our future, but even if we decided today to go full throttle on nuclear, the time to ramp would be far longer than solar/wind/battery.

If the above is true, the world is going to need huge amounts of batteries. We have noted in other chapters just how large this market will be. We are at a loss to find a single expert on this subject who believes that there will be enough batteries to meet the demand in 2026, much less later in the decade. At some point between now and 2026, some automakers and utilities are going to be screaming about a supply chain problem. It won't be semiconductors or wiring harnesses as in 2021-2. It will be batteries.

As this chapter is written in July 22, Tesla is ramping up their new 4680 cell production lines. Panasonic, CATL and others are also ramping up this form factor primarily to service Tesla. Once the 4680 has been successfully ramped (late 2022 or early 2023), Tesla will be in a position to cookie-cutter the factories to produce by far the most batteries of any company. This will provide them with leadership in production knowledge, probably cost, and…merely having a supply.

Meanwhile Tesla is also sourcing battery materials, improving mining, and processing methods, and working to bring mining and processing in proximity to cell manufacturing to reduce costs of transport.

We discuss some of the details about the Tesla lead in battery sourcing in other chapters. Consider this case study. Toyota gets it wrong. They do little to set up any supply chain or cell manufacturing of their own. But in 2025, they see the handwriting on the wall, and realize they are in deep trouble if they don't switch to BEVs. They go looking for supplies. GM, Ford, and VW are all making some cells and buying from OEMs. They barely have enough for their own needs. Smaller companies who don't have the ability to make their own cells are also at a huge disadvantage when attempting to purchase cells from OEMs when much larger companies are trying to place huge, long-term orders.

Toyota and the smaller makers will be looking for batteries, finding none, other than Tesla. Maybe even Tesla is unable to come to their rescue. We suspect that Tesla will be the supplier of last resort, if they have any to sell. If they do, then the profit potential is huge.

But, just maybe, if the raw materials issue has been addressed, Toyota might just need the recipe to make great batteries themselves. Tesla will have just such a recipe. Another royalty opportunity. Smaller companies would also be interested in buying the batteries.

Dojo - Tesla has undertaken to build one of the largest computers in the world. At AI Day2, the world got its first look at a single Dojo cabinet. Tesla plans to have four of those cabinets running in Q1 2023, and 10 cabinets later in the year. Four cabinets will be the equivalent of 16 racks of their current system.

The purpose of Dojo is to train its AI deep neural networks and Machine Learning algorithms. In other words, when data comes in from the cars cameras and other monitors (acceleration, braking, and much more), an AI training system looks to add to its understanding of the world as seen by those inputs. It then reviews the new data in light of the information already in the database and arrives at updated conclusions regarding how the car should respond under those circumstances.

The ability of any such system to process the data and produce new behaviors is the available space to do computations and the speed with which it can do those computations. Dojo is designed to be able to handle vast amounts of data and do so quickly.

Elon has mentioned that Dojo and other related Tesla capabilities might one day be offered as a service to others who need to handle huge data loads to train other such neural networks. Tesla could charge for computer use as Amazon does with their hugely profitable AWS. Amazon makes more money from AWS (Amazon Web Services) than it does from their online retail business. This Dojo aaS business opportunity was mentioned by Elon at the recent AI Day2. At the Q3 earnings call, Dojo aaS was mentioned as a possible revenue source. Elon said they would know in 2023 if Dojo was competitive.

There are other potential OEM and royalty income streams that may enhance Tesla's bottom line in the future…in fact, too many to list or describe. Then there would be dozens or hundreds that are not known at this time by the general public.

CHAPTER 39

Energy Storage - Home, Business, Local, and Utility Battery Storage

by Randy Kirk

Elon Musk quote re: Master Plan Part 3:

> "If you assume battery life of approximately 20 years before it gets recycled then you need 15 TWh per year of annual battery production to reach steady state."

As noted elsewhere in this book, we have about 1,000 GWh, or 1 TWh now.

Elon continued: "How do we scale to get to that fully sustainable energy economy and what tonnage do we need of what materials and what is the best way to get those materials and turn them into batteries?"

It is becoming increasingly clear that solar/wind/battery will be the dominant methods of producing and storing energy in the future, and that future is not multiple decades, but only years away.

Elon has also noted that the Tesla energy business will eventually be about the same size as the automotive business.

Assuming the production ramp of battery factories in Austin and Berlin go according to plan, Tesla will be the second largest battery factory in the world by the end of 2023, and this is true if no other Tesla battery factories are built or brought online by that time.

Tesla's largest 3rd party battery supplier, CATL will likely maintain their leadership position, with current capacity being ramped at this time of 260 GWh. The expected annual battery run rate for Fremont, Austin, and Berlin is 210 GWh.

CATL is currently in the planning stages to increase capacity to 690 GWh.

Tesla says they will announce their expansion plans by the end of 2022, but all eyes are on Indonesia. Moreover, most expect Austin and Berlin to eventually produce far more than the 100 GWh currently ramping.

Panasonic is building two additional 40GWh factories in the US, and another factory in Japan.

A quick back-of-the-napkin number crunch tells us that these two leaders will still be producing less than 5% of the needed power circa 2023 to get to Elon's version of steady state, much less the 300 TWh needed as the underlying supply before we can even talk about steady state.

Elon clearly intends to be a leader in batteries, and while he states that bots and robotaxis will be bigger revenue generators than cars or energy, the company's mission will be advanced in large measure due to batteries. Undoubtedly, this is why the 3rd master plan is about ramping batteries.

Now, to be clear, energy is not as S3XY as family sedans doing 0-60 in 2 seconds flat. Thus, Tesla fans, followers, and wall street pay far less attention to energy than they do to cars, robotaxis, AI and bots. A huge future catalyst to $TSLA stock will be the day Wall Street realizes the shocking profits that will come from the energy side of the company.

A Bit of Back Story

Today, the world's energy sources are widely carbon based. Massive amounts of wood (charcoal), coal, oil, and natural gas heat our homes, run our factories, propel our vehicles, and light up everything. In terms of adding CO^2 and particulates to the atmosphere the list above is also from worst to least worse.

Elon Musk intends to swap all of these sources to electricity produced by wind, solar, and batteries.

> *"Master Plan Part 3 is all about achieving very large scale.* ***In order to shift the entire energy infrastructure and transport infrastructure of earth****, there has to be a very high scale. We have to ask what is the actual tonnage? If we work backward from let's say about 300 TWh of installed capacity in vehicles and stationary [battery packs] then how do you achieve that tonnage from a mining and refining standpoint, but also do so in a sustainable way."*

As of this writing, this is all we know about Master Plan Part 3. If we have updates prior to publication, we will provide those here or in a suffix.

However, we do know the building blocks of the energy grid planned by Tesla, and we do know the components necessary to get the job done. And no company other than Tesla is working the plan in the way they are. So, as usual, no competition at all for the ultimate plan.

The New Grid

New home building projects in Texas and Australia are the testing grounds for the new way of managing distribution of electricity. Huge new projects in California, Hawaii, Europe, and Australia are already proving that utility size projects combining solar and/or wind generation with battery storage are the cheapest way to produce grid level energy, bar none.

Put these two ideas together and you have a distributed energy solution which only relies on utility-sized installations as a backup. On the other hand, in the transition, the distributed energy sources are actually backing up the utilities.

For most of the world today, and for most of human history everywhere, the primary point of energy production was the location where it would be used. Various types of oil, wood, or coal were burned in the home or factory, producing heat or light. With the advent of electricity, this has changed for 1st world economies. Large utilities burn coal, oil, or gas at central locations to generate energy, then move the electricity to where it is needed by the electrical grid. Of course, we also produce natural gas and gasoline that is piped or trucked to distribution points or right to the home.

Under the Tesla plan, we would have a hybrid system. Many, or maybe eventually all, homes would produce electricity from the sun using solar power on their roof or even possibly from the windows and even house paint. This energy would be used immediately for all aspects of HVAC, lighting, appliances, to charge cars, boats, and other adult toys, and more. Any excess energy would be stored in one or more battery packs in the home or other building.

If there was even more excess energy produced on some days or during some periods of the day, that energy would be routed to a larger grid to be stored or used where there might be less production than needed.

In a perfect world, there would be a very large local battery for every neighborhood that would act as additional backup for days when the sun was not producing all that was needed. This larger battery would likely be an underground unit.

Either the individual homes or buildings would be attached to the regional grid system, or the neighborhood battery would be attached, or possibly both. The regional grid would use multiple types of energy production, including solar, wind, hydro, thermal, and even nuclear to produce any additional backup to the distributed system. Batteries would be used for solar and wind facilities to take up excess production, and release needed energy for peak demand or low production times.

Tony Seba has stated that this type of system will eventually make electricity too cheap to meter. So individual households in the future will likely be billed for some type of subscription amount to be part of the overall grid. In other words, your future gas and electricity bill will be a tenth of what it is today.

Tesla Battery Storage Business Moats

While Tesla is a leading supplier of wall mounted batteries for the home, larger batteries for factories, and some of the largest batteries in the world for utilities, they are not alone in these markets.

However, the demand in 2022 is so huge that Tesla's order book is filled beyond 2023.

So, the first moat is that Tesla is already one of, if not the, leader in the home, factory, and utility battery business.

Secondly, Tesla is vertical. They make the batteries or buy them as an OEM and sell them to the end user in most cases. They do have some distributors and OEMs buying from them, as well.

Their cost, as best as anyone seems to be able to determine, is as low or lower than any other maker or supplier. Due to their overwhelming dominance in the battery business, they are able to buy batteries or raw materials to build their own at the very lowest possible cost.

They have a technology lead. As noted in the auto section moats, Tesla's engineering prowess has resulted in their being well in the lead technologically. They are experts at material science, battery science, and building the product (factories) that make the product (batteries.)

They have a huge lead in installed capacity. Other than CATL, no other battery company is close to Tesla in factory capacity. But unlike CATL and others, they are also purchasing batteries from virtually every serious battery maker.

As usual, their flexibility allows them to change up chemistries on the fly. The major components of lithium-ion batteries are fairly fluid. In fact, even the lithium part is potentially replaced by sodium, and CATL is working on this solution. Another alternative is carbon on carbon, which Elon mentioned in a 2022 interview. Watch that space.

Tesla is lining up the upstream supplies. There will be shortages of many of the raw materials that need to be mined for this 40X total current worldwide production ramp up. Elon has repeatedly said that he doesn't want to get into mining but will if he has to. Tesla already has mineral rights in Nevada where it seems likely they will test a direct-from-clay method discussed on Battery Day.

In an interview in June 2022, Elon seemed to imply that he is ever more likely to have a bigger role in processing mined products prior to being added to the battery lines. The processing seems to be the biggest major limiting factor in the long term, and the quality of those refined materials must be exact. Plans for a lithium refining plant seem to be under way in South Texas.

Tesla has, on the mining side, entered into dozens of contracts with the world's largest extractors for multi-year production.

The Software

Sales and installations of batteries at all levels is a decent business, but not necessarily one that includes high margins. However, Tesla has lined up long term, high margin business to service their utility sized installations and provides the magic dust that makes these systems so profitable.

I am going to pull a large section of information directly from Tesla's website, as I think most of it is quite necessary for understanding how significant this part of the business is and will become. According to the Tesla website:

> "Autobidder provides independent power producers, utilities, and capital partners the ability to autonomously

monetize battery assets. Autobidder is a real-time trading and control platform that provides value-based asset management and portfolio optimization, enabling owners and operators to configure operational strategies that maximize revenue according to their business objectives and risk preferences. Autobidder is part of Autonomous Control, Tesla's suite of optimization software solutions.

Autobidder is successfully operating at Hornsdale Power Reserve (HPR) in South Australia, and through market bidding, has added competition to drive down energy prices."

Value Stacked Monetization

Batteries are highly flexible assets, but they require smart strategies and software to realize their full value. Autobidder allows owners to realize this value by handling the complex co-optimization required to successfully stack multiple value streams simultaneously, including:

- Wholesale markets, including energy, ancillary services, and capacity
- Transmission & Distribution-level grid services
- Renewable firming and shaping
- Bilateral contractual arrangements
- Other portfolio needs

In wholesale markets, Autobidder includes participation in the following, where regionally applicable:
- Day-ahead markets
- Real-time markets
- Continuous markets

Real-time Market Operations

Autobidder has hundreds of megawatt-hours of assets under management that have supplied gigawatt-hours of grid services globally. Autobidder operates at every scale: from aggregations of behind-the-meter residential systems to 100MW utility-scale installations. With seamless integration between hardware and software, Autobidder can be trusted to capture revenues immediately after project energization and 24/7 in dynamic environments.

Autobidder is hosted on Tesla's highly reliable and secure cloud infrastructure that is engineered to perform large-scale complex computation and is capable of interfacing with market operators, network providers and customer networks via secure web APIs.

Machine Learning and Optimization Algorithms

Tesla's team of experienced machine learning engineers, optimization engineers and market trading experts have created a library of sophisticated algorithms that drive the complex optimal dispatch behavior behind Tesla's batteries.

The algorithms are based on numerous mathematical techniques including classical statistics, machine learning and numerical optimization. The library includes the functionality to perform:

- Price forecasting
- Load forecasting
- Generation forecasting
- Dispatch optimization
- Smart bidding

Autobidder's algorithms are adaptable to new markets and services, and continuously improve through experiential data to maintain high financial performance in dynamic market environments.

Autobidder was designed to collaborate with and augment the capabilities of human operators. Autobidder continuously executes transactions in the market using a numerical optimization model that is based on the parameters set and adjusted by a human operator, reflecting the preferences of the trading desk."

Also from Tesla's website:

> "Opticaster is Tesla's intelligent software designed to maximize economic benefits and sustainability objectives for distributed energy resources. As the fundamental machine learning and optimization engine for Tesla energy software, it forecasts and optimizes energy in real-time. Facility managers, business owners and renewable developers use Opticaster to reduce energy spend, increase renewable energy consumption, and deliver clean power to the grid during times of need. Opticaster is part of <u>Autonomous Control</u>, Tesla's suite of optimization software solutions.
>
> Opticaster has accumulated over a hundred million hours of operational experience, delivering tens of millions of dollars in value from OPEX savings and grid service revenue to thousands of Tesla customers globally."

Automated Utility Savings

Opticaster puts managing energy spend on autopilot by autonomously shifting energy usage to less expensive times and reducing peak demand charges. It intelligently navigates complicated rate structures across many utility territories and energy markets.

Additionally, Opticaster ensures that energy consumers adhere to operational constraints for capturing energy storage incentive value.

Current supported rate structures include but are not limited to:
- Daily, monthly, and annual demand charges
- Time-of-use energy and demand rates
- Real-time energy rates
- Grid-level demand charges

Grid Service Participation

In addition to optimizing site-level energy spend, Opticaster enables customers to use their energy assets to provide valuable services to the grid. Opticaster solves complex use cases that combine multiple revenue streams while also respecting site export limits, throughput, and backup constraints.

Once a site is enrolled in an aggregation or grid service program, Opticaster ingests special price signals sent to site over-the-air. For example, a demand response dispatch may be called 24 hours ahead of time. The dispatch signal is sent to the local site controller where Opticaster will ingest it and adjust the day's optimal dispatch schedule to generate the most value through co-optimized dispatch. Opticaster is fundamental to Tesla-controlled Virtual Power Plant (VPP) operations in Massachusetts and South Australia.

Reliable Performance
Every Tesla site comes Opticaster-enabled across Powerwall, Powerpack and Megapack product lines. Opticaster enables highly efficient edge computing, which ensures high availability and fast

response of autonomous control regardless of cellular connectivity. Performance improvements and customized price schedules can be seamlessly pushed down to site from "Tesla's secure cloud infrastructure if necessary. Through its coordinated local and server-side architecture, Opticaster offers a very flexible, reliable solution in an ever-changing energy landscape."

These system maintenance, management services and SaaS designed to maximize revenues and profits for all battery owners give Tesla a huge moat that will provide steady profits for decades into the future."

Tesla as a Utility

Tesla clearly intends to use their ability to arbitrage energy in other interesting ways. They are already approved as a utility in England and Texas. They are in discussions with Arizona. They have teamed with Octopus Energy in Germany. We can be reasonably certain that these very quiet forays are just the tip of future forays into the utility business.

Bottom line on batteries for the energy side of Tesla: The real question is how fast they and their third-party OEM suppliers can ramp production. There doesn't seem to be any possible time in the next decade when battery supply will be greater than demand, a problem every business would love to have. Every battery not needed for a car will be employed for semi-trucks, roadsters, and energy storage. The energy division will likely be using a different chemistry, which should allow for more production that couldn't go into vehicles. We will do the math in the final section of the book when we look at future profits.

Solar - the Forgotten Tesla Product Line

Tesla has a lot on its plate. Cars, other vehicles, autonomy, energy storage, AI, insurance, and robots, just to name a few. As Elon has mentioned more than a few times, sometimes there just isn't enough bandwidth (his personally, or corporate) to deal with even fantastic opportunities. Here are just a few that have been mentioned, but are definitely not being given much attention:

HVAC for the home using Octovalve heat distribution concept.
VTOL (Vertical Lift Off and Landing jet aircraft)
AI training as a service (Brief mention at AI Day2)
Ride sharing
Food and/or other services at supercharger stations (Some minor tests)

AND Solar
SolarCity was founded in 2006 by Musk's cousins, Peter and Lyndon Rive. It was backed by Musk who served as chairman of the board at both Tesla and SolarCity. Musk's aerospace company, SpaceX, had also purchased tens of millions of dollars' worth of solar bonds from SolarCity.

"The goal is to make solar roofs that look better than a normal roof, generate electricity, last longer, have better insulation, and actually have an installed cost that is less than a normal roof plus the cost of electricity. Why would you buy anything else?" Quote from SolarCity's Inside Energy Summit in New York.

On August 1, 2016, Tesla announced that it would be acquiring the company in an all-stock $2.6 billion transaction. The addition of solar to the energy division of Tesla seemed like an obvious move that would enhance the mission of moving the world towards sustainable energy.

Solar City had a singular focus on leasing units to residential users. While Tesla would continue this sales approach, the focus shifted to solar glass roof tiles. The idea was well received by Tesla fans, but the execution has been slow to mature, and retail prices have increased beyond the level where the roof makes a clear financial benefit for the average homeowner.

What might the future hold for the solar business? Very little has been said about solar, but we do know that engineering continues to be the focus. Installation costs need to come down. Methods need to be found to cut the total cost. Such improvements are right in the sweet spot of the Tesla skill set. It is hard to get away from the thought that the focus is not on solar.

At some point, the focus will undoubtedly shift, and when it does, the solar division has potential to make a solid contribution to the bottom line. The US alone replaces 5,000,000 roofs per year and builds 1,000,000 or more new homes and apartment buildings. In addition, there are roofs for industrial and government applications.

Tesla, of course, also manufactures and installs solar panels on existing roofs, which adds millions of potential installations to the overall addressable market. There is currently precious little being said by Tesla or written about by journalists or other pundits regarding the future of the solar division. What can be said without reservation: The total market is huge, and, if Tesla decided to dominate this market, they have the products, factories, and people to do so.

CHAPTER 40

He who has the BIGGEST Battery, Wins

by Randy Kirk

Tesla Valuation as Only an Energy Storage Company

The Tesla energy storage business is the least understood of the Tesla divisions. The average consumer or investor can easily understand cars, insurance, robots, and solar. It might be a bit harder for the world to get their head around the potential for autonomous driving and robotaxi, but these two are still something the consumer can imagine wanting or using.

No one gets up in the morning and thinks: I need to add energy storage to my list of needs or wants. The average Joe has no idea that energy storage is a key component of utility level solar and wind efforts. In fact, even so-called experts in energy fail to realize that Tesla batteries combined with solar/wind is already the cheapest new energy generation facility a utility can create.

So, you could say that Tesla energy storage is the least S3XY of all the divisions. On the other hand, Elon Musk has often stated that energy will be equal in sales revenue to cars or even larger than the auto business. It is our opinion that the ramp for energy, like the ramp for trucks has only been constrained by lack of battery capacity, and that this constraint will be largely in the rear-view mirror in 2023.

The base projection in this chapter takes Elon at his word. Energy will equal auto. Total battery production in 2030 will be 3TWh. Tesla will make 20M cars in 2030.

The simple math. 20M vehicles (we'll assume some of these are semi-trucks) will require about 70KWh each, or 1.4TWh total. That would leave 1.6TWh for energy storage. We will project total deployed energy in 2022 at 5GWh, as this would seem to be the minimum likely number. From there, what will it take to get to 1.6TWh by 2030? 100% per year compounded would do the trick.

Breaking News

By the time you read this, it won't be breaking anymore, but it might still be flying under the radar.

Newsflash 1 - Tesla made a public pronouncement that they are no longer battery constrained for cars OR energy. It is hard to overstate the importance of this announcement, but The Street may still be asleep on this issue through the end of 2022, and into 2023. It is likely they will wake up when **quarterly profits for energy pass $2B in early 2023.**

Newsflash 2 - Tesla seems likely to refine raw lithium and other metals in a plant they plan to start building in late 2022. Production is slated for 2024.

Newsflash 3. The IRA bill passed by congress will provide Tesla with massive subsidies for their production of batteries and application of those batteries to cars and storage. At $45 per MWh, the potential income for 2023 alone is 160,000,000 KWh X $45 or

Making The Future Awesome | 236

over $7B. No one is counting this in Tesla's stock valuation as this is written.

I have created a chart, below, that projects likely revenues and profits from energy storage by quarter through 2023. Increasing profits beyond these estimates in 2024 and beyond will require additional capacity at Lathrup, Reno, or somewhere else in the world. Currently, the Lathrup factory is said to have a capacity of 40 GWh per year, and this is expected to be fully ramped in 2023. Reno appears to be fully ramped on panels and packs unless more lines are added, which may or may not require more space.

	Q2'22	Q3'22	Q4'22	Q1'23	Q2'23	Q3'23	Q4'23
Energy storage GWh	1.1	2	4	6	8	10	12
Revenue ($B)	0.866	2	5	8	10	12	15
COG ($B)	0.769	1.8	4	6.4	7.5	8	10
Profit ($B)	0.097	0.2	1	1.6	2.5	4	5

If this estimate is correct, and if the PE for Tesla is at 50, the street is currently underestimating Tesla's value by about $655B. That underestimation is only for battery storage. We don't have enough information right now to generate a true value for solar, but there is every reason to believe that this ramp is also about to take off.

Battery storage is not the only income stream for Tesla energy. Other revenues will be derived from maintenance contracts for the utility scale batteries. Then there is arbitrage using AI to buy and sell electricity when opportunities arise during the ebb and flow of demand vs supply. Tesla is setting themselves up as a utility that will sell energy to consumers and industry. And then there is the sleeper, VPP, or virtual power plants.

Tesla is using their software prowess to cobble together the resources of hundreds or even thousands of Powerwalls in a region that together can give the grid instant power when the demand is too much for the utility to manage. VPP's have been around for many years, but not in the organized way that Tesla is managing the idea. Just this past Summer, VPP's have been successfully used in Northern and Southern California and Japan. The homeowner is paid about $2 per Kw during these peak situations. Of course, Tesla makes money on those same Kw's, but also sells the equipment to the homeowner and the utility that makes the VPP possible.

So, while the estimate of Tesla's earnings for battery storage is possible to model (even with a huge dose of humility for guessing margins), the real numbers are far greater, and the public is far from having the information necessary to guess the future value of the other related products and services in this division.

CHAPTER 41

How Tesla Uses Artificial Intelligence to Move Further and Further Ahead

by John Gibbs

Artificial Intelligence – call it Machine Learning if you want better nerd street cred – is as old as computers themselves. From the dawn of the computer age in the 1950s, AI has grown from very rudimentary early products to a state where it is changing our world so quickly that it's hard for any of us to keep up. As it turns out, two companies that Elon Musk founded, Tesla and OpenAI, are helping to create this brave new world!

Computer based AI started in the 1950s and made great strides during the 50s and 60s. In a move that has repeated several times since then, however, the progress of AI was overstated in the press. When walking, talking robots didn't appear by the late 1960s, people lost hope that AI would achieve anything very useful.

Then in the 1970s and early 80s the first AI winter happened (A time when AI scientists were stumped and had few breakthroughs). Another AI spring happened in the late 80s and early 90s, but it too returned to winter in the late 1990s. This second AI winter lasted until a very specific date: September 11, 2012. This was the date a George Hinton lead team which was responsible for building AlexNet, which handily won the ImageNet 2012 contest. This breakthrough destroyed any previous success rates using a Convolutional Deep Neural Network (or CNN).

Interestingly enough, it was just after this date that, by insider accounts, Tesla began to seriously ramp up their efforts to use image based Neural Networks like CNNs, in conjunction with more "old school" AI techniques, to improve performance in their factory in Fremont, California. While most people know about Tesla's Full Self Driving Beta (FSD Beta) software and how impressive it is on North American roads today, Tesla's AI effort really started around 2013. Their effort was focused on making Tesla factory production much more agile and lean than is possible without AI involved. FSD is, in fact, a byproduct of Tesla's factory AI – a byproduct that could someday garner Tesla trillions of dollars in robotaxi fares!

To begin with, let's discuss the ways in which Tesla uses Machine Learning in their factories. While a good deal of this is a closely guarded secret (Tesla, after all, doesn't want to give away their 'secret sauce' to the competition), there are things we outsiders have learned over the years, and especially in the past year or so.

Tesla has a system they call Digital Self Management, or DSM, which has replaced traditional middle management with AI software. As Tesla is a highly agile company, the ability to make changes and pivot to doing other tasks almost instantly is critical to company culture. As anecdotal stories tell it, Tesla makes up to 27 changes PER DAY in their factories! Compare this to traditional automakers who might make 27 changes per year (or longer), and you can see the insane pace of change that Tesla is able to maintain.

The pace of change, which Elon Musk has referred to as the only thing that matters, is enabled by DSM as DSM provides almost

Making The Future Awesome | 240

instantaneous feedback to workers on the floor. Imagine a manager who can see everything and understand everything all at once, and who can always focus on you (and the person next to you, and the person next to them, etc.). This digital manager can provide nearly instant feedback concerning how well a human worker is doing their work, and this impressively fast feedback frees workers to experiment. Rather than waiting around for a human manager to eventually come over and look at each employee's results, the employees can manage themselves via this AI-based software.

They can try something out and find out immediately if it improved things, made no difference, or made matters worse. If the change made things better, even by a small amount, the change can be incorporated into production immediately (even the very car being experimented on can continue through production and be sold!) Each subsequent car can be improved with the same design or build changes. Of course, to keep track of all this, cars need what is termed their digital double, a virtual Tesla that exactly matches the physical one being built.

Consider how freeing it must be for employees to be able to make changes and find out if they work or not, immediately, without needing to have meetings, impress a manager, or expend the energy needed to convince others of the value of this change. DSM thus brings the cost of change to mere pennies, rather than hundreds of thousands or millions. As you might imagine, this level of agility is hugely disruptive, and one of the biggest reasons Tesla is ahead of all other auto manufacturers and increasing their lead.

Now let's turn to Tesla's FSD and especially FSD Beta, the cutting-edge AI based software that is driving Teslas around in the US and Canada as we speak. Here we have much more data. In fact, about 160,000 Tesla owners, including all four authors, are currently driving FSD Beta around city streets, parking lots, and highways all across North America!

As noted, Tesla's autonomous driving efforts were originally an outgrowth of their factory DSM system. DSM relies heavily on computer vision and recognition of objects in the real world (this is a table, this is a box, this is a human being, etc.), and Musk and others realized this could transfer effectively to the world of autonomous driving. Originally partnering with NVidia and MobilEye,

Tesla has since developed its own hardware (Hardware 3) and of course the software that runs on it. The current version of FSD Beta is almost entirely based on Deep Neural Networks that take in video images from each of Tesla's eight cameras, processes the video into one 360° surround video, creates a depth map of the world using pseudo-lidar, parses that world into a series of objects (this is a car, this is a human, this is a light pole, etc.) and then acts upon that knowledge to drive through the world.

If this sounds complex, you have no idea. Autonomous driving is by far the most complex task ever attempted by machine learning. As a benchmark, consider that we landed on the moon some 53 years ago, but to date no car has ever driven fully autonomously– until Teslas that is!

A major part of that complexity is the all-too-real fact that the world is simply chock full of exceptions (for example, this is a stop sign, except that a human is holding it, which means it might be a stop sign depending on if she is holding it upright or down at her side.)

Tesla's amazing engineers have created Neural Networks using the latest techniquest like RNNs, LSTMS, and now Transformers, that are able to recognize the world under most conditions, recognize what they see around them, estimate paths, kinematics, and trajectories, and act (acceleration, braking, steering) to maneuver through the complex roadways around us.

One other important factor when it comes to FSD is the rule of thumb that technologies follow an exponential curve. In other words, new technology like autonomous driving does not improve in a straight line, but in an upward bending curve, or an exponential curve.

Another way to think about exponentials is this: if you take 30 linear steps (at about 1 meter per step) you will walk about 30 meters, or about the length of a basketball court. If, instead, ou take 30 exponential steps (1 meter, 2 meters, 4 meters, etc.) you'll travel 1,073,741,824 meters, or more than 1 million kilometers, or more than enough to travel to the moon and back!

When it comes to technology and specifically machine learning, exponential growth means that the past is a poor predictor of the future. Although autonomous driving has been pursued seriously since the 1990s, and by Tesla since about 2014, the results have been slow to improve, which makes many people believe quite strongly that Tesla's FSD is at least a decade away from being better than human. If we think that the advances follow an exponential rather than linear curve, however, the decades that have been devoted to autonomous driving up until now have filled out the bottom, flatter part of the curve, and we are now hitting the suddenly steep upward sloping part.

Tesla has the brilliant engineers, the computer hardware, the elegant neural network architecture, and above all the data collected together to hit the steep part of the curve any day now. What could this mean?

It could mean that Tesla's FSD Beta software, which is currently at "beginner student driver" level of competence, could become as good as the best human drivers, not years from now, but in *months!* Yes, that's correct. It might only be a matter of months from now when FSD Beta could be as good as a very safe human driver. And if this happens, what happens a year after that? Tesla's FSD could be far better than the best human driver by then. This sounds crazy even as I write it, but I remind myself that we humans think in linear, not exponential, terms. Thus, we had better pay attention to the numbers rather than our intuition, and the numbers indicate that autonomous driving from Tesla is getting better and better at an astonishing pace.

Between the rapidly advancing state of autonomous driving with FSD Beta and the ability to evaluate changes nearly instantly using DSM, it is no wonder that Tesla is often considered an AI company first. From manufacturing cars to self-driving cars, Tesla uses Machine Learning to pull further and further away from the competition, to make their cars better and safer, and to delight FSD Beta users with the amazing performance of Teslas that can almost drive themselves!

CHAPTER 42

Tesla Solar and Home Battery Storage

by Brian Wang

Tesla sells solar panels, solar roofs, and home battery storage, representing huge potential for Tesla. Solar power is currently a lower priority for Tesla's business, though this could change. In October '22 Tesla is showing large increases in hiring for solar.

Tesla has competitive solar power offerings, but solar panels are sourced mainly from the dominant Chinese suppliers. This makes regular solar panels a relatively undifferentiated commodity. In residential solar and batteries, Tesla is working to innovate with Powerwall batteries, energy management software, and an integrated solar roof.

There are some problems to be solved with the installation processes of solar roofs. Version 3 has been tested on employee homes, and Tesla is beginning to switch their emphasis to new homes. They are getting a good test as part of a 2,400-home development near Austin where the Tesla Solar Roof is an option home buyers can select.

Solar costs about $3 per watt and Tesla installed 106 MW in Q2 of 2022. This is about $300M of solar. The overall US residential solar market is over 5 GW in a year or 1.2 GW in a quarter. Solar is growing at about 30% per year. An average home solar installation is about 5 KW. Tesla installed about 20K out of a total of 240K installations. Clearly, there is market growth potential.

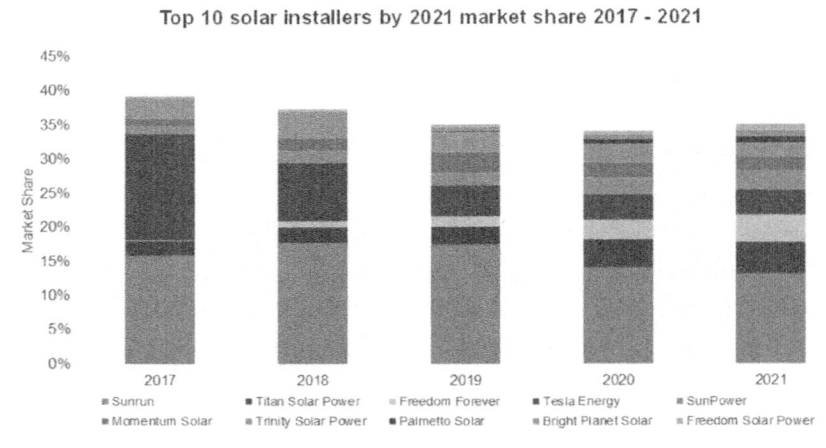

Top 10 solar installers by 2021 market share 2017 - 2021

- Sunrun
- Titan Solar Power
- Freedom Forever
- Tesla Energy
- SunPower
- Momentum Solar
- Trinity Solar Power
- Palmetto Solar
- Bright Planet Solar
- Freedom Solar Power

Source: Wood Mackenzie US PV Leaderboard

Sunrun, Titan Solar Power, and Freedom Forever have over 20% of the US solar residential market. Tesla uses subcontractors for solar installations and shifted its business model to focus on being seen as the best solar, battery and software technology offering.

Tesla has not solved the integrated solar roof. They are on their third iteration of trying to combine a roof with solar power. The challenge is that homes tend to have different floor plans and different roof shapes. Tesla wants to factory-produce the non-power roof tiles and the power generating roof tiles and put them together at the home. The puzzle pieces of roof tiles do not all fit together precisely, and tiles need to be cut and adjusted to get the final roof put together.

Figuring out this puzzle has been the major hang-up among several that has kept the Solar Roof from achieving success. With a switch

Making The Future Awesome | 246

in emphasis to the much easier job of installing roofs on new homes, this division should begin to ramp.

Virtual Power Plant

Owners of Tesla Solar Power and Tesla Powerwalls who have opted into Tesla's Virtual Power Plant program get $2 per KWh when their local power utility uses the Tesla Virtual Power Plant. Basically, Tesla pulls together hundreds or thousands of Powerwall owners in a region, uses software to manage their capacity, then, when called upon, can provide critical energy to the grid.

Pacific Gas and Electric (PG&E) in Northern California had ten emergency energy event days in late August and September of 2022 during a heat wave. This resulted in participants in the VPP making $10 per hour for about 1-3 hours during each of the events or about $250 in compensation. PG&E and Tesla expect that over the hot months of May to October there could be 20-60 hours' worth of emergency events, so the potential payouts could rise significantly.

A properly sized solar installation can almost eliminate the monthly electric bill for a house. The VPP program can add another 15-30% of financial benefit to the homeowner. There is also net metering in many locations, which is trickling power to the grid during the day when it is cheaper to buy the electricity from a homeowner. Net metering can add another 10-15% financial benefit to the Powerwall owner.

Tesla solar and battery offerings with extra software management can provide a faster payback period of 6 years instead of 10 years for those without a similar VPP program.

The Virtual Power Plant for home Powerwall batteries and Tesla Autobidder software with Megapacks enable superior energy grid stabilization and more energy revenue for Tesla.

Megapacks plus VPP can provide a more reliable energy grid (particularly for less well-maintained utilities like PG&E), lower cost emergency power options, and replacement of less utilized peaker plants. A win for the homeowner, the utility, the community, and Tesla.

The Utility gets a big potential win

A CAISO study calculates a massive price differential to ensure local reliability in the face of future power plant closures. CAISO is the California Independent System Operator. It is a non-profit Independent System Operator serving California. It oversees the operation of California's bulk electric power system, transmission lines, and electricity market.

California has almost 80 peaker plants, totaling 7GW of power. Ten percent of these are used less than 1% of the time (less than 80 hours per year).

An $800 million natural gas peaker plant currently needs to be kept online even if it was not used. Using a VPP at 25 MW would be about 10% of a full natural gas peaker plant. However, there may not be the full need for the entire output of the peaker plant. PG&E would not have to pay the $1,000-$2,700 per KW to support the construction of the peaker plant. PG&E would not have to pay for the natural gas power when the peaker plant is used.

Tesla solar power on homeowners' roofs and Powerwalls acting as a replacement for these peaker plants are all paid for and installed

Making The Future Awesome | 248

by the homeowners. Such a system would likely cost a collective $90-$130 million. If the program expands to 32,000 homes, then this VPP would be able to come close to offsetting a 270 MW peaker plant. It would cost the homeowners $1.45B-2B to install. The homeowners would be doing it anyway. They get repaid for the energy shortage events.

Tesla with Megapacks, Powerwalls, VPP and Autobidder is helping to support or replace the most expensive and weakest parts of the electrical grid.

Power outages can cost billions of dollars in lost business. The American Society of Civil Engineers reports that power outages cost the US about $28 to $169 billion each year. The PG&E-Tesla VPP helped Northern California avoid even more severe power outages during the last heat wave. Similar projects were in use by SCE in Southern California.

Commercial Solar

Tesla also has commercial solar installations. Their largest customer is Tesla's own charging stations.

They are installing solar power and batteries at 4,000 charging stations. V4 Supercharger is coming soon to Yuma County, Arizona. 40 stalls, plus two 4,500 square foot solar arrays and a Megapack. This would be about two hundred, 400-watt solar panels for a total of 80Kw of solar power. That total would be about 16 times an average residential solar installation. 4,000 charging stations with solar is equal to almost one year of Tesla residential solar power installations.

While the future seems bright for Tesla solar, there doesn't seem to be enough emphasis on this division to get a serious ramp any time soon.

On the other hand, the Powerwall business is booming. We have included the total expected sales in the energy section.

CHAPTER 43

Valuing Tesla as a Robot Company Only

by Randy Kirk

Optimus is coming. Elon plans to be manufacturing humanoid robots as early as 2023. At AI Day2, he said deliveries could begin between late 2024 and 2027. For once, there is a good chance Elon is sandbagging. Here are some questions we will try to answer in this chapter:

- Why is a humanoid robot-like Optimus a game changer?
- How would Wall Street value The Optimus Company if it was a stand-alone, startup company...right now?
- What is the total addressable market, TAM, for Optimus?
- How does general, real world AI play into the equation?
- How much will Optimus cost?
- Will Tesla sell robots or rent them out?
- How quickly will Tesla ramp full production, and for what use cases?

Robots have been around for a very long time, especially if using the Merriam Webster definition:

1: a machine that resembles a living creature in being capable of moving independently (as by walking or rolling on wheels) and performing complex actions (such as grasping and moving objects)

2a: a device that automatically performs complicated, often repetitive tasks (as in an industrial assembly line)
2b: a mechanism guided by automatic controls

One of the most famous, and funniest, few minutes in all of television history shows Lucille Ball on an assembly line trying to wrap chocolates as they stream by.

The conveyor belt is, of course, a sort of robot. We can imagine today how easy it might have been to create a robotic arm or other device that might have slid Lucy's chocolates into an envelope, then sealed the envelope before having another arm place the chocolates in a box. In fact, if you search on YouTube for "packaging line for candy," you'll see dozens of examples of such automated lines.

Here's how Optimus changes everything. Like a human, he can pick up the candy, inspect the candy for visual flaws, place the candy into a wrapper, then insert the candy into a box. Optimus could even place a lid on the box when it is full, then move full boxes into master packs that might be behind the robot. When the master pack is filled, Optimus could walk the box over to a shelf for storage or place it on a pallet to be moved later.

Complexity could easily be added. Multiple feeders could bring a variety of candies into the workspace. Customizing the assortments would be a breeze for Optimus.

To automate all of these functions today, you would need multiple stations, robots, and computer management systems, which would take up enormous amounts of room. A human or an Optimus can do all the work in a small space. An Optimus can do work faster and more precisely than a human and do so almost 24/7.

An argument could be made that current systems might be faster than Optimus, but the answer for that is merely to use more humanoid robots.

The savings in total cost of equipment and space is the game changer, and this candy line example is a simple operation that doesn't require strength, isn't dangerous, and can be performed in a controlled environment. Optimus becomes even more valuable when the Bot works in dangerous, inclement, environments...like, say, space or Mars.

How Much will Optimus Cost?

Elon has proposed that the robot should cost less than a small car, or around $20,000. Dozens of experts and pundits have estimated the cost to produce Optimus at scale might be between $5k-$10k. The costs associated with programming and the research and development costs related to the artificial intelligence portion could be in the multiple $B's. Assuming the production of even 10M units per year, a billion in R & D only adds $100 to the raw cost.

Many in the Tesla community ask the question, Will Tesla ever actually sell these bots? Renting them may be the way to go.

For the analysis, let's go back to the candy packing line. We are going to assume a boutique candy company who can't spend $Ms to automate packing. In this case, we will posit a single employee who works eight hours each day removing finished candy from molds, placing them in packages, assorting them in a box, placing the lid on the box, and then packing the boxes in a master.

This little factory is in Indonesia, so the cost for the employee is just $3 per hour with no benefits. This is roughly $6,000 per year.

If Tesla were to provide an Optimus at $5,000 per year, this should be a no-brainer decision for the owner. The bot always shows up, never tires, doesn't create any drama, and will work overtime without any issue. If the sales pick up to the point where it would have taken another half time worker, Optimus can work faster or longer at no additional cost.

If Tesla asked the owner to pay $30,000 for the robot, the owner might not have a way to pay that amount. But if Tesla is happy to take $400 a month, any smart owner is going to say yes.

Of course, this was the extreme case regarding the wage comparison. The more realistic case might be a candy maker in Los Angeles paying $20 an hour and employing 3 packers. Optimus replaces two of those, the third one gets a raise to $30 an hour to manage the robot. The savings are now $60,000 per year, and the remaining employee can probably take on additional tasks, as well. If Tesla would rent an Optimus to this owner for $2,000 a month, the owner would gladly sign up, pocketing an extra $36k per year in the process.

Of course, if the Robot costs $5K to build, the $2,000 per month pays the full cost within 2.5 months, and from that point forward Tesla earns $2,000 per month with no outlay.

What Is the Total Addressable Market (TAM) for Optimus?

When marketers and financial types ask this question about most products and services, the answer is some percentage of the local, regional, national, or world population. What is the TAM for smartphones? At least one smartphone per person between ages 5 and 85 worldwide. Maybe you'd need to limit that number by income or access to electricity.

The TAM for Optimus is well beyond the total population on earth and is truly unknowable. The more "intelligent" and capable Optimus becomes, the more use cases smart business owners, governments, and homeowners will find. Like the gentry of old, a family of three might want one Optimus for each family member, and another one to stay home and watch the house and dog when everyone is out.

How Does Artificial Intelligence (AI) Play into the Optimus Question?

Without AI, automated equipment can only perform very specific and limited tasks. Those tasks are sometimes "baked in" to the mechanical way that the machine works. You push a button, the motor turns on, and it moves a lever in a certain repetitive way until the system turns it off.

Sometimes the function of automated equipment is much more sophisticated. Many cars today have sensors that automatically apply the brakes if the car gets too close to an object in front of it. A computer has analyzed the situation based on human programming of that computer, to perform various functions based on input.

When AI joins the game, the computer programming is designed to accumulate data of certain types. The data then changes how the program responds in the future.

If we take that same automatic braking system and apply AI, the data might show that the sun reflection off of the paint of silver cars renders those cars invisible until too late to respond. Possibly the programming was set up to allow a change in the way incoming light is analyzed, since the engineers knew that there might be many issues of how incoming light might affect performance. Then the AI would automatically attempt to correct for the problem.

For Optimus there is an almost infinite set of variables to consider, especially as the environment becomes more and more variable. If Optimus is used in a closed space in the candy factory, it really doesn't need to know how to walk on uneven surfaces, as it will always be on a flat hard surface. But if we want to take our bot to the beach, the walking, running, jumping, and falling skills are exponentially more difficult.

Your personal robot, to be really useful, needs to be able to understand a long list of commands, interact with those commands, and then go somewhere and manipulate objects of varying dimensions and materials. The whole idea of having something like C-3PO in real life starts to seem implausible.

According to the experts, Optimus will soon have those capabilities. The entire issue seems to be one of data gathering, huge amounts of storage, and the computational power to manage the data. One thing that seems certain. Some level of C-3PO is possible.

How Should or Would Investors and Wall Street Value the Optimus Product if it were a Stand-alone Startup?

How can we compare the potential value of Optimus with other startups in the past? To begin with, there is no possible comparison as no product has ever had a TAM of this size. Therefore, it would seem that the immediate issue is how fast can Tesla make robots that have a usable functionality greater than the cost to manufacture plus a profit?

YouTuber, Warren Redlich, has suggested that even if the first 10,000 Optimus robots cost $50,000 each to make, the public would happily pay $100,000 for such a toy, even if it had limited functionality. Under a rental plan, possibly a rent of $10,000 or more per month would find a very willing market.

If after 10,000 were produced on a pilot line, Tesla was able to start making the robots at scale using one or more lines, the cost of goods (COGs) would seemingly fall to $10,000 or less, even considering the cost of the "robots" to make the robots. *Or would much of the work be done by Optimus bots?*

So, how do we compare this to any other startup? Maybe we could look at the valuations of some "next Teslas." Investors are looking under every rock, hoping to find the next Tesla. They are willing to give some of these company's valuations of 10's of $Bs well before they have a proven ability to ever make a profit.

>Rivian - Currently valued at $36B. Highest was over $100B
>Lucid - Currently $27B. Highest was $91B
>Nikola - Currently $2B. Highest was $34B
>XPeng - Currently $12.5. Highest was over $60B
>Nio - Currently $33B. Highest was $99B

Do you think any wall street analyst currently values Optimus at $100B? $33B? And yet, it seems far more likely that Optimus will be adding many, many $Bs to the Tesla bottom line than any of these fine automakers.

In fact, Rivian, Lucid, and Nikola are burning through massive amounts of cash with first profits not likely for years to come. I (Randy) think that it is very possible that Optimus will be a big part of the Tesla bottom line well before those three auto companies are showing even a dollar of profit.

As noted above, the potential is also far greater than any other product ever offered. It is clear that once ramped, Tesla could be deploying 10M, 100M, or more robots per year. At $24,000 per year in profit, the numbers become staggering, but please provide an argument for why Optimus would be worth less than $2,000 per month. The truth is, Optimus would be worth far more than that.

So, which day does Wall Street wake up to this potential? What happens to Tesla's stock price when that happens?

After AI Day2

I (Randy) follow about 20 online pundits daily. You can find the list in the Appendix under resources. I'm writing this the morning after AI Day2 and there is universal dancing in the streets. The Tesla robotics team was able to show off an amazingly capable Optimus 1 walking, doing functions that required navigating a room, and using humanoid hands.

They also showed Optimus 2, which was a more refined, custom-built robot, designed to be mass produced. These capabilities were ready for showtime in much less than a year. The Tesla community was awestruck by the possibilities in the very near future if this amount of progress could be achieved in such a short window.

What might the real bottom line look like for the near term? Actual production at scale in late 2024 with 1M or more bots produced in 2025 at $20,000 each seems possible. This rather conservative estimate would produce $20B in revenue in 2025. Why would the profit margin be less than 50% if the robots were sold, rather than rented? So, the robots should bring $10B in profit in 2025.

It is unimaginable that Tesla would sell these without an ongoing subscription for future updates. $1,200 a year would be the minimum imaginable. This would add $1.2B each year.

Ramping seems simple enough. If the ramp to 1M units is successful, the ramp to 5M would seemingly take far less work than going from 1M to 5M cars. This new division of the Tesla company will be one that eclipses all the others.

CHAPTER 44

The Biggest Moat - Flexibility

by Randy Kirk

As noted elsewhere in the book, Berkshire Hathaway's oft quoted chair, Warren Buffet, places a huge amount of weight on a company's moat(s) when determining whether or not he will invest. To that end we have provided a very long list of Tesla and SpaceX moats that should make any Buffet fan happy.

Over the last weeks of diving deeper and deeper into the Tesla story, a moat of historic proportions has emerged. I doubt whether even the 4D chess expert, Elon Musk truly planned this mile-wide, mile-deep moat. More likely, it has materialized due to the first principles approach being applied to every aspect of the business.

What Is the Flexibility Moat, and Why is it Worthy of a Second and Separate Chapter?

Let's start from the simplest, but maybe the most profitable example - the Model Y. In 2022, the Model Y will become the best-selling car in the world by both sales and profits. In 2023, it will become the best-selling car by units. Some will argue that selling more than one or two million of the same model cars per year is impossible due to the law of large numbers. Others will merely argue that the competition is coming, and that similar models will put a cap on potential sales. Finally, there is the argument that people want to feel unique, not see themselves coming and going at every intersection.

How will flexibility destroy the law of large numbers, destroy any serious competition, and make people forget about whether their car is unique enough?

Tesla has double the industry standard for margins, and these are only growing as Tesla makes more vehicles, thereby creating ever-increasing economies of scale. Using China as an example, since BYD is probably the best competitor at the moment, we can imagine a time when Tesla's China sales start to slow due to a confluence of events: The Chinese economy slows, BYD undercuts Tesla on the basic value proposition, and five other made-in-China vehicles provide good value and different, compelling styles.

There are dozens of marketing options Tesla could take under such circumstances, and these have also been outlined in great detail in this book. The short version, ship any excess to other markets, create incentives to sell a Tesla to your friend, lower prices as much as necessary, chase fleet sales, advertise, and more.

Other car makers don't have all these tools available to deploy, as they are already advertising, and don't have the margins to undercut Tesla on pricing or to add free features.

How about the car itself? New colors, free wraps, upgraded wheels, tires, etc., longer range, free supercharger miles, lower cost for FSD, add a plaid version, or create a version with lower range and reduced features that completely undercuts the market.

Other car companies don't have the margins to offer free wraps and upgraded wheels. They don't have a $15,000 FSD software product that costs almost nothing to produce. They can't lower range, as their range is generally below Tesla already.

But there's more! The China design factory has been in business for at least two years. Does anyone reading this think they have failed to provide Elon with multiple designs of completely different models that might sit on the current drive train, or even require a new drive train? At a bare minimum there are already complete prototypes built for a $25,000 car, a small truck, a commercial van, and a robotaxi. You can probably add others. With Tesla's modular approach to manufacturing, existing lines that lack demand can relatively easily switch to new products.

While it might be hard to hide the creation of actual tooling for some of these optional models, it isn't impossible. There could already be test tooling for many of the most difficult parts of some of these models.

Other factories use the traditional line approach in their manufacturing process and take years to bring a new design to market.

Robotaxis

There has been a raging debate over whether Tesla will stop selling cars when the robotaxi fleet needs millions of cars per year. Here is another way to think about it. Flexibility would suggest that you start making robotaxis as fast as your factories can make them, but you don't stop selling other products if there is still demand.

Elon has always said that part of the robotaxi fleet would be made up of individual owners or fleet owners having a taxi business. The most flexible approach would be to hold onto that thinking for at least 3-5 years as the new design is ramped. The market will dictate if there is a time when it makes sense to slow down the manufacturing of cars for individual ownership.

There will continue to be a need for cars and trucks that are specifically outfitted for various uses and businesses. Some folks will just prefer to own rather than ride in a "public" taxi. Tesla will truly be the only company with the flexibility to do both.

Batteries

Tesla provided clickbait to many journalists and YouTubers when they defied the chip shortage and increased production while every other car company had to shut down production. That same flexibility is going to become increasingly evident in Tesla's battery strategy.

Several pundits have begun to notice the unorthodox way that Tesla is acquiring battery cells and raw materials years into the future. They have purchased land for a potential mine. They are considering refining lithium in Texas (as of this writing). They have created long term contracts directly with mining and refining companies all over the world. They have publicly declared on many occasions that they will buy all the scarce raw material and batteries that anyone will sell them.

In addition, they are ramping up 210 GWh of battery production in California, Texas, and Berlin. Many feel that Berlin and Texas will eventually be 200 GWh each. No one thinks Tesla will stop with these three facilities.

Now, here is where the flexibility plays out. Tesla is already using 18650, 2170, and 4680 cylindrical cells. Rumor has it that they will soon be using blade cells from BYD. There is no evidence that they will use pouches, as these do seem to be outmoded.

Making The Future Awesome | 264

Tesla uses a wide variety of chemistries in their cathode and anode. You might say they are chemistry and form-factor agnostic to a point. The result is that they can switch chemistries based on which raw materials are plentiful and/or inexpensive. They can buy batteries from almost any cell manufacturer, as they have designed their cars to use what is available, to a point.

No other car company has designed their vehicles to have this flexibility. AND Tesla has an energy storage business that we argue will be using as many batteries as the car business within 2-3 years. *This means that the combined purchasing power of cells and raw materials are multiple times the competition far into the future.*

The Skate plus the Gigacastings

A few electric car companies have intimated that they will have a basic drivetrain "skate," and that this foundational part of the car can then be outfitted with various models on top of the skate. This seems brilliant.

Tesla has this same option ready to go if they can ever make enough model 3s and Ys to satisfy demand. But Tesla has gone one step further.

The Gigacasting idea has captivated the imaginations of the nerds and engineers of the world. Using a die cast approach for the front and rear structures of the underbody has eliminated 173 parts and two-thirds of the robots necessary to assemble the structure of the car. That is a breakthrough that saves money, complexity, factory space, and speeds production. It also reduces multiple potential quality issues.

But I haven't heard anyone talking about the next level of this development. You've already proven the concept, now you change the molds to fit the passenger compartments that will sit on top. You aren't re-engineering the entire structure, just changing those few necessary points where the new model will connect with the structure. Flexibility on steroids.

One last flexibility moat - Massive Capital

Almost every company, and certainly every legacy automotive company, has limits on their ability to spend money. A company might want to spend money on R & D, new products, additional capacity, acquisitions of companies, patents, other assets, or talent.

But according to pundits like Gary Black and others, Tesla already appears to have a problem. They can't spend the cash they are going to generate. It is hard to imagine any expenditure they might like to make that they are not able to make. If they can't buy what they need with the cash in the bank or the cash they are going to generate in the next few quarters, they can go to the capital markets where they will have no problem selling more shares. They also have no debt, so they can borrow from banks, institutions, or float bonds.

Of course, if I had that kind of capital available, it might turn out I'd make at least a few less-than-wise investments. But between Elon and the think tank he has at his elbow, they have shown an almost uncanny ability to invest capital with stunning returns.

Maybe the competitive advantage of this huge difference in available capital is obvious. Maybe it isn't.

In normal times it means that, if Tesla decided to, they could build the 10 Gigafactories they need for 20M cars per year in two or three years. Mental bandwidth might stand in the way, but cash would not.

That cash means you can make huge mistakes with little impact. Maybe one day Model 3 sales crater. Maybe the company spends $3B on the humanoid robot, but it never comes to market. Can you think of another company who has spent $billions on projects that never materialize, and it isn't even a rounding error on the balance sheet. Like, maybe, Apple.

One last example. As this chapter is being written, Tesla has announced a plan to refine lithium somewhere on the Gulf Coast. They have also just announced that they are no longer battery constrained for cars or energy storage. I rest my case.

CHAPTER 45

Coming Attractions - Dojo aaS, Used Cars, HVAC, and VTOL

by Randy Kirk

As noted elsewhere and reiterated by Elon at AI Day2, Tesla is made up of multiple startup companies. We have identified the following:

- Tesla Vehicles
- Energy Storage
- Solar
- Electric Utility - VPP
- Supercharger Network
- Car Insurance
- Used cars
- SaaS
- Robot
- Dojo aaS
- HVAC
- TaaS robotaxis
- e-VTOL

As of this moment, the vehicle business is in profits, which are substantial and climbing. There are good reasons to believe that energy storage is also profitable when divided from solar. Similarly, the Supercharger network very likely has operating earnings that might be offset by depreciation, since the rate of build is so great. Almost nothing is known about the profits for insurance, used cars, or electric utility efforts, though all three would seem to be high margin, low overhead operations. SaaS is a very small business thus far. Solar is probably still losing a lot of money, but once it turns, it could easily become another money printing business.

So, after disrupting the auto business, the electric power business, the fuel station business, the car insurance industry, becoming a major player in used cars, and potentially completely changing human life as we know it with robots on two legs, what could possibly be left?

Dojo aaS

Did you know that Amazon makes far more profit from its cloud storage business, AWS, than it does from all other Amazon businesses? The total revenues are stretching towards $100B. So, if Tesla has the very best computer hardware and software engineers of any company and has just gone live on the largest and fastest neural network training device ever made; and if Tesla plans to manufacture more Dojo units in 2023…a lot more; and if Elon Musk said on AI Day2 that Tesla has plans to sell time on these units in the future, I suppose this could be a fairly decent startup.

It is hard to know when revenue will begin to flow from this venture, but 2024 would seem like a reasonable guess.

Used Cars

Tesla announced a few weeks ago that their income from used car sales puts it in the class of other national, stock exchange listed, used car sales companies, possibly comparing their business to Carvana or Autonation. Each company has a market cap of around $4B.

According to Jimmy Douglas, director of sales and delivery operations at Tesla:

> *Most people don't realize that Tesla runs its own vertically integrated, nationwide online used car retailer. It's as big as some publicly traded used car retailers you've definitely heard of, despite no Super Bowl commercials or wacky waving inflatable arm flailing tube men.*

Since their used car sales are directly tied to trade-ins and returned lease vehicles, the used car business should continue to ramp at about the same rate as the underlying new car business.

Tesla doesn't have a separate line item for used car sales on the income statement. These sales are combined with other services, including insurance, repairs, and even the Supercharger network. So, it is impossible to know what the total sales or profits are from this division.

What is probably a dead certainty is that no financial guru is including $4B in market cap for this activity, nor are they contemplating that at 50% per year growth, the value of just the used car sales could be over $10B by 2025, depending on the PE.

HVAC

Elon Musk has teased more than a few times that an HVAC (heating, ventilation, and air conditioning) system might be coming in 2023. Offering a home heating, air conditioning, water heater, air filtration system using a sophisticated heat pump approach, has been on the table ever since the company invented the octovalve to move air and fluids around the cars.

Here is an Elon Tweet on October 22

> **Elon Musk replied**
>
> **Elon Musk Quotes** @muskQu0tes · 16h
> "We will make super-efficient home hvac with hepa filters one day."
> @elonmusk on Tesla
>
> 💬 264   🔁 282   ♥ 3,725
>
> **Elon Musk** ✓ @elonmusk · 1h
> Replying to @muskQu0tes
> It will happen
>
> 💬 800   🔁 332   ♥ 5,483

The concept is so cool that I have been holding off on a new HVAC system for my home in hopes of being one of the first to install this product.

The market, of course, is huge. Similar to roofs, you have replacements for water heaters and HVAC systems ranging around 15-25 years. You also have the new home business.

e-VTOL

Elon says that he has a great drawing for an electric, Vertical Lift Off and Landing craft (VTOL). He also says that he doesn't have the bandwidth to develop this product right now. The current ratio of the battery energy density to weight ratio is also part of the issue, but it seems that the current specs are close to good enough.

Elon has also stated that his vision of the future transportation of the world would see:

Underground tunnels with electric autonomous vehicles in the cities.

Autonomous vehicles or hyperloops handling much of the mid-range trips.

VTOL and hyperloops taking over for the longer trips - I'm thinking 200-1,000 miles.

Starship would handle the cross-continent and cross-ocean trips. I can't find a reference, but I think current airlines would handle the trips between VTOL range and Starship range.

It isn't clear whether Elon's idea is significantly better than other e-VTOL ideas that are under development, but one suspects it is.

CHAPTER 46

The Value of SpaceX

by Brian Wang

In August 2022, SpaceX completed a stock sale that valued the company at $127B, making it the 2nd largest privately held company in the world by value. Here is a chart from https://www.cbinsights.com/research-unicorn-companies

List of unicorn companies

Company	Valuation ($B)
ByteDance	$140
SpaceX	$127
SHEIN	$100
Stripe	$95

SpaceX has two primary income streams. The first is the business of charging companies, universities, governments, and others to launch their satellites into orbit. This includes an ever-growing number of contracts with NASA for transporting material and astronauts to the ISS, and for an upcoming moon landing.

> *One reason SpaceX's valuation has proven more resilient than other unicorns: high demand, not just for its shares, but for seats on its rockets. Earlier this week, a company director said at an industry conference that SpaceX had nearly fully booked its rocket payloads through 2024 and was already accepting bookings in 2025.* Forbes https://www.forbes.com/sites/alexkonrad/2022/08/11/austr alian-south-korean-investors-pour-more-cash-into-spacex-at-125-billion/?sh=da3f91e4163b

The second source of income is Starlink. Starlink's mission is providing broadband Internet services to poorly served regions, to moving objects such as ships, trains, and planes, and to anyone needing very fast and very reliable service. They will also serve to replace cell towers for cell phone connectivity.

Starlink has recently started shipping receiver dishes to individual consumers that gives them excellent Internet connectivity for $110 per month. By the end of 2022, well over 1M users will have signed up and purchased the dish and service.

In addition, Starlink now offers a premium tier with a scan array that's twice as big as the standard plan and with download speeds ranging from 150-500Mbps. That tier costs $500 per month compared to $110 for the standard plan. The dish will set you back $2,500 compared to the smaller disc at $599.00

The next rung up the ladder of service options takes Starlink to sea and in the air. Connectivity to your yacht or cruise ship starts at

$10,000 to set it up and $5,000 per month. Royal Caribbean International has already started installing Starlink on its cruise ships. Hawaiian Airlines has purchased the service for their passengers.

There is great excitement in the Elon Musk community about the portability of the dish. These are already being used for camping.

Various militaries may also be lined up to buy after Starlink showed its power in the Ukraine conflict. Trucks bearing the dishes were able to be deployed in the field, allowing troops to communicate even after Russia had tried to block their more traditional communication systems.

All communication satellites in the future will speak to one another using lasers, according to many pundits. But Starlink is already there. Here is the basic reason, according to Elon: "Starlink inter-satellite laser links should be operational by end of year. This will dramatically reduce global latency. Light travels ~40% faster in vacuum/air than in fiber optic cables & satellite path length is shorter (cables follow coastlines)".

Hot off the presses as this book is wrapping up in mid-September (date?) 2022, T-Mobile has inked a deal with Starlink to provide limited email and text services to customers who are out of range of towers. Elon says that talks are being held with Apple for some kind of use case, though he offered no details. One suspects it would be similar to the T-Mobile deal. See much more on this in a separate chapter on the ramifications of the T-Mobile deal and cell-phone connectivity.

The potential future for Starlink is likely unknowable since other potential use cases seem to be popping up every month. But for the purpose of valuing the Starlink division of SpaceX, we will use what we can be relatively certain of.

We'll look just a couple of years out when the global network should support 40M global subscriptions with the 12,000 satellites. We will project $50B per year (an average of $1,250 per user), with the assumption being that the price per month for regular users may actually decrease, but that there will be plenty of premium users.

The ground cost for customer service, repairs, bookkeeping, etc., is a complete guess, but we'll call it 5% or $2.5B.

The fleet of satellites will need to be replaced at the rate of 20% per year or 2,400 units per year. We will assume that the new, much less expensive rocket, Starship, will be deploying much less expensive satellites (mass production), resulting in each deployed satellite costing no more than $500,000, and maybe, much less. This would result in an ongoing cost of $1.2B per year.

If you've been keeping up with the math, you will begin to see that this project prints money like no other company, ever. $50B in revenues producing $46.3B in profit per year.

To make matters even more interesting, the actual potential market for users is much closer to 1B or even more, as there are at least that many underserved people. So, revenues could reach $1.2T. Or possibly, the monthly cost to some of those individuals would be half or even less than half of the $110 per month. The total addressable market is still likely to approach $1T, given all the use cases.

So, what will the value of Starlink be with profits at $46B? At least $1T and probably more. What would the value be with net profits approaching $1T? It seems preposterous to consider, but on the order of $20T - $40T.

How fast will this valuation move up towards these astronomical (pun intended) numbers? The satellite launch part of the project is publicly available, and the speed will depend on Starship getting to low earth orbit successfully.

How quickly Starlink intends to build subscribers would be tied to how fast they can manufacture the antennae dishes. It would appear that they are now building 30,000 terminals per week, or 1.5m per year. This production level could allow Starlink to hit 5m subscribers by 2025, a far cry from the 22.7M subscribers and $40B in revenue projected by SpaceX. But if you can make 30,000 a week, how hard is it to go to 130,000?

In truth, no one knows if the market for this service will result in 100,000 or more signing up per month. And getting that kind of response may require some lowered monthly subscription fees. However, the margins are obviously there to do so.

Using our earlier analysis, the cost per month could drop to $10 and the company would still be profitable. We can guess the number will, on average, be somewhere between $10 and $110.

Back to the question of SpaceX valuation, short term. The company is valued at $127B with only about $2B in revenues largely from the other businesses. With even 1M subscribers the revenue should grow to $3B. If Elon is right and revenues reach $40B in 2025, the company would surely be worth over $1T. So, between now and then, we might suspect a very fast ramp of the SpaceX stock doubling each year.

We can easily project these huge valuations without considering other businesses that SpaceX intends to enter, such as space tourism, city-to-city transportation, space junk removal, or asteroid demolition.

CHAPTER 47

Mechazilla Launch Towers are Giant Rocket Catching Robots

by Brian Wang

Many people have difficulty understanding the scale of Elon Musk's ambitions. They do not understand how all of the different parts are critical to the master plan. For Tesla, Elon has written out two master plans and will soon reveal a third plan.

However, even the average person who knows something about Elon Musk's SpaceX commonly only knows about the million-person City on Mars goal. Elon's most ambitious and outrageous plan to make Humanity multi-planetary is S3XY and beyond audacious. A large percentage of the population might also be aware that SpaceX is shooting off a lot of rockets and they have some concepts that SpaceX has reusable boosters and/or rockets.

The focus around Mars and very cool rockets is only a small part of the picture.

However, rocket launches are only about 3% of today's space business. The rockets enable the business, but rocket launches themselves are only $10B of a $330B business. The real revenue source of the space business is the satellites. This is why Starlink, the placement of 14,400 satellites in low earth orbit, is so important. The goal is to provide outstanding broadband service to folks in areas that have typically had no service at all, or very poor service at best.

Taking satellites into space for other companies or governments, making trips to the International Space Station, and upcoming missions to the Moon are some of the other contracts that SpaceX currently has in order to generate revenue and profits. The future will see many other revenue sources.

Reaching the primary goals of SpaceX requires fast, inexpensive, launches of big rockets. For Elon Musk's ambitions around rockets, space, and the Earth. Mechazilla is critical.

What is a Mechazilla?

When the uninitiated look at the launch tower, they don't understand how it will transform our world. They think it is just the place where you launch the rockets. All of the big developments around SpaceX clearly show what is planned along the way. We will show how all of the pieces fit together into a symphony of radical change and improvement.

Mechazilla is a 50-story tall stationary robot that will catch 200-ton rockets with its chopstick like "arms."

This sounds impossible, but the size of the chopstick arms is almost the size of the drone ships SpaceX has been using to land rockets at sea. SpaceX has landed over 100 times on these drone ships. SpaceX has shown that they can guide returning rockets to that target, precisely every time.

The arms of Mechazilla can move up and down at 1 meter per second.

SpaceX will mass produce the Mechazilla launch towers. They will put them onto converted oil rigs. How's that for recycling? Taking outdated, useless oil rigs and turning them into platforms for launching and landing massive rockets.

When the space shuttle was in operation, it could launch a payload of 27,500 kilograms for $1.5 billion, or $54,500 per kilogram. For a SpaceX Falcon 9, the rocket that is used to access the ISS, the cost is just $2,720 per kilogram.

Elon has projected the fully reusable Starship Super Heavy will bring cargo costs to $10 per kilogram (2.2 pounds.) That is less than it currently costs to get a package weighing 1kg from Los Angeles to NYC.

There are multiple steps necessary to get to that cost.

Bring the cost of each Raptor 2 engine down to $250,000. There are 40 engines on the booster and the Starship. This would be $10 million for the engines and say $10 million for the rest of the rocket plus double for labor to get to a cost of about $40 million per rocket. NASA's new SLS rocket will cost $1.6B for a comparison.

It will take about $900,000 worth of fuel to launch the Super Heavy Starship. SpaceX is looking for ways to lower the cost of the fuel.

Critically, SpaceX needs to use the booster thousands of times. They want to refuel and fly them every hour. The super heavy boosters will boost the rocket, then break away and fly back to the tower within about 10 minutes. The booster would be refueled while a new rocket is loaded on top. This high rate of use would mean each tower would be dedicated to its booster. There would be multiple Starships for each booster as a Starship going to orbit might not return for a couple of days.

Taking Over Air Cargo and then Passenger Travel is the Future

Some towers would be dedicated for just Starship missions without boosters. Those would be to move passengers or cargo around the world. The US military has already awarded SpaceX two $150 million contracts for the first under one hour delivery anywhere in the world.

Launching 1 million satellites into orbit at 100 satellites per launch is 10,000 launches over say six years. This would be a huge number. SpaceX is making a Raptor rocket engine factory to make 4000 engines every year. SpaceX is already producing at a rate of about 400 Raptors every year and this rate is increasing every month.

The 4000 engines are enough for 40 boosters and 400 Starships every year. This means there is a need for 40 to 80 launch towers. If SpaceX is heading toward launching Starships three times per day and Boosters once an hour, then, in one year of full production, the fleet would fly 400-1000 times per day. All of the most ambitious satellite launch demand would be handled in one to two weeks.

The launch capabilities need to move up to delivering cargo at massive scale around the world. It would connect continents first so that we shave off 12-16 hours on the longest flight packages. Megacities like New York, LA, and Tokyo would then get direct connections. 100,000 to 350,000 flights per year would be the capacity of the system with the first year of production of fully used boosters and Starships.

SpaceX air/space cargo delivery would improve and provide clear demonstrated evidence for the safety of the rockets. Future passengers would want to see large numbers of successful flights before they'll be ready to transition to rocket passengers.

Passenger flights around 2030 would be different. You would be strapped in a semi-reclined position and then experience a roller coaster-like ride. You'll go up for a few minutes with moderate G forces followed by weightlessness, and then less than a G deceleration for landing.

The capabilities and costs of the Super Heavy Starship require capturing the long-range Earth based air cargo market. Space business will not develop that quickly even with super-aggressive transformation of the internet, GPS, and communication.

Passengers and cargo will go to their local Spaceports, each with several launch towers. The launch towers are like the future runways of the new airports.

Traveling Anywhere on Earth in 30 Minutes is Close to Teleportation

Traveling around the world will almost always be faster than the drive to the Spaceport.

The cost of large airplanes is $100-300 million. The Starship is all that is needed for point-to-point transportation. The Starship alone will cost about $5 to $10 million each in mass production and only uses about $250,000 of fuel per flight. Starship will fly twenty times faster than airplanes and deliver four times the payload per flight.

The fuel and operating costs per flight will be similar to an airline covering the same distance, and could ultimately be better for Starship, because Starships could make ten to twenty trips per day while an airplane flying long distances makes only one to four flights per day.

Mechazilla is central to the entire operation. Mechazilla catches the returning rockets and/or boosters and rockets. Then the rockets or boosters are repositioned for the next flight. As needed, Mechazilla lifts the rocket on top of the booster and then becomes the stabilizer until launch.

The changes and plans that Elon has are not incremental. They are transformational changes where a product or system gets 10 to 20 times better, but then works together with other products or system improvements that combine to be thousands of times better at their function and/or multiples less expensive to provide.

CHAPTER 48

Starlink as a Stand-Alone Profit Center

by Randy Kirk

Starlink is a constellation of satellites in low earth orbit which have the capacity to provide those who need Internet broadband services with fast, reliable connections. As of this writing, over 2,000 satellites are operational and serving 35 countries. On July 7, 2022, Starlink announced that they have a receiver that will work for airplanes, ships at sea and other vehicles.

By the time this book is published about half of the projected 5,000 satellites in earth orbit will be owned by SpaceX, and this percentage will continue to grow dramatically over the next few years.

How Does Starlink Work?

Consumers connect to the satellite using a small dish that self-orients to the closest satellite system. The current cost for the dish is under $600, and the subscription fee is $110 per month for residential service. A new larger dish has just been introduced. It seems likely that more products will be introduced over time.

Starlink has much bigger plans for the potential constellation. They currently have FCC permission to place 12,000 satellites in orbit. The eventual goal is to have 40,000. Some of those would be orbiting at even lower altitudes in order to provide faster speeds.

However, those currently using the system seem to be quite satisfied with both speed and latency.

The Mission and the Addressable Market

It is impressive to think that just 30 years after the advent of a public internet, 65% of the world's population has access to the critical opportunities offered by online information, tools, and communication. The huge challenge for internet service providers (ISPs) is to reach those other 35% or 2.8B people. That is the mission of Starlink.

But the addressable market is not just those with no access to cable, satellite, or other services, another billion or so have slow or intermittent service.

Additionally, millions of folks with access at home have limited or no access when traveling by trains, planes, ships, or recreational vehicles. Starlink is now offering services to all of these moving objects and at substantially higher prices, thus profits.

Every military needs field access to the Internet as we have just witnessed in the Ukraine.

Financial institutions and other businesses will pay substantial subscription fees to move information around the world at lightning speeds. Starlink satellites have the ability to speak with one another using lasers. Once fully activated, data will be able to move from satellite to satellite at the speed of light, resulting in the fastest possible data pack deliveries.

Starlink has recently announced that, pending FCC approval, the service will become available to mobile devices. SpaceX says it can achieve this capability due to its acquisition of Swarm, last August. The company is a nano-satellites technology company providing data for Internet-of-Things devices.

According to a SpaceX FCC filing, SpaceX stated it would attach new modules to Starlink satellites and produce a small mobile device for users to connect to on the ground. This increases functionality and adds more reasons to subscribe.

And finally, while Starlink sort of denies it, the existing 65% of the world who have access might prefer the faster speeds and dependability of the Starlink service at some point, making the total addressable market just about every human, business, and government entity on earth.

For the purposes of this book, we will assume that Starlink would be perfectly happy to have 1-2B of the folks with no or poor access as individual users or small businesses, and a few hundred million of those who need special services.

The Moats

The moats on Starlink are particularly impressive. It is hard to imagine how any competitor will be able to come close to Starlink's capabilities in the foreseeable future.

Cost to deploy - Starlink has multiple moats when it comes to cost to deploy. First, they have an Elon Musk factory making the satellites at scale, currently about 45 per week. Of course, as noted elsewhere regarding the Tesla auto factories, there is constant iteration to improve both the quality and the cost of the satellites. Like Tesla cars the satellites are also able to be updated over-the-air with improvements.

Whether you are laying cable, stringing telephone lines, or setting up Wi-Fi towers, there is a very high cost to create the infrastructure. This is certainly true with satellites. But here again, the leadership is unassailable. Starlink's cost per kg to deliver satellites into orbit is orders of magnitude lower than their peers or even their nascent competitors. As discussed in much greater detail in the section about SpaceX rockets, Tesla also mass produces rockets, reuses most of the rocket parts, and is about to drop the cost per kg even lower with the deployment of Starship.

Starship will have a capacity to carry 150 tons to orbit. Starlink will be sending a 2nd generation satellite which will, according to Musk, have 10 X the capability of the current version, into orbit on Starship about 120 at a time. This compares to 50 on board the Falcon currently. With a cost of about $2M per flight, the delivery cost of the Starlink Gen2/V2.0 will be just $17,000 each. The satellites cost about $200K each.

While there are some other ISPs creating constellations, they are filling other niches. Some countries, like China, seem to feel they need to have their own satellite communication systems. If broadband from space becomes fast enough with low enough latency, there might be room for competition to cover some of the market. At this point, it would seem foolhardy for any other company to attempt to compete worldwide on the scale of Starlink.

Sophistication of Starlink Satellites - Elon often refers to his 5-step approach to factory production. The core of those five steps is to produce enough products so that you can iterate often. No other company is mass producing satellites. They are generally hand built like a Ferrari, not created on assembly lines like a Tesla Model Y. The mass production of the satellites allows Starlink to continuously improve the product with small changes, then from time-to-time, bring a completely new version to the market.

Availability of Capital - Investors want to be a part of Elon Musk companies. When you watch a rocket land on the target of a drone vessel at sea, you are inspired and drawn to the prospect of being a part of something big. The interest in Starlink specifically is seemingly almost limitless. The offers for private placements into SpaceX are gobbled up as soon as offered. Any online discussion of an eventual Starlink public stock offering generates huge amounts of chatter on social platforms.

Starlink is the largest communication system ever contemplated. What would a competitive company mission need to offer that would provide investors the prospect of taking a significant bite out of the addressable market for space-based connectivity. Other than sovereign nations desiring to "own their own," the only likelihood would be niche opportunities or some incredible breakthrough in methods for providing broadband.

There are other new players in this space. Some of those are actually using SpaceX to deliver their satellites into orbit. These are niche players who believe their value-added proposition will be different enough compared to Starlink that they can prosper. But there is no company at this time attempting to build a massive satellite array with 1-2 billion customers as the goal.

CHAPTER 49

Starlink and your Smartphone

by Brian Wang

Elon Musk has virtually no limits to his belief that the biggest industries in the world are all ripe for disruption. If you thought that Starlink would never expand beyond providing broadband Internet services to remote, poorly served consumers, you would be wrong. Elon has just inked a deal that will take SpaceX into the smart phone communication business.

The Global satellite phone market generates over $4 billion per year in revenue. There are several major global satellite phone competitors (Iridium, Globalstar, Inmarsat).

T-Mobile and SpaceX Starlink just announced a competing service that will enable regular cell phones to access Generation 2 Starlink satellites directly.

The Starlink Generation 2 satellites will be 7 meters across and will have 25 square meter antennas, so regular cell phones will communicate with the satellites for text and voice. Each Gen 2 Starlink satellite will have 2 to 4 megabits per second of communication speed.

Iridium has 66 satellites in orbit but at higher altitudes. Each Iridium satellite can support up to 1,100 concurrent phone calls at 2.4Mbps. Each Starlink Generation 2 satellite will match or double the data rates of an Iridium satellite. SpaceX, Starlink and the phone companies could improve data rates and reliability with dedicated hardware and software in future mobile phones. SpaceX Starlink will eventually have 30,000 Generation 2 satellites. This will be almost 500 times more than Iridium.

Satellite phones from Iridium (IRDM), Globalstar (GSAT), Inmarsat, or Thuraya cost about $375 to $1,295 plus there is a yearly service fee varying from $348 to $750. Additionally, depending on the provider, voice calls vary from $0.99 to $1.30 per minute.

Starlink-T-Mobile service will work with your regular phone. Customers will not need to buy a custom satellite phone.

One SpaceX Super Heavy Starship could deploy 80 to 120 Generation 2 satellites in a single launch. There could be about 12-16 mini-Generation 2 satellites launched with each Falcon 9 launch.

Making The Future Awesome | 294

SpaceX will have about 100 Falcon 9 launches in 2023. Those launched in 2023 will primarily fill out the 12,000 Generation 1 Starlink network but some will be for mini-generation 2. The first few launches in 2023 will have SpaceX Starlink Generation 2 satellites and this will surpass the Iridium satellite network.

AST Mobile is a startup that has a 64-meter folding antenna for direct satellite to cell phone communication. Larger foldout antennas will enable higher speed direct cell phone to satellite communication.

Larger antennas will enable satellites to provide 30Mbps or greater communication rates. The initial 25 square meter antennas for Gen 2.0 Starlink will have 2-4Mbps of communication speed. Iridium satellites have 2.4Mbps of speed. Iridium satellites can each support 1,100 simultaneous voice conversations. Each voice conversation takes 2,400 bits per second to support.

The direct to ground communication antennas will fold out like the existing solar power arrays on Starlink satellites.

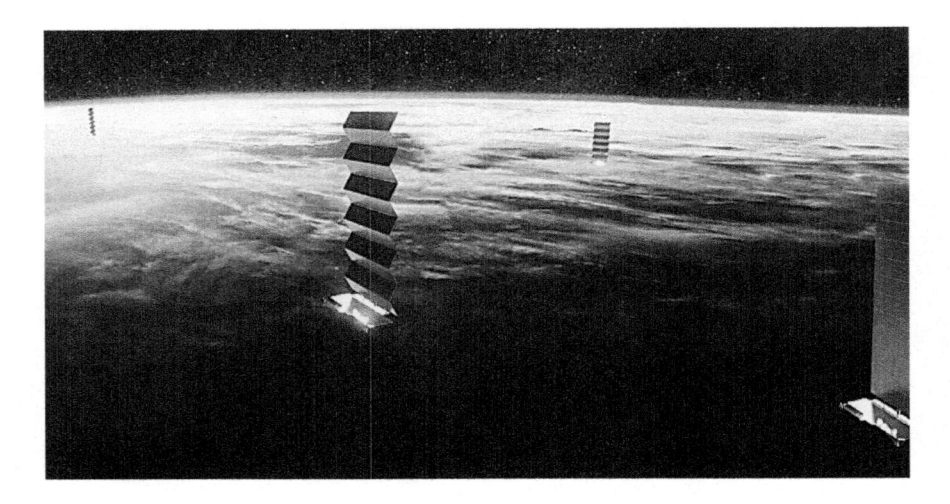

If SpaceX was forced to only use Falcon 9, they would still be able to launch 6,000 mini-Generation 2 Starlink satellites by 2025. If SpaceX gets the fully reusable Super Heavy Starship operational, then they will be able to launch the entire 30,000 generation 2 satellite network within 6-18 months after Super Heavy Starship is flying on a regular basis.

T-Mobile provides mid PCS cellular spectrum for SpaceX Starlink to use for this service. T-Mobile will be able to retire, and avoid paying for, 40% of remote cellular towers. Cellular towers cost about $50,000 and need to be replaced about every ten years and the cellular company must pay rent of about $1,500 to $3,500 per month to rent space for their towers.

There are 5 million cell towers in the world. Replacing 2 million of them with SpaceX Starlink satellites would save $120 billion per year. T-Mobile could save $5-10 billion per year from 2025 onwards and get half of the satellite service revenues which could reach $8 billion per year in 2024.

I expect Apple, Samsung and the non-T-Mobile cellphone service providers will work with SpaceX Starlink. It will provide incremental revenue and superior remote service at lower cost.

SpaceX will be able to backhaul the entire internet. There are estimates that the need for internet data movement (backhaul) for network providers will reach 22Tbps and $25 billion per year in 2030. The complete Gen 2 satellite network will be able to have laser communication between each satellite to move over 600Tbps.

In 2021, Satellite backhaul was 470Gbps of traffic carried; the total addressable market in 2030 will be 22Tbps.

Direct Cell Phone to Satellite Market

For a premium service, you will pay about $500 per year. A hypothetical lower service is $100-200 per year. An emergency text service is $60 per year or per use basis. Assuming 3% share of the revenue of T-Mobile for the $500 per year customers, plus 10% for the $100 per year users, then the Serviceable Addressable Market (SAM) is $2.5B.

Multiply this by 10 if SpaceX is able to sign up carriers reaching North America, Europe and the wealthier Asian markets. (ATT, Verizon, German, Vodaphhone. UK etc...) Now you have a SAM of $25B.

The TAM, if SpaceX can sign up all cell phone networks, would 5X the above SAM or $125B.

These increases are possible with full Gen 2 satellites or strong Gen 3.

Now, you might also modify the phones with larger fractal antennas and better software. This would improve the transmission rate to 10Mbps per second per satellite. 30,000 gen 2 satellites would provide 300Gbps towards the total world capacity for direct phone to satellite.

Gen 3 satellites with larger antennas times 120k satellites would allow an improvement in transmission rate to 30Mbps per second per satellite or 3,600Gbps total capacity.

The direct cell phone to satellite business has several other players in addition to the existing global satellite phone companies. SpaceX will have more capacity than all of them when they reach 200+ Gen2 or mini-Gen2 Starlink satellites.

SpaceX will get the Gen-2 with direct to cell phone satellite network completely deployed by late 2024 or 2025. It will provide text, voice, and internet of things on a global basis, providing SpaceX with a separate and significant revenue stream.

SpaceX's primary rocket development and Starlink deployment costs stabilize at about $10B per year in expenses. SpaceX getting to over 10 million Starlink customers will enable SpaceX to become profitable. By the end of 2024 with the full Generation 1 Starlink network deployed and significant Generation 2 also deployed, SpaceX will have 60-80% profit margins from $35B in revenue.

Below is a chart of how deploying Generation 1 and Generation 2 satellites and scaling to 150 million customers globally translates to $318B in revenue. The profit margins will be high.

Making The Future Awesome | 298

In 2025, with $97B in annual revenue and $70B in profit, SpaceX can have a company valuation of $4-6T with a PE of 60 to 90.

	2022	2023	2024	2025	2026	2027
					30K Gen 3	120K Gen 3
		120 Gen 2	4000 Gen 2	30K Gen 2	30K Gen 2	30K Gen 2
		9K Gen 1	12K Gen 1	12K Gen 1	12K Gen 1	12K Gen 1
		No Super Hea	Super Heavy	Super Heavy		
Falcon 9 Launch Revenue	2.5B	3B	3B	2B	2B	1B
Falcon Heavy Launch revenue	1B	1B	1B			
Super Heavy Starship Launch Revenue				5B	10B	12B
Starlink Internet Revenue	1B	5B	15B	40B	70B	150B
Premium Starlink		0.5B	5B	10B	15B	
Direct to Phone		2B	6B	20B	30B	40B
Backhaul Revenue		1B	5B	15B	30B	50B
Cargo - Twice day continent connection				5B	30B	60B
Cargo City- City						5B
TOTAL	4.5B	12.5B	35B	97B	187B	318B

The primary driver of SpaceX revenue is the rate that they can produce Starlink dishes and then sell the dishes and services to customers. They are at 150k per month now in late 2022 which is 1.8M per year but are increasing the speed of sales. They would need to average 450k per month in 2023 to hit the targets in the chart. They would need to average 1.2 million dishes per month in 2024. The direct phone revenue is determined by how many cellphone customers choose to buy global satellite text and voice from T-Mobile and any other new SpaceX cellphone partners.

September 25, 2022, Elon Musk tweeted that over 1 million dishes had been manufactured. SpaceX will end 2022 with over 1.5 million Starlink customers.

During the 2020s Starlink Will Integrate with 5G and 6G Systems

The conventional terrestrial communication networks will be expanded to include low earth orbit (LEO) satellite access, as this will be necessary to achieve truly global coverage. Starlink will dominate 90+% of the LEO satellites. LEO satellite access will be tightly integrated with terrestrial networks using 6G networks. There will be seamless mobility between terrestrial and LEO satellite networks. LEO satellite access will be designed into 6G systems from day one. 6G standardization will start in 3G around 2025 and 6G commercialization will occur around 2030.

Designing a flexible network architecture for the integrated terrestrial and LEO satellite access will mean:

- support efficient load balancing
- seamless mobility
- dynamic resource allocation between the terrestrial and LEO satellite access.

In addition, the architecture should be flexible enough to support ease of constellation management and the diverse LEO satellite deployment scenarios with Intersatellite Links (ISLs), multi-link connectivity, and backhauling.

SpaceX will undoubtedly be the dominant player in global communication and data with about a 10-30% global share.

CHAPTER 50

The Boring Company – Taking Transportation into 3D Space

by Randy Kirk

An often-overlooked aspect of the Elon Musk persona is his charm. At times it is the awkward, halting speech that implies that he shares the human tendency towards lack of self-esteem. But for many, this personality quirk speaks to his actual humility. He knows that he doesn't know everything about everything and maybe even not much at all about many things.

His boyish charm impresses another group of fans. It is not a stretch to say that his sense of humor and playfulness suggests he is a teenager trapped in a middle-aged man's body. This quirky humor is particularly noted on Twitter and in his naming regimens throughout the various companies and even his many children.

The Boring Company is in the business of boring tunnels, not audiences or wives. The company was founded out of Elon's frustration with the iconic "LA traffic." While those who are knowledgeable about the traffic in Rome, DC, Mumbai, Taipei, or NYC might argue that LA traffic is not even close to the worst in the world, Musk's experience was based on the 405 Fwy in West LA and the East/West corridor streets Wilshire, Santa Monica Blvd, Olympic, and Pico, a section of LA County where the only solution to the gridlock would seem to be going up or burrowing down. In effect, going from traveling in 2D to 3D.

Elon says that there are real problems with flying taxis, so he imagined a world where traffic would be neither seen nor heard by those on the surface. His concept of running all traffic through underground tunnels is based on the idea that there is almost unlimited capacity for tunnels in a 3D space.

Part two of his tunnel concept was to create small diameter tunnels that would be faster and cheaper to construct than those currently used for subways. He has proven that you can build these types of tunnels for a small fraction of the cost of the larger diameter versions.

Part three was possibly the most ingenious and inventive part of the plan. The boring machines that bore out these tunnels are designed to build out the walls of the tunnels while they are boring. This means that the boring machines work continuously as compared to industry standard machines that must stop every so often while laborers work to build out the walls.

The final idea was to run autonomous pods in the tunnels, not large trains. As of today, the pods have not made it to prime time. Instead, the current tunnel system in Las Vegas has Tesla cars moving people from station to station. While these cars are currently moving at relatively slow speeds and still driven by a human, they are expected to be running autonomously in the very near future, and the speeds are intended to move up substantially.

The Las Vegas system has been a proof of concept and is now moving conventioneers and vacationing families between the convention center and local hotels. Millions of wealthy and influential individuals are seeing the efficacy of the tunnel system and getting their first experience in a Tesla automobile. Soon, this experience will also be a robotaxi experience.

So, with no advertising needed, The Boring Company and Tesla are sending visitors home from their Las Vegas vacations with an experience that might apply to their city, their families, or their companies. And this free advertising will continue to grow with the growth of the tunnel system in Vegas.

Multiple other cities in Texas and Florida are close to breaking ground on tunnels. YouTuber Warren Redlich is a huge fan of The Boring Company. He sees a future where thousands of boring machines will be building tunnels in cities and between cities all over the world.

Whether or not Warren's expectations get met, it seems likely that the Boring company will be building a lot of tunnels. The revenues may come from governments paying a fee for the actual building of tunnels and cars to outfit the systems. Currently the revenues are derived from passenger payments to The Boring Company and some contributions from hotels in Vegas to build out the specific stop at their hotel.

Other future revenues could include tunnels for other purposes, including utilities, sewage, etc. Advertising or concessions might be set up at the stations. The cars themselves could have advertisements running during the trips.

Freight can also be moved through the tunnels but would likely need to do so on automated pods. Containers would be loaded onto these pods. Once they reach their destination, trucks would offload the containers and take the cargo to the final destination.

It appears that Elon wants to attempt a full-scale hyperloop in a tunnel by the end of 2022. A hyperloop is a 700-mph train that travels through a tube that is near vacuum using magnetic propulsion. Musk recommended the concept years ago, but said he had no time to develop it. Therefore, he made all his ideas and drawings public and suggested others develop it. While there have been serious efforts to get the concept to market, Elon appears to have lost patience. Moreover, the other concepts were above ground, and he intends to go through Boring tunnels.

Elon's hope for hyperloop has always been to eliminate short haul (under 1 hour) air travel. Once again, the potential addressable market is very large, indeed.

But hyperloop can also be a freight solution for short to medium length trips. The cost would be far less than by air.

The promise of The Boring Company goes way beyond making trips faster, safer, and less stressful. There is also the futuristic idea of eliminating almost all surface roads. The only surface roads that would be necessary would be for pedestrians, bicycles, and small freight haulers. Autonomous cars will also eliminate parking. The Boring Company will eliminate almost all roads. Our cities and suburbs will be quieter, prettier, and have far less particulates in the air from fumes and tire dust.

Will The Boring Company become the largest Elon Musk enterprise? Tesla will have cars, energy, robotics, and AI. It might be hard to top that. SpaceX will have space transportation and long-haul passenger and freight business, internet, mobile phone connectivity, plus military contracts. That's another huge business. Neuralink will be curing brain diseases and helping make superhumans. Will every human on earth eventually want to get hooked up? Another large business.

But replace the entire highway transportation network worldwide, and possibly be the go-to company for underground utilities and sewage? Maybe this will turn out to be the giant among giants.

CHAPTER 51

In the Room with Elon Musk - AI Day2, 2022 Reflections

by John Gibbs

For the second time in less than two months, I was "this" close to Elon Musk. On September 30, 2022, only one row of chairs and a short gap lay between me and one of the brightest entrepreneurial and engineering lights in the US, and indeed the world.

While my chance to see Elon was all about seeing Elon and being energized by his words, my attention was much more divided than it had been at Investor Day. This time not only was Elon presenting, but so were some of the greatest minds in the Artificial Intelligence and Machine Learning communities. Needless to say, I was in nerd heaven!

Only ten days prior to the event, I didn't believe I would be in Palo Alto for this event. Fortunately for me though, my YouTube channel has finally developed enough of a reputation that some people at Tesla know about it, and I was granted an invitation about 8 days prior to the event.

Amazingly, there I was at 6 PM on a Friday evening in Tesla's main Machine Learning headquarters in Palo Alto, getting ready to see the main event. Elon would soon introduce a fantastic team of engineers, and show off the latest TeslaBot prototypes, named BumbleCee and
AI-2.

The first stop for early arrivals was at least as exciting as the event itself. Ringing the main hall were around 20 stations. Each one was staffed by a couple of Tesla engineers. Here we could ask questions and hear what they were allowed to tell us, which was often frustratingly cut off with "I wish I could tell you more." But we could dig into the specifics of Dojo hardware, Full Self Driving vision systems, occupancy networks, simulation, Quality Assurance, and much more.

Then came the main event, a presentation that lasted nearly three and a half hours! Starting with Elon himself introducing BumbleCee and AI-2, the presentation reviewed the Tesla AI team's amazing work during the past year:

- Three TeslaBot prototypes were shown
- The hardware, from actuators to joints to hands, was discussed
- TeslaBot software was dissected
- Full Self Driving Beta (or fully autonomous driving) was explored in great detail
- Dojo, the star of last year's AI Day, was updated, including the likely completion date
- An extended Q&A session specifically set aside for students to ask questions of Elon and the team.

If you'd like to dive more deeply into some or all of the above, you can watch it. I highly recommend doing so though you might want to break it up into smaller segments. 203 minutes is a lot of time to sit and absorb such high-level information!

https://www.youtube.com/watch?v=ODSJsviD_SU

After the presentation, it was so late that people ate the delicious catered food, had a drink or two, and headed home–or to Tesla's test track to get a test ride in a Model S Plaid!

What was my reaction to the evening? It felt like an amusing cross between a high school science fair (the stations around the hall), a massively compressed academic conference (the presentations) and a peek inside a top-secret laboratory (the "I wish I could tell you more" moments that festooned the evening). All in all, I had an absolutely fantastic time, but there were many at the event who found it a bit overwhelming due to the length and the level of detail of the presentations.

This general reaction brings me to an important insight I've recently had about Elon Musk: he is radically honest. Of course, this is a rare trait, and one which most misunderstand when it comes to Elon.
For example, prior to AI Day2, Elon repeatedly told people this was a recruiting event for the best AI practitioners in the world. He further noted that it wasn't a press event, and that most people who weren't best-in-class AI software, hardware, or robotics experts would find it mind numbingly boring.

In the leadup to the event, however, many people, including me to some extent, were thinking of this as a new product announcement similar to the Cybertruck or Model 3 introductions in years past. Certainly, one could be forgiven for this misunderstanding as the first AI Day did introduce the Dojo supercomputer and a design concept for the TeslaBot, but still Elon tried very hard to warn everyone this was not going to be a demo for the masses.

Our speculation about the many possible new things we might see were somewhat dashed, but we should have known better: Elon is a very precisely honest person, and he also loves to tell us what he can. In fact, the entire reason AI Day 2022 was pushed back to September rather than August was because Elon announced that they wanted a working prototype of the TeslaBot. In fact, we got multiple prototypes rather than just one! While many were a bit disappointed not to see more new toys, I was pretty ecstatic to have a chance to dig into some of the details concerning how Tesla's hardware and software advances are going.

My second takeaway is that Tesla is a bit of an "anti-Apple" when it comes to demos. The main live demo of the evening was BumbleCee walking out on stage right at the beginning, waving to the crowd, and walking off stage, followed immediately by its sibling, AI-2. (Two more prototypes have been built according to inside sources, including Bumblebee, who is the robot featured in the videos shown during AI Day). This demo was done straight away at the beginning of the presentation, rather than building to Steven Jobs's famous "one more thing" at the end of the presentation.

Additionally, AI-2 had to be wheeled out awkwardly, and its torso tipped over a bit as the team was moving it to the side of the stage. This foible elicited a wonderful "Tesla demos, coming in hot!" quip from Musk. In fact, this moment recalled the much more embarrassing moment when Franz von Holzhausen shattered the window of the CyberTruck by throwing a steel ball into it during the truck's unveiling back in 2019. Tesla has a bit of a reputation for doing things that could fail miserably in their live demos. In fact,

Making The Future Awesome | 310

they were taking a big chance when they had BumbleCee walk out on stage and wave. This was in fact the first time the bot had ever walked without a tether to be sure it didn't fall over!

Tesla's presentations are certainly lacking in polish, but they make up for it in the excitement of something that could fail in a pretty spectacular way right in front of us. All in all, what Tesla AI Day lacked in polish it more than made up for in rawness, depth, and detail.

This leads me to my third observation: Tesla's team is not only some of the most brilliant people one could meet, but Tesla also actually lets them talk about what they're working on! Of course, I have to say that many of the really deep details I wanted to know about weren't covered, for the very good reason that it would be a bad move to let the competition know every detail about what you're working on.

Given this factor, however, the team was allowed to speak at great depth both during their presentations and at their stations around the outside of the hallway. The chance to hear people at the top of their respective disciplines go into some degree of detail about their work is always exciting for me and getting to hear people who are working hard to change the world was doubly so.

The best parts of the presentations, in my mind, were the unscripted moments when one of the team (who sat on stools on the stage left side awaiting their turn to speak) would interrupt, and then they and the presenter would talk excitedly about a specific point they were researching. I thought to myself, what an amazing experience it must be to walk the halls of this building any day of the week!

My final take away from AI Day 2022 is that Tesla should consider multiple AI Days. The event was incredible, but it had so much information packed into such a limited amount of time that even for a highly interested person like me it was a bit overwhelming. Tesla could have one Dojo event, one TeslaBot event, one Full Self Driving and vision event, and even a data collection and infrastructure event.

Near the end, I think Elon realized the length and depth were tough on the audience. He mentioned that Tesla should consider monthly podcasts about AI topics. In my mind this could be a fantastic way to continue recruiting but be able to focus on a particular topic in more depth each month.

Given that the AI Day is primarily a recruiting event for students who are often not very wealthy, and who live all around the world, it would make sense to have a virtual event that is available by invitation only so that students can get more detailed presentations and also ask questions. The podcast can then be broadcast later for more general consumption.

While I very much hope that Tesla will continue to have AI Days each year - and that I will be invited to them in the future! - Elon is right that a monthly podcast would take some of the pressure off the big yearly event.

What are my big picture thoughts about seeing Elon Musk at Telsa's AI Day 2022?

The TeslaBot will absolutely change the world–and soon!

The Full Self Driving Vision team is already changing the world with their incredible Neural Network architecture and training. No one will catch Tesla on Full Self Driving because Tesla keeps improving the ways in which they capture and label data.

Dojo is a reality this year, rather than a vision. I got to look inside a functional exopod and see results of operations it can perform on a monitor, proving it is a beast of a computer.

The team should strongly consider Elon's suggestion that they have a more targeted monthly podcast.

Elon Musk is a huge presence in any room—as soon as he walks into a room with his massive size and personality, people turn to him as if he's magnetic. Yet at an event like AI Day 2022, he can be incredibly generous, ceding focus to the team leaders who work hard every day and very much deserved the attention they got at this event.

In short, after AI Day, I am even more convinced that Elon Musk and Tesla are changing the world. I am even more excited to be a part of this amazing future!

CHAPTER 52

Neuralink - Improving Brains

by Randy Kirk

"If Arkk is correct, then by 2025, Elon Musk will be a trillionaire. Elon currently has 241 million shares of Tesla and will get eight more CEO compensation bonuses totaling another 12 million shares," according to a report in the blog NextBigFuture.
Arkk said that at $1,333 per share, those 759 million shares would be worth $1.012 trillion. "Elon's net worth would also be boosted by the future value of his 54% ownership of SpaceX, 80% share of Boring Company and 90% share of Neuralink."

Read more at:
https://economictimes.indiatimes.com/markets/stocks/news/tesla-bull-predicts-elon-musk-could-be-a-trillionaire-in-four-years/articleshow/81691899.cms?utm_source=contentofinterest&utm_medium=text&utm_campaign=cppst

Currently the smallest market cap of Elon's companies, Neuralink is only valued at $1B, based on a recent private stock offering. Elon is believed to own 90% of the company after that capital injection.

But how much value would you place on a company who reached only the first level of their aspirations if those aspirations were as described on their website:

> "We're designing the first neural implant that will let you control a computer or mobile device anywhere you go.
>
> "Micron-scale threads are inserted into areas of the brain that control movement. Each thread contains many electrodes and connects them to an implant, the Link.
>
> "The threads on the Link are so fine and flexible that they can't be inserted by the human hand. Instead, we are building a robotic system that the neurosurgeon can use to insert these threads exactly reliably and efficiently where they need to be.
>
> "These threads are then attached to a quarter sized implant in the skull. The design of the implant is such that after surgery, the implant would not be visible. The implant would communicate with the Neuralink app.
>
> "The Neuralink app would allow you to control your iOS device, keyboard, and mouse directly with the activity of your brain, just by thinking about it.
>
> "The Neuralink app would guide you through exercises that teach you to control your device.
>
> "With a Bluetooth connection, you would control any mouse or keyboard, and experience reality — unmediated and in high fidelity.

"The initial goal of our technology will be to **help people with paralysis to regain independence through the control of computers and mobile devices. Our devices are designed to give people the ability to communicate more easily via text or speech synthesis, to follow their curiosity on the web, or to express their creativity through photography, art, or writing apps.**

"The Link is a starting point for a new kind of brain interface. As our technology develops, **we will be able to increase the channels of communication with the brain, accessing more brain areas and new kinds of neural information. This technology has the potential to treat a wide range of neurological disorders, to restore sensory and movement function, and eventually to expand how we interact with each other, with the world, and with ourselves.**"

Should Neuralink reach even the first level of those goals, the valuation would immediately move into the tens of $billions. With each new ability to overcome some failure of the brain, the resulting good that could be done would be almost without precedent.

But the website does not fully encapsulate Elon's vision. For instance, Elon has stated: "I mean this is obviously sounding increasingly like a black mirror episode but yeah essentially if you have a whole brain interface everything that's encoded in memory **you could upload or basically store your memories as a backup and restore the memories. Then ultimately you could potentially download them into a new body or into a robot body** the future is going to be a weird one!"

"We are already a cyborg to some degree," Musk told Joe Rogan in an interview:

"You have your phone, laptops, and devices. I mean today, if you don't bring your phone along, it is like you have missing limb syndrome. We are already partly a cyborg."

Elon went on to explain the possibilities: "Even if you lost your optic nerve, and return hearing sense to deaf individuals. If you have severe epilepsy, it could detect it in real-time and stop it from occurring. […] There is a whole list of injuries — for example, if a person has a stroke, that could also be fixed if you lose muscle control." Adding that if you have Alzheimer's, Neuralink will be able to help you with restoring memory.

"It could, in principle, fix anything that's wrong with the brain."

"Over time, we will see a closer merger of biological intelligence and digital intelligence. It is all about the bandwidth of the brain, "he said.
"Some high-bandwidth interface to the brain will be something which helps achieve symbiosis between human and machine intelligence, which solves a control and usefulness problem."

"From a long-term existential standpoint, that's, like, the purpose of Neuralink, to create a high-bandwidth interface to the brain such that we can be symbiotic with AI. Because we have a bandwidth problem. You just can't communicate through your fingers. It's just too slow."

So how does one begin to value this product if it achieves some or all of these results? We could start with the value of curing some brain malfunctions that interfere with the use of our physical bodies or overcome injuries to our bodies. How many millions of people could be helped?

Another area of low hanging fruit is helping folks with neurological disorders that contribute to depression, anxiety, addiction, or other disabling emotional and psychological disorders. The total addressable market (TAM) would be everyone but you and me, and I'm not sure about you.

Once Neuralink has disposed with all of those human problems, they can turn to augmenting the human to a superhuman. One merely has to contemplate the incredible efficiency with which we already manage information and communication. It was only 170 years ago when the fastest way to get a message to someone was a pony. It was only 25 years ago that most research required a visit to the library. The future might provide research and communication without moving a muscle.

For instance, we can all get a translation of words in a foreign language, measurements in other measures, value in other currencies, and definitions of any word in far less than a minute. But we often don't bother. How lazy we are. But with Neuralink, the information would be automatic depending on your settings. Imagine an immediate translation in a conversation. In fact, there might not be any conversation as such, but merely sending your thoughts.

Apple and others are working hard to turn external products like watches into medical tools that monitor your vitals and report problems. With Neuralink, most of this would become automatic and not even require looking at an app.

At some point, every human will want this product. Elon says he believes the surgery will be like Lasik in cost, time, and comfort. So, what would the monthly subscription be $10? $100? Multiply by most of the world's population.

How fast will Neuralink be worth many $Bs or even $Ts? This one is the hardest to predict. The governments of the world will need to approve these medical processes. I suspect that it will be at least 3-5 years before we'll see any large-scale sales. Human trials, however, are imminent.

CHAPTER 53

How Much Is $1,000,000,000,000

by Randy Kirk

Keep in mind that Elon Musk doesn't care about being a trillionaire. He cares about his missions. If it were about money or the things money can buy, he wouldn't be living in a $40K home near SpaceX.

However, many reading this book love to watch their favorite team's stats. From the age of seven, I was the one who went after the morning newspaper before anyone else. My interest was not in the news headlines or the funny papers. I wanted to see if Stan the Man had improved his batting average, was still leading the league in hits and doubles, and if the Cardinals were still in the run for the pennant.

In that same way, Bloomberg and others chart the net worths of billionaires, and People Magazine tells us about the wealth of our movie stars. We still check out the stats on our sports heroes, including if their new contract was the biggest in history.

Therefore, for a bit of fun, we thought we'd add up all the values of the various enterprises, then project into the future. We are not interested in whether Elon will hit 62 home runs, but when will Elon become a trillionaire?

So how much is a trillion of anything, anyway. It is really quite outside our ability to comprehend. Here are some ways to make it more real…maybe.

- If you stretched out millionaires (each with a net worth of $1M) head-to-toe from Austin to Cape Canaveral, their combined net worth would be $1T dollars. (One million millionaires.)
- In 1987, the total US National Budget crossed $1T for the first time.
- The US military budget is under $1T
- Only 16 countries and four US states have a GDP of more than $1T
- $1T is enough to buy any US company except the top 6. And it is enough to buy every major car company with plenty to spare.

John D Rockefeller became the first person with a nominal net worth of over $1B. That was on Sept 29, 1916 (how do they know??) Depending on who's counting that would give him a $250-$450B net worth in 2022 dollars.

The first thing we will look at is "Why Now?" Why is there even the potential for a person to reach $1T in wealth? What are the conditions that make such an achievement possible? We will look at the convergence of technologies and human needs and wants that are driving disruptions in energy, auto, space, robotics, AI, and medicine.

We will also explore "Why Elon Musk?" Some think he is an alien. Others think he is a villain. He thinks he might be part of a simulation. We think he is a once-in-a-lifetime genius with a long list of skill sets that combined with passion, persistence, and hard work, position him to run companies that are leading the disruptions in energy, auto, space, robotics, AI, and medicine.

Since these industries represent the largest industries in the world, being number one in any of them would make you a multibillionaire. Leading in most or all of them? That would be the "Why?" of the trillion-dollar story we are telling.

How will Elon Musk Reach $1T in Net Worth

In order to determine the "How?" question, we will pull apart each and every division of SpaceX and Tesla in detail, then apply some reasonable estimate of revenues to each. Some will be easier than others. But even the BEV (battery electric vehicle) business valuation, seemingly the easiest to project, could shift radically for any number or reasons.

We will not be digging into the weeds about these valuations. There are plenty of others online who can provide you with quarter-by-quarter estimates of every little detail. We will provide a list of resources in the Appendix of this book.

The final section of the book is "When?" Once we have determined the various income streams, the last step will be to determine the stock price, which is loosely based on current income and future expected income. We will look down the road and project the stock price for Tesla and the street estimate of SpaceX (a privately held corporation) in the next several years. Ultimately, we'll reach my estimate for the day that Elon becomes the first Trillionaire.

We will apply the stock price of each company to Elon's total stock ownership in each company to come up with his personal worth. For instance, he owns about half of SpaceX and 16% of Tesla. If Tesla reaches $6.25T in market cap, Elon's percent of that would be about $700B. If SpaceX were to be worth $600B, Elon's part would be worth $300B. Together that would get us to $1T.

The case will hinge on the execution of projects that are already producing tangible results. As an inventor, Musk always has another idea close at hand that he is eager to produce. However, he doesn't need to start manufacturing anything new to reach $1T.

When will Elon Musk surpass the trillion-dollar mark? You can join the pool we have started that includes a $1,000.00 prize for the person who comes closest to the date that Bloomberg says Elon has passed $1T.

https://www.freebusinesshelpnow.com/

CHAPTER 54

When will Elon Musk Reach $1T in Personal Net Worth?

by Randy Kirk

As you may or may not know, we have created a game around this question. The object of the game is to "guess" the day that Elon passes three milestones of net worth: $420B, $690B and $1T. The winner of each correct estimate will receive $420, $690, and $1,000 respectively.

Why the game? Elon says: *"The thing we call money is just an information system for labor allocation. What actually matters is making goods & providing services. We should look at currencies from an information theory standpoint. Whichever has least error & latency will win."*

For fans of Elon Musk, his wealth is a method of scoring the underlying successes that the world is watching with awe. We get that he is much more concerned with reaching his lofty goals that he believes will do good for humans than he is about owning anything. This is why it is so interesting to watch this measure of the story of Elon Musk.

The Rules:

You may only enter the contest once. Duplicate entries will be discarded.

Determination of the date on which Elon Musk's net worth reaches the contest amounts will be Bloomberg.com as seen at https://www.bloomberg.com/billionaires/

The tiebreaker will be that entry that comes closest to estimating the actual total wealth on the day Elon passes that milestone. For instance, he might pass the $420B milestone on March 20, 2023, and the total wealth might be $425B on that day. If there is more than one correct guess, the winner will be the one who guessed closest to $425B. If this tiebreaker does not narrow the winner down to a single entry, the winning amount will be divided between all winning entries.

All decisions are final and at the sole discretion of the contest owners.

The contest is open to anyone, including Tesla, SpaceX, Neuralink, The Boring Company, and Twitter employees, friends and family members of the contest owner, and Elon Musk.

Entries for various levels of the contest will be cut off when Elon's wealth is within $50B of each level. In other words, we will no longer accept entries for the $420B level when Elon's worth reaches $370B according to Bloomberg. We reserve the right to reopen entries for any level if Elon's worth falls more than $20B below that level until that level is regained.

So, When Indeed?

While many see it as a foredrawn conclusion that Elon Musk will one day be worth at least $1T, the law of large numbers (business version) is nothing to scoff at. Apple is a great example. Their iPhone and SaaS (app store) business generate so much profit that the computer businesses seem puny by comparison. So, for Apple to grow much beyond its current valuation, it might need some kind of product that will throw off similar kinds of profits to the phone and apps.

The reality is that those don't come around every day.

On the other hand, Elon seems destined to blaze past $1T because his companies are dealing in businesses that have much larger addressable markets than Apple. A Smart phone costs $1,000. A Tesla costs an average of $50,000. Starlink has the potential to generate $100 per month per customer. No Apple app or combination will allow Apple to reach that kind of revenue per customer.

Apple is looking at cars and virtual reality systems as their way to grow at levels seldom seen by large cap companies. Tesla is looking at humanoid robots and robotaxis as avenues to market caps higher than any company in history ON TOP of becoming the largest company by market cap from cars alone.

The other helping factor for Elon is that he owns just under 20% of Tesla and around 50% of SpaceX. It is historically unprecedented for one human to own this percentage of two huge companies.

Roughly speaking, a good estimate of the timing for the $1T mark would be about the time that Tesla hits $4T in market cap. This would give Elon about $800B in worth. If SpaceX was worth about $400B ($127B now) at that time, he would have $200B worth of SpaceX stock. Those, taken together, would equal $1T.

Neuralink is possibly worth $1B at this time and The Boring Company is worth around $5B. So, while this is not chump change, these companies may not materially affect the contest results. However, don't discount those entirely. SpaceX may spin off Starlink in an IPO. If Starlink has 1B customers by then at $1,200 each per year, the revenue would be $1.2T, giving Starlink a very high valuation. The Boring Company is very likely just about to ramp up production of the boring machines. It wouldn't take too many significant contracts to create some significant increases in The Boring Company's valuation.

We will now endeavor to take each company and attempt to provide some kind of projection of earnings and likely market cap number for each quarter into the future. We will invite some well-known Tesla pundits from YouTube and the Twitter community to help play the game.

As with any company, large or small, these projections are not worth very much except by way of some guesses as to the percentage potential for achieving them. A new breakthrough in technology, a new product added to the mix, a difficult economic climate, or any one of hundreds of contingencies could alter any of these projections by an order of magnitude.

So, without too much stressing over the methodology, sit back and enjoy the process.

You read it here first. Tesla will earn $60B in 2023! How in the world do I reach that figure? Three significant metrics will drive that result.

1. **Tesla vehicles - $40B**
   Tesla will sell 2,700k vehicles in 2023. Yes, that is far more than a 50% increase. In fact, close to 100%. I think you'll see that this number is very reasonable.

TOTAL GROSS PROFIT (ASSUMED): $39.75B + $13B +$7.2B + $5B = $64.75B

Giga-Factory	Assumed Annual Production Run-Rate	Average Weekly Production
Fremont	650,000	13,000
Shanghai	1,200,000	24,000
Austin	375,000	7,500
Berlin	375,000	7,500
Nevada (Semi-Truck)	30,000	600
Austin (Cybertruck)	20,000	400
TOTALS:	2,650,000	53,000

Average selling price (overall) @ $50,000 per vehicle = $132.5B revenue.
Average profit @ $15,000 per vehicle (overall) = $39.75B

2. **Energy Storage**.
   Sales of 36 GWh at an ASP of $1M/GWh = $36B revenue.
   Profit on Energy Storage @ 36% = **$13B**
   Add: Inflation Reduction Act (IRA) Incentives from U.S. battery production –
   Estimated 160M kWh @ $45/kWh = **$7.2B**

3. **Other Revenues.** Services, Used Cars, Solar, Insurance, Other = **$5B**

Keeping in mind that this is napkin math, we will assume that certain other incomes will offset operating expenses and settle in at $60B in EBIDTA or about $19 per share. If Tesla were to have a 65 P/E, the share price would reach $1,235 split adjusted, resulting in a market cap of about $3.86B

As much as I feel that this is a conservative, realistic analysis for 2023, and one that is almost baked in, based on known factory capacities and expected ramps, the 2024 picture is much fuzzier.

We should certainly expect another 125k Model Ys from both Berlin and Austin to complete the 500k per factory first phase. Cybertruck should be hitting its stride with at least another 220k units, and Semi is slated to increase by 30K per year to 60K. If Austin doesn't begin Model 3 production, and Shanghai stays at roughly '23 levels, this would give us a 500K unit increase on vehicles. 500K x $15,000 per vehicle increases 2024 over 2023 by **$7.5B**.

A small additional ramp of Megapacks in Lathrop should also increase sales in energy storage. That total would be a meager increase, but in keeping with the 45% per year average. The huge increase in 2023 offset by a smaller increase in 2024.

Tesla would need to start new Gigafactories soon to get much more production increase in 2024, but another Megapack factory would be faster to jump start.

For now, I'm going to leave it at 3.2M vehicles in 2024 with another explosion in growth in 2025 coming from at least two new Gigafactories and at least two new Megapack factories.

If Tesla stock reaches $1,235 next year (2023), Elon will be worth very close to $1T when you include Twitter. My guess is that he'll hit that magic number on May 4, 2024.

Watch for our next book, *The Elon Musk Magic*, due in August 2023.

APPENDIX
Author Biographies & Contact Information

RANDY KIRK

Inc Magazine declared: "What separates this book (When Friday Isn't Payday) from the pack is its relentless practicality...an experienced small business owner figuratively at your side, keeping panic at bay with practical applications." When Friday Isn't Payday was selected by Inc. as one of the three best small business books of 1994.

After spending 26 years building a plastics manufacturing business to become the largest manufacturer of bicycle style water bottles in the world, the company AC Technologies, was sold to a small conglomerate. Taking almost 40 years of experience from running, writing about, and speaking about small business, Randy Kirk & Associates was formed in 2008 to help owners of entrepreneurial companies with their marketing efforts.

In addition to AC Technologies, businesses in distribution, advertising, import-export, guarantee assurance, and independent sales representation filled out decades of sales and marketing experience.

Outside pursuits include the raising of four, now adult, children and eight grandchildren, membership at Immanual Baptist Church, extensive writings on various issues, and the presidency of a local business group.

Randy has a BS and JD from UCLA

LARS STRANDRIDDER

Lars Strandridder is 42 years old and lives in Denmark with his wife and their two kids.

He worked as a team leader in one of Denmark's biggest travel agencies when Covid hit!

When he got sent home, he started working on his hobby project, a YouTube Channel called BestInTESLA which he started back in July 2019. The goal of the channel was to help people better understand Tesla and the EV revolution. That effort included fighting all the fear, doubt and uncertainty that was being spread about the electric car, Tesla and Elon Musk.

As he has been following Tesla and the EV adoption closely since 2015, he could see the massive gap between what the mainstream media was reporting, and what was actually going on.

Today his Channel has more than 18 million views and has become his full time job.

JOHN GIBBS

Dr. John Gibbs has a BA in Physics from Princeton University, a Ph.D. in English Literature from The Ohio State University, and an MS in Artificial Intelligence from The University of Georgia.

John teaches 3D animation, design, writing, and AI-related topics at UGA, where he is Associate Professor, Head of Dramatic Media, and Faculty Fellow in The Institute for Artificial Intelligence (IAI). John has published 11 books on 3D animation, and has written numerous articles on varied topics, including AI and Machine Learning.

John is also co-founder and CEO of Artimatic.io, a company that is applying Machine Learning techniques to 3D animation problems.

Finally, John is the creator of the Dr. Know-It-All channel on YouTube (http://youtube.com/drknowitallknowsitall), a channel that explains what's going on with technology, AI, and Elon Musk's companies. The channel has more than 600 videos, many of which focus on AI, Tesla, Full Self Driving, and cutting edge AI topics.

BRIAN WANG

Brian Wang is a futurist, speaker, and successful blogger who covers a wide range of bleeding edge science and technology topics.

His blog at Nextbigfuture.com receives 5+ million annual readers and is ranked as a top Science News Blog worldwide by Alexa, an Amazon company. The blog covers disruptive technology trends including Space, Energy, Robotics, Artificial Intelligence, Quantum Computing, Medicine, Anti-aging Biotechnology, and

Nanotechnology. His work has been cited by futurist, Peter Diamandis and by marketing guru Seth Godin.

Brian has made hundreds of predictions at the prediction tracking website Metaculus and has a proven 80% forecasting accuracy. Being a future enthusiast, he is currently a startup co-founder, Angel Investor, as well as advisor to several technology companies.
Prior to blogging and lecturing on the future, Brian was a founder & CEO of a multi-million dollar technology consulting firm designing IT systems.

He received a BS in Computer Science from University of Regina, and MBA from University of Calgary.

Resources

If you would like to keep up to date on all things Elon Musk, the following YouTubers and active Twitter community members have helped us to expand our understanding.

Lars Strandridder - Best in Tesla   @TeslaBest

John Gibbs   - Dr. Know-It-All Knows It All @DrKnowItAll16

Brian Wang   – Next Big Future   @nextbigfuture

Rob Mauer   - Telsa Daily   @TeslaPodcast

Steven Mark Ryan - Solving the Money Problem   @stevenmarkryan

Dave Lee   - Dave Lee on Investing   @heydave7

Sandy Munro   - Munro Live   @MunroAssociates

Warren Redlich - Warren Redlich   @WR4NYGov

Jordan Giesige -The Limiting Factor   @LimitingThe

Brian White   - My Tesla Weekend   @4Kpodcast

Sam Evans   - The Electric Viking   @theevking

Farzad Mesbahi - Farzad Mesbahi   @farzyness

Dillon Loomis   - Electrified   @DillonLoomis22

James Stephenson -James Stephenson   @ICannot_Enough

Jon Stewart   - CleanerWatt   @cleanerwatt

Alexandra Merz	@TeslaBoomerMama
Gary Black	@garyblack00
Ross Gerber	@GerberKawasaki
Troy Teslike	@TroyTeslike
Sawyer Merritt	@SawyerMerritt
Elon Musk	@elonmusk

41 Best Elon Musk Quotes

1. "I love the thought of a car drifting apparently endlessly through space and perhaps being discovered by an alien race millions of years in the future."
2. "I think it is possible for ordinary people to choose to be extraordinary."
3. "The key test for an acronym is to ask whether it helps or hurts communication."
4. "To make an embarrassing admission, I like video games. That's what got me into software engineering when I was a kid. I wanted to make money so I could buy a better computer to play better video games. Nothing like saving the world."
5. "The path to the CEO's office should not be through the CFO's office, and it should not be through the marketing department. It needs to be through engineering and design."
6. "You could power the entire United States with about 150 to 200 square kilometers of solar panels, the entire United States. Take a corner of Utah... there's not much going on there, I've been there. There's not even radio stations."
7. "I'm nauseatingly pro-American. I would have come here from any country. The U.S. is where great things are possible."
8. "Any product that needs a manual to work is broken."
9. "It's OK to have your eggs in one basket as long as you control what happens to that basket."
10. "When Henry Ford made cheap, reliable cars people said, 'Nah, what's wrong with a horse?' That was a huge bet he made, and it worked."

11. "If you go back a few hundred years, what we take for granted today would seem like magic -- being able to talk to people over long distances, to transmit images, flying, accessing vast amounts of data like an oracle. These are all things that would have been considered magic a few hundred years ago."
12. "I've always wanted to be part of something that would radically change the world ... People forget the power of inspiration. All of humanity went to the moon with the Apollo missions. The issue was cost. There was no chance to build a base and create frequent flights. That's the problem I would like to solve."
13. "Entrepreneurship is like eating glass and walking on hot coals at the same time."
14. "Failure is an option here. If things are not failing, you are not innovating enough."
15. "And we need things in life that are exciting and inspiring. It can't just be about solving some awful problem. There have to be reasons to get up in the morning."
16. "I'm actually making history tonight as the first person with Asperger's to host SNL. Or at least the first to admit it. So I won't make a lot of eye contact with the cast tonight. But don't worry, I'm pretty good at running human and emulation mode."
17. "Some people don't like change, but you need to embrace change if the alternative is disaster."
18. "I think life on Earth must be about more than just solving problems ... It's got to be something inspiring, even if it is vicarious."
19. "I don't spend my time pontificating about high-concept things; I spend my time solving engineering and manufacturing problems."

20. "Nobody wants to buy a $60,000 electric Civic. But people will pay $90,000 for an electric sports car."
21. "I think that's the single best piece of advice: Constantly think about how you could be doing things better and questioning yourself."
22. "If humanity doesn't land on Mars in my lifetime, I would be very disappointed."
23. "I'd like to dial it back 5% or 10% and try to have a vacation that's not just e-mail with a view."
24. "Engineering is the closest thing to magic that exists in the world."
25. "An asteroid or a supervolcano could certainly destroy us, but we also face risks the dinosaurs never saw: An engineered virus, nuclear war, inadvertent creation of a micro black hole, or some as-yet-unknown technology could spell the end of us."
26. "I would like to die on Mars. Just not on impact."
27. "For my part, I will never give up, and I mean never."
28. "Failure is an option here. If things are not failing, you are not innovating enough."
29. "People work better when they know what the goal is and why. It is important that people look forward to coming to work in the morning and enjoy working."
30. "My biggest mistake is probably weighing too much on someone's talent and not someone's personality. I think it matters whether someone has a good heart.
31. "Work like hell. I mean you just have to put in 80 to 100 hour weeks every week. [This]_improves the odds of success. If other people are putting in 40 hour workweeks and you're putting in 100 hour workweeks, then even if you're doing the same thing, you know that you will achieve in four months what it takes them a year to achieve."
32. "I've actually not read any books on time management."

33. "Don't delude yourself into thinking something's working when it's not, or you're gonna get fixated on a bad solution."
34. "If something has to be designed and invented, and you have to figure out how to ensure that the value of the thing you create is greater than the cost of the inputs, then that is probably my core skill."
35. "I always have optimism, but I'm realistic. It was not with the expectation of great success that I started Tesla or SpaceX... It's just that I thought they were important enough to do anyway."
36. "You want to have a future where you're expecting things to be better, not one where you're expecting things to be worse"
37. "Good ideas are always crazy until they're no
38. "I came to the conclusion that we should aspire to increase the scope and scale of human consciousness in order to better understand what questions to ask. Really, the only thing that makes sense is to strive for greater collective enlightenment."
39. "Why do you want to live? What's the point? What inspires you? What do you love about the future? And if the future's not including being out there among the stars and being a multi-planet species, it's incredibly depressing if that's not the future we're going to have."
40. "You get paid in direct proportion to the difficulty of problems you solve."

Printed in Great Britain
by Amazon